Wilkie Collins

Antonina - the fall of Rome

Wilkie Collins

Antonina - the fall of Rome

ISBN/EAN: 9783742848758

Manufactured in Europe, USA, Canada, Australia, Japa

Cover: Foto ©Andreas Hilbeck / pixelio.de

Manufactured and distributed by brebook publishing software (www.brebook.com)

Wilkie Collins

Antonina - the fall of Rome

EACH VOLUME SOLD SEPARATELY.

COLLECTION
OF
BRITISH AUTHORS

TAUCHNITZ EDITION.

VOL. 679.

ANTONINA BY WILKIE COLLINS

IN TWO VOLUMES.

VOL. 2.

LEIPZIG: BERNHARD TAUCHNITZ.
PARIS: C. REINWALD, 15, RUE DES SAINTS PÈRES.

COLLECTION OF BRITISH AUTHORS
TAUCHNITZ EDITION.
Each volume 1/2 Thaler = 54 Xr. Rhen. = 2 Francs (1s. 6d.)

ADAMS: Sacred Allegories 1 v.
AGUILAR: Home Influence 2 v. The Mother's Recompense 2 v.
Rita 1 v. Carr of Carrlyon 2 v. The Days 2 v.
AINSWORTH: Windsor Castle 1 v. Saint James's 1 v. Jack Sheppard (w. portr.) 1 v. The Lancashire Witches 2 v. The Star-Chamber 2 v. The Flitch of Bacon 1 v. The Spendthrift 1 v. Mervyn Clitheroe 2 v. Ovingdean Grange 1 v. The Constable of the Tower 1 v. The Lord Mayor of London 2 v. Cardinal Pole 2 v. John Law 2 v. The Spanish Match 2 v. The Constable de Bourbon 2 v. Old Court 2 v. Myddleton Pomfret 2 v.
ALL FOR GREED 1 v.
MISS AUSTEN: Sense and Sensibility 1 v. Mansfield Park 1 v.
NINA BALATKA 1 v.
REV. R. H. BAYNES: Lyra Anglicana 1 v.
CURRER BELL: Jane Eyre 2 v. Shirley 2 v. Villette 2 v. The Professor 1 v.
E. & A. BELL: Wuthering Heights, and Agnes Grey 2 v.
LADY BLESSINGTON: Meredith 1 v. Strathern 2 v. Memoirs of a Femme de Chambre 1 v. Marmaduke Herbert 2 v. Country Quarters (w. portr.) 2 v.
BRADDON: Lady Audley's Secret 2 v. Aurora Floyd 2 v. Eleanor's Victory 2 v. John Marchmont's Legacy 2 v. Henry Dunbar 2 v. The Doctor's Wife 2 v. Only a Clod 2 v. Sir Jasper's Tenant 2 v. The Lady's Mile 2 v. Rupert Godwin 2 v.
BROOKS: The Silver Cord 3 v. Sooner or Later 3 v.
BROWN: Rab and his Friends 1 v.
TOM BROWN'S School Days 1 v.
BULWER (LORD LYTTON): Pelham (w. portr.) 1 v. Eugene Aram 1 v. Paul Clifford 1 v. Zanoni 1 v. Pompeii 1 v. The Disowned 1 v. Ernest Maltravers 1 v. Alice 1 v. Eva, and the Pilgrims of the Rhine 1 v. Devereux 1 v. Godolphin and Falkland 1 v. Rienzi 1 v. Night and Morning 1 v. The Last of the Barons 2 v. Athens 2 v. Poems of Schiller 1 v. Lucretia 2 v. Harold 2 v. King Arthur 2 v. The New Timon; Saint Stephen's 1 v. The Caxtons 2 v. My Novel 4 v. What will he do with it? 4 v. Dramatic Works 2 v. A Strange Story 2 v. Caxtoniana 2 v. The Lost Tales of Miletus 1 v. Miscellaneous Prose Works 4 v.
SIR HENRY LYTTON BULWER: Historical Characters 2 v.
BUNYAN: The Pilgrim's Progress 1 v.
MISS BURNEY: Evelina 1 v.
BURNS: Poetical Works (w. portr.) 1 v.
BYRON: The Works (w. portr.) compl. 5 v.
"THE LAST OF THE CAVALIERS," AUTHOR OF: The Last of the Cavaliers 2 v. The Gain of a Loss 2 v.

T. CARLYLE: The French Revolution 3 v. Frederick the Great 13 v. Oliver Cromwell 4 v.
"CHRONICLES OF THE SCHÖNBERG-Cotta Family," AUTHOR OF: Chronicles of the Schönberg-Cotta Family 2 v. The Draytons and the Davenants 2 v.
S. T. COLERIDGE: The Poems 1 v.
WILKIE COLLINS: After Dark 1 v. Hide and Seek 2 v. A Plot in Private Life 1 v. The Dead Secret 2 v. The Woman in White 2 v. Basil 1 v. No Name 3 v. Antonina 2 v. Armadale 3 v.
"COMETH UP AS A FLOWER," AUTHOR OF: Cometh up as a Flower 1 v. Not wisely, but too well 2 v.
FENIMORE COOPER: The Spy (w. portr.) 1 v. The Two Admirals 1 v. Jack O'Lantern 1 v.
THE TWO COSMOS 1 v.
MISS CRAIK: Lost and Won 1 v. Faith Unwin's Ordeal 1 v. Leslie Tyrrell 1 v. Winifred's Wooing and other Tales 1 v.
MISS CUMMINS: The Lamplighter 1 v. Mabel Vaughan 1 v. El Fureidîs 1 v. Haunted Hearts 1 v.
DE FOE: Robinson Crusoe 1 v.
CHARLES DICKENS: The Pickwick Club (w. portr.) 2 v. American Notes 1 v. Oliver Twist 1 v. Nicholas Nickleby 2 v. Sketches 1 v. Martin Chuzzlewit 2 v. A Christmas Carol; the Chimes; the Cricket 1 v. Master Humphrey's Clock 3 v. Pictures from Italy 1 v. The Battle of Life; the Haunted Man 1 v. Dombey and Son 3 v. Copperfield 3 v. Bleak House 4 v. A Child's History of England (2 v. 8" 27 Ngr.). Hard Times 1 v. Little Dorrit 4 v. A Tale of two Cities 2 v. Hunted Down; the Uncommercial Traveller 1 v. Great Expectations 2 v. Christmas Stories 1 v. Our Mutual Friend 4 v. Somebody's Luggage; Mrs. Lirriper's Lodgings; Mrs. Lirriper's Legacy 1 v. Doctor Marigold's Prescriptions; Mugby Junction 1 v. No Thoroughfare 1 v.
B. DISRAELI: Coningsby 1 v. Sybil 1 v. Contarini Fleming (w. portr.) 1 v. Alroy 1 v. Tancred 2 v. Venetia 2 v. Vivian Grey 2 v. Henrietta Temple 1 v.
DIXON: Lord Bacon 1 v. The Holy Land 2 v. New America 2 v.
MISS A. B. EDWARDS: Barbara's History 2 v. Miss Carew 2 v. Hand and Glove 1 v. Half a Million of Money 2 v.
MRS. EDWARDS: Archie Lovell 2 v.
ELIOT: Scenes of Clerical Life 2 v. Adam Bede 2 v. The Mill on the Floss 2 v. Silas Marner 1 v. Romola 2 v. Felix Holt 2 v.
THE STORY OF ELIZABETH 1 v.
ESSAYS AND REVIEWS 1 v.
FRANK FAIRLEGH: or, Scenes from the Life of a Private Pupil 2 v.
"PAUL FERROLL," AUTHOR OF: Paul Ferroll 1 v. Year after Year 1 v. Why Paul Ferroll killed his Wife 1 v.
FIELDING: Tom Jones 2 v.

COLLECTION

OF

BRITISH AUTHORS.

VOL. 679.

ANTONINA BY WILKIE COLLINS.

IN TWO VOLUMES.

VOL. II.

ANTONINA;

OR,

THE FALL OF ROME.

A ROMANCE OF THE FIFTH CENTURY.

BY

WILKIE COLLINS,
AUTHOR OF "THE WOMAN IN WHITE."

IN TWO VOLUMES.
VOL. II.

LEIPZIG

BERNHARD TAUCHNITZ

1863.

ANTONINA;

OR,

THE FALL OF ROME.

CHAPTER I.

The Famine.

THE end of November is approaching. Nearly a month has elapsed since the occurrence of the events mentioned in the last Chapter, yet still the Gothic lines stretch round the city walls. Rome, that we left haughty and luxurious even while ruin threatened her at her gates, has now suffered a terrible and warning change. As we approach her again, woe, horror, and desolation have already gone forth to shadow her lofty palaces and to darken her brilliant streets.

Over Pomp that spurned it, over Pleasure that defied it, over Plenty that scared it in its secret rounds, the spectre Hunger has now risen triumphant at last. Day by day has the city's insufficient allowance of food been more and more sparingly doled out; higher and higher has risen the value of the coarsest and simplest provision; the hoarded supplies that pity and charity have already bestowed to cheer the sinking people, have reached their utmost limits. For the rich, there is still corn in the city — treasure of food to be bartered for treasure of gold. For the poor, man's natural nourishment exists no more; the season of famine's loathsome feasts, the first days of the sacrifice of choice to necessity, have darkly and irretrievably begun.

It is morning. A sad and noiseless throng is advancing over the cold flagstones of the Great Square, before the Basilica of St. John Lateran. The members of the assembly speak in whispers. The weak are tearful — the strong are gloomy — they all move with slow and languid gait, and hold in their arms their dogs or other domestic animals. On the outskirts of the crowd march the enfeebled guards of the city, grasping in their rough hands rare, favourite birds of gaudy plumage and melodious note, and followed by children and young girls vainly and piteously entreating that their favourites may be restored.

This strange procession pauses, at length, before a mighty cauldron slung over a great fire in the middle of the Square, round which stand the city butchers with bare knives, and the trustiest men of the Roman legions with threatening weapons. A proclamation is then repeated, commanding the populace who have no money left to purchase food, to bring up their domestic animals to be boiled together over the public furnace, for the sake of contributing to the public support.

The next minute, in pursuance of this edict, the dumb favourites of the crowd passed from the owner's caressing hand into the butcher's ready grasp. The faint cries of the animals, starved like their masters, mingled for a few moments with the sobs and lamentations of the women and children, to whom the greater part of them belonged. For, in this the first stage of their calamities that severity of hunger which extinguishes pity and estranges grief was unknown to the populace; and though fast losing spirit, they had not yet sunk to the depths of ferocious despair, which even now were invisibly opening between them. A thousand pangs were felt, a thousand humble tragedies were acted in the brief moments of separation between guardian and charge. The child snatched its last kiss of the bird that had sung over its bed; the dog looked its last entreaty for protection from the mistress who had once never met it without a caress. Then came the short interval of agony and death, then the steam rose fiercely from the greedy cauldron, and then the people for a time dispersed; the sorrowful to linger near the confines of the fire, and the hungry to calm their impatience by a visit to the neighbouring church.

The marble aisles of the noble Basilica held a gloomy congregation. Three small candles were alone lighted on the high altar. No sweet voices sang melodious anthems or exulting hymns. The monks, in hoarse tones and monotonous harmonies, chanted the penitential psalms. Here and there knelt a figure clothed in mourning robes, and absorbed in secret prayer; but over the majority of the assembly, either blank despondency or sullen inattention universally prevailed.

As the last dull notes of the last psalm died away among the lofty recesses of the church a procession of pious Christians appeared at the door and advanced slowly to the altar. It was composed both of men and women bare-footed, clothed in black garments, and with ashes scattered over their dishevelled hair. Tears flowed from their eyes, and they beat their breasts as they bowed their foreheads on the marble pavement of the altar steps.

This humble public expression of penitence under the calamity that had now fallen on the city was, however, confined only to its few really religious inhabitants, and commanded neither sympathy nor attention from the heartless and obstinate population of Rome. Some still cherished the delusive hope of assistance from the Court at Ravenna; others believed that the Goths would ere long impatiently abandon their protracted blockade, to stretch their ravages over the rich and unprotected fields of southern Italy. But the same blind confidence in the lost terrors of the Roman name, the same fierce and reckless determination to defy the Goths to the very last, sustained the sinking courage and suppressed the despondent emotions of the great mass of the suffering people; from the beggar who prowled for garbage, to the patrician who sighed over his new and unwelcome nourishment of simple bread.

While the penitents who formed the procession above described were yet engaged in the performance of their unnoticed and unshared duties of penance and prayer, a priest ascended the great pulpit of the Basilica, to attempt the ungrateful task of preaching patience and piety to the hungry multitude at his feet.

He began his sermon by retracing the principal occurrences in Rome since the beginning of the Gothic blockade. He touched cautiously upon the first event that stained the annals of the besieged city — the execution of the widow of the Roman general Stilicho, on the unauthorised suspicion that she had held treasonable communication with Alaric and the invading army; he noticed lengthily the promises of assistance transmitted from Ravenna, after the perpetration of that ill-omened act. He spoke admiringly of the skill displayed by the government in making the necessary and immediate reductions in the daily supplies of food; he lamented the terrible scarcity which followed, too inevitably, those seasonable reductions. He pronounced an eloquent eulogium on the noble charity of Læta, the widow of the emperor Gratian, who, with her mother, devoted the store of provisions obtained by their imperial revenues to succouring, at that important juncture, the starving and desponding poor: he admitted the new scarcity consequent on the dissipation of Læta's stores; deplored the present necessity of sacrificing the domestic animals of the citizens; condemned the enormous prices now demanded for the last remnants of wholesome food that were garnered up; announced it as the firm persuasion of every one that a few days more would bring help from Ravenna; and ended his address by informing his auditory that as they had suffered so much already, they could patiently suffer a little more, and that, if after this they were so ill-fated as to sink under their calamities, they would feel it a noble consolation to die in the cause of Catholic and Apostolic Rome, and would assuredly be canonised as saints and martyrs by the next generation of the pious in the first interval of fertile and restoring peace.

Flowing as was the eloquence of this oration, it yet possessed not the power of inducing one among those whom it addressed to forget the sensation of his present suffering and to fix his attention on the vision of future advantage, spread before all listeners by the fluent priest. With the same murmurs of querulous complaint, and the same expressions of impotent hatred and defiance of the Goths, which had fallen from them as they entered the church, the populace now departed from it, to receive from the city officers the stinted allowance of repugnant food, prepared for their hunger from the cauldron in the public square.

And see, already from other haunts in the neighbouring quarter of Rome their fellow-citizens press onward at the given signal, to meet them round the cauldron's sides! The languid sentinel, released from duty, turns his gaze from the sickening prospect of the Gothic camp, and hastens to share the public meal; the baker starts from sleeping on his empty counter, the beggar rises from his kennel in the butcher's vacant outhouse, the slave deserts his place by the smouldering kitchen fire — all hurry to swell the numbers of the guests that are bidden to the wretched feast. Rapidly and confusedly, the congregation in the Basilica pours through its lofty gates; the priests and penitents retire from the altar's foot, and in the great church, so crowded but a few moments before, there now only remains the figure of a solitary man.

Since the commencement of the service, neither addressed nor observed, this lonely being has faltered round the circle of the congregation, gazing long and wistfully over the faces that met his view. Now that the sermon is ended, and the last lingerer has quitted the church, he turns from the spot whence he has anxiously watched the different members of the departing throng, and feebly crouches down on his knees at the base of a pillar that is near him. His eyes are hollow, and his cheeks are wan; his thin gray hairs are few and fading on his aged head. He makes no effort to follow the crowd and partake their sustenance; no one is left behind to urge, no one returns to lead him to the public meal. Though weak and old, he is perfectly forsaken in his loneliness, perfectly unsolaced in his grief; his friends have lost all trace of him; his enemies have ceased to fear or to hate him now. As he crouches by the pillar alone, he covers his forehead with his pale, palsied hands, his dim eyes fill with bitter tears, and such expressions as these are ever and anon faintly audible in the intervals of his heavy sighs: — "Day after day! Day after day! And my lost one is not found! my loved and wronged one is not restored! Antonina! Antonina!"

Some days after the public distribution of food in the square of St. John Lateran, Vetranio's favourite freedman might have been observed pursuing his way homeward, sadly and slowly, to his master's palace.

It was not without cause that the pace of the intelligent Carrio was funereal, and his expression disconsolate. Even during the short period that had elapsed since the scene in the Basilica already described, the condition of the city had altered fearfully for the worse. The famine advanced with giant strides; every succeeding hour endued it with new vigour, every effort to repel it served but to increase its spreading and overwhelming influence. One after another the pleasures and pursuits of the city declined beneath the dismal oppression of the universal ill, until the public spirit in Rome became moved alike in all classes by one gloomy inspiration — a despairing defiance of the famine and the Goths.

The freedman entered his master's palace neither saluted nor welcomed by the once obsequious slaves in the outer lodge. Neither harps nor singing boys, neither woman's ringing laughter nor man's bacchanalian glee, now woke the echoes in the lonely halls. The pulse of pleasure seemed to have throbbed its last in the joyless being of Vetranio's altered household.

Hastening his steps as he entered the mansion, Carrio passed into the chamber where the senator awaited him.

On two couches, separated by a small table, reclined the lord of the palace and his pupil and companion at Ravenna, the once sprightly Camilla. Vetranio's open brow had contracted a clouded and severe expression; and he neither regarded nor addressed his visitor, who, on her part, remained as silent and as melancholy as himself. Every trace of the former characteristics of the gay, elegant voluptuary and the lively, prattling girl seemed to have completely vanished. On the table between them stood a large bottle, containing Falernian wine, and a vase, filled with a little watery soup, in the middle of which floated a small dough cake, sparingly sprinkled with common herbs. As for the usual accompaniments of Vetranio's luxurious privacy, they were nowhere to be seen. Poems, pictures, trinkets, lutes, all were absent. Even the "inestimable kitten of the breed most worshipped by the ancient Egyptians" appeared no more. It had been stolen, cooked, and eaten by a runaway slave, who had already bartered its ruby collar for a lean parrot and the unroasted half of the carcase of a dog.

"I lament to confess it, oh estimable patron, but my mission has failed," observed Carrio, producing from his cloak several bags of money and boxes of jewels, which he carefully deposited on the table. "The Prefect has himself assisted in searching the public and private granaries, and has arrived at the conclusion that not a handful of corn is left in the city. I offered publicly in the market-place five thousand sestertii for a living cock and hen, but was told that the race had long since been exterminated, and that, as money would no longer buy food, money was no longer desired by the poorest beggar in Rome. There is no more even of the hay I yesterday purchased to be obtained for the most extravagant bribes. Those still possessing the smallest supplies of provision guard and hide them with the most jealous care. I have done nothing but obtain for the consumption of the few slaves who yet remain faithful in the house this small store of dogs' hides, reserved from the public distribution of some days since in the square of the Basilica of St. John."

And the freedman, with an air of mingled triumph and disgust, produced as he spoke his provision of dirty skins.

"What supplies have we still left in our possession?" demanded Vetranio, after drinking a deep draught of the Falernian, and motioning his servant to place his treasured burdens out of sight.

"I have hidden in a secure receptacle, for I know not how soon hunger may drive the slaves to disobedience," rejoined Carrio, "seven bags of hay, three baskets stocked with salted horse-flesh, a sweetmeat-box filled with oats, and another with dried parsley; the rare Indian singing birds are still preserved inviolate in their aviary, there is a great store of spices, and some bottles of the Nightingale Sauce yet remain."

"What is the present aspect of the city?" interrupted Vetranio, impatiently.

"Rome is as gloomy as a subterranean sepulchre,"

replied Carrio, with a shudder. "The people congregate in speechless and hungry mobs, at the doors of their houses and the corners of the streets; the sentinels at the ramparts totter on their posts; women and children are sleeping exhausted on the very pavements of the churches; the theatres are emptied of actors and audience alike; the baths resound with cries for food and curses on the Goths; thefts are already committed in the open and unguarded shops; and the barbarians remain fixed in their encampments, unapproached by our promised legions from Ravenna, neither assaulting us in our weakness, nor preparing to raise the blockade! Our situation grows more and more perilous — I have great hopes in our store of provisions; but —"

"Cast your hopes to the Court at Ravenna, and your beasts' provender to the howling mob!" cried Vetranio with sudden energy. "It is now too late to yield; if the next few days bring us no assistance, the city will be a human shamble! And think you that I, who have already lost in this public suspension of social joys my pleasures, my employments, and my companions, will wait serenely for the lingering and ignoble death that must then threaten us all? No! it shall never be said that I died starving with the herd, like a slave that his master deserts! Though the plates in my banquetting hall must now be empty, my vases and wine-cups shall yet sparkle for my guests! There is still wine in the cellar, and spices and perfumes remain in the larder stores! I will invite my friends to a last feast; a saturnalia in a city of famine; a banquet of death, spread by the jovial labours of Silenus and his fauns! Though the Parcæ have woven for me the destiny of a dog, it is the hand of Bacchus that shall sever the fatal thread!"

His cheeks were flushed, his eyes sparkled; all the mad energy of his determination appeared in his face as he spoke. He was no longer the light, amiable, smooth-tongued trifler; but a moody, reckless, desperate man, careless of every obligation and pursuit which had hitherto influenced the easy surface of his patrician life. The startled Camilla, who had as yet preserved a melancholy silence, ran towards him with affrighted looks and undissembled tears. Carrio stared in vacant astonishment on his master's disordered countenance; and, forgetting his bundle of dog skins, suffered them to drop unheeded on the floor. A momentary silence followed, which was suddenly interrupted by the abrupt entrance of a fourth person, pale, trembling and breathless, who was no other than Vetranio's former visitor, the Prefect Pompeianus.

"I bid you welcome to my approaching feast of brimming wine-cups and empty dishes!" cried Vetranio, pouring the sparkling Falernian into his empty glass. "The last banquet given in Rome, ere the city is annihilated, will be mine! The Goths and the famine shall have no part in my death! Pleasure shall preside at my last moments, as it has presided at my whole life! I will die like Sardanapalus, with my loves and my treasures around me, and the last of my guests who remains proof against our festivity, shall set fire to *my* palace, as the kingly Assyrian set fire to *his!*"

"This is no season for jesting," exclaimed the Prefect, staring round him with bewildered eyes and colourless checks. "Our miseries are but dawning as yet! In the next street lies the corpse of a woman, and — horrible omen! — a coil of serpents is wreathed about her neck! We have no burial-place to receive her, and the thousands who may die like her, ere assistance arrives! The city sepulchres outside the walls, are in the hands of the Goths. The people stand round the body, in a trance of horror, for they have now discovered a fatal truth we would fain have concealed from them;" here the Prefect paused, looked round affrightedly on his listeners, and then added in low trembling tones:

"The citizens are lying dead from famine in the streets of Rome!"

CHAPTER II.

The City and the Gods.

WE return once more to the Gothic encampment, in the suburbs eastward of the Pincian Gate, and to Hermanric and the warriors under his command, who are still posted at that particular position on the great circle of the blockade.

The movements of the young chieftain from place to place, expressed, in their variety and rapidity, the restlessness that was agitating his mind. He glanced back frequently from the warriors around him to the remote and opposite quarter of the suburbs, occasionally directing his eyes towards the western horizon, as if anxiously awaiting the approach of some particular hour of the coming night. Weary at length of pursuing occupations which evidently irritated rather than soothed his impatience, he turned abruptly from his companions, and advancing towards the city, paced slowly backwards and forwards over the waste ground between the suburbs and the walls of Rome.

At intervals he still continued to examine the scene around him. A more dreary prospect than now met his view, whether in earth or sky, can hardly be conceived.

The dull sunless day was fast closing, and the portentous heaven gave promise of a stormy night. Thick, black layers of shapeless cloud, hung over the whole firmament, save at the western point; and here lay a streak of pale, yellow light, enclosed on all sides by the firm, ungraduated, irregular edges of the masses of gloomy vapour around it. A deep silence hung over the whole atmosphere. The wind was voiceless among the steady trees. The stir and action in the being of nature and the life of man seemed enthralled, suspended, stifled. The air was laden with a burdensome heat; and all things on earth, animate and inanimate, felt the oppression that weighed on them from the higher elements. The people who lay gasping for breath in the famine-stricken city, and the blades of grass that drooped languidly on the dry sward beyond the walls, owned its enfeebling influence alike.

As the hours wore on and night stealthily and gradually advanced, a monotonous darkness overspread, one after another, the objects discernible to Hermanric from the solitary ground he still occupied. Soon the great city faded into one vast, impenetrable shadow, while the suburbs and the low country around them, vanished in the thick darkness that gathered almost perceptibly over the earth. And now the sole object distinctly visible was the figure of a weary sentinel, who stood on the frowning rampart immediately above the rifled wall, and whose drooping figure, propped upon his weapon, was indicated in hard relief against the thin, solitary streak of light still shining in the cold and cloudy wastes of the western sky.

But as the night still deepened, this one space of light, faded, contracted, vanished; and with it disappeared the sentinel and the line of rampart on which he was posted. The rule of the darkness now became universal. Densely and rapidly it overspread the whole city with startling suddenness; as if the fearful destiny now working its fulfilment in Rome, had forced the external appearances of the night into harmony with its own woeboding nature.

Then, as the young Goth still lingered at his post of observation, the long, low, tremulous, absorbing roll of thunder afar off became grandly audible. It seemed to proceed from a distance almost incalculable; to be sounding from its cradle in the frozen north; to be journeying about its ice-girdled chambers in the lonely poles. It deepened rather than interrupted the dreary mysterious stillness of the atmosphere. The lightning, too, had a summer softness in its noiseless and frequent gleam. It was not the fierce lightning of winter, but a warm, fitful brightness, almost fascinating in its light, rapid recurrence, tinged with the glow of heaven, and not with the glare of hell.

There was no wind — no rain; and the air was as hushed as if it slept over chaos in the infancy of a new creation.

Among the various objects displayed, instant by instant, by the rapid lightning to the eyes of Hermanric, the most easily and most distinctly visible was the broad surface of the rifted wall. The large, loose stones, scattered here and there at its base, and the overhanging lid of its broad rampart, became plainly though fitfully apparent in the brief moments of their illumination. The lightning had played for sometime over that structure of the fortifications, and the bare ground that stretched immediately beyond them, when the smooth prospect which it thus gave by glimpses to view, was suddenly checquered by a flight of birds appearing from one of the lower divisions of the wall, and flitting uneasily to and fro at one spot before its surface.

As moment after moment the lightning continued to gleam, so the black forms of the birds were visible to the practised eye of the Goth — perceptible, yet evanescent, as sparks of fire, or flakes of snow —

whirling confusedly and continually about the spot whence they had evidently been startled by some unimaginable interruption. At length, after a lapse of some time, they vanished as suddenly as they had appeared, with shrill notes of affright which were audible even above the continuous rolling of the thunder; and immediately afterwards, when the lightning alternated with the darkness, there appeared to Hermanric in the part of the wall where the birds had been first disturbed, a small red gleam, like a spark of fire lodged in the surface of the structure. Then this was lost; a longer obscurity than usual prevailed in the atmosphere, and when the Goth gazed eagerly through the next succession of flashes, they showed him the momentary and doubtful semblance of a human figure, standing erect on the stones at the base of the wall.

Hermanric started with astonishment. Again the lightning ceased. In the ardour of his anxiety to behold more, he strained his eyes with the vain hope of penetrating the obscurity around him. The darkness seemed interminable. Once again the lightning flashed brilliantly out. He looked eagerly towards the wall — the figure was still there.

His heart throbbed quickly within him, as he stood irresolute on the spot he had occupied since the first peal of thunder had struck upon his ear. Were the light and the man — one seen but for an instant; the other, still perceptible — mere phantoms of his erring sight, dazzled by the quick recurrence of atmospheric changes through which it had acted? Or, did he indubitably behold a human form; and had he really observed a material light? Some strange treachery, some dangerous mystery, might be engendering in the besieged city, which it would be his duty to observe and unmask. He drew his sword; and, at the risk of being observed through the lightning, and heard during the pauses in the thunder, by the sentinel on the wall, resolutely advanced to the very foot of the fortifications of hostile Rome.

He heard no sound, perceived no light, observed no figure, as, after several unsuccessful attempts to reach the place where they stood, he at length paused at the loose stones which he knew were heaped at the base of the wall. The next moment he was so close to it, that he could pass his sword-point over parts of its rugged surface. He had scarcely examined thus, a space of more than ten yards, before his weapon encountered a sharp, jagged edge; and a sudden presentiment assured him instantly, that he had found the spot where he had beheld the momentary light, and that he stood on the same stone which had been afterwards occupied by the figure of the man.

After an instant's hesitation, he was about to mount higher on the loose stones, and examine more closely the irregularity he had just discovered in the wall, when a vivid flash of lightning, unusually prolonged, showed him, obstructing at scarcely a yard's distance his onward path, the figure he had already distantly beheld from the plain behind.

There was something inexpressibly fearful in his viewless vicinity, during the next moment of darkness, to this silent, mysterious form, so imperfectly shown by the lightning that quivered over its half-revealed proportions. Every pulse in the body of the Goth seemed to pause as he stood, with ready weapon, looking into the gloomy darkness, and waiting for the next flash. It came — and displayed to him the man's fierce eyes glaring steadily down upon his face — another gleam; and he beheld his haggard finger placed upon his lip in token of silence — a third; and he saw the arm of the figure pointing towards the plain behind him; and then in the darkness that followed, a hot breath played upon his ear, and a voice whispered to him, through a pause in the rolling of the thunder: — "Follow me."

The next instant Hermanric felt the momentary contact of the man's body, as with noiseless steps he passed him on the stones. It was no time to deliberate or to doubt. He followed close upon the stranger's footsteps, gaining glimpses of his dark form moving onward before, whenever the lightning briefly illuminated the scene, until they arrived at a clump of trees, not far distant from the houses in the suburbs that were occupied by the Goths under his own command.

Here the stranger paused before the trunk of a tree which stood between the city wall and himself, and drew from beneath his ragged cloak a small lantern, carefully covered with a piece of cloth, which he now removed, and holding the light high above his head, regarded the Goth with a steady and anxious scrutiny.

Hermanric attempted to address him first, but the appearance of the man, barely visible though it was by the feeble light of his lantern, was so startling and repulsive, that the half-formed words died away on his lips. The face of the stranger was of a ghastly paleness; his hollow cheeks were seamed with deep wrinkles; and his eyes glared with an expression of ferocious suspicion. One of his arms was covered with old bandages, stiff with coagulated blood, and hung paralysed at his side. The hand that held the light trembled, so that the lantern containing it vibrated continuously in his unsteady grasp. His limbs were lank and shrivelled almost to deformity, and it was with evident difficulty that he stood upright on his feet. Every member of his body seemed to be wasting with a gradual death, while his expression, ardent and forbidding, was stamped with all the energy of manhood, and all the daring of youth.

It was Ulpius! The wall was passed! The breach was made good!

After a protracted examination of Hermanric's countenance and attire, the man, with an imperious expression, strangely at variance with his faltering voice, thus addressed him: —

"You are a Goth?"

"I am," rejoined the young chief; "and you are —"

"A friend to the Goths," was the quick answer.

An instant of silence followed. The dialogue was then again begun by the stranger.

"What brought you alone to the base of the ramparts?" he demanded, and an expression of ungovernable apprehension shot from his eyes as he spoke.

"I saw the appearance of a man in the gleam of the lightning," answered Hermanric. "I approached it, to assure myself that my eyes had not deluded me, to discover —"

"There is but one man of your nation who shall discover whence I came, and what I would obtain," interrupted the stranger fiercely; "that man is Alaric, your King."

Surprise, indignation, and contempt appeared in the features of the Goth, as he listened to such a declaration from the helpless outcast before him. The man perceived it, and motioning to him to be silent, again addressed him.

"Listen!" cried he, "I have that to reveal to the leader of your forces, which will stir the hearts of every man in your encampment, if you are trusted with the secret after your King has heard it from my lips! Do you still refuse to guide me to his tent?"

Hermanric laughed scornfully.

"Look on me," pursued the man, bending forward, and fixing his eyes with savage earnestness upon his listener's face. "I am alone, old, wounded, weak, — a stranger to your nation, — a famished and a helpless man! Should I venture into your camp — should I risk being slain for a Roman by your comrades — should I dare the wrath of your imperious ruler without a cause?"

He paused; and then still keeping his eyes on the Goth, continued in lower and more agitated tones:—

"Deny me your help, I will wander through your camp till I find your King! Imprison me, your violence will not open my lips! Slay me, you will gain nothing by my death! But aid me, and to the latest moment of your life you will rejoice in the deed! I have words of terrible import for Alaric's ear, — a secret, in the gaining of which I have paid the penalty thus!"

He pointed to his wounded arm. The solemnity of his voice; the rough energy of his words; the stern determination of his aspect; the darkness of the night that was round them; the rolling thunder that seemed to join itself to their discourse: the impressive mystery of their meeting under the city walls, all began to exert their powerful and different influences over the mind of the Goth, changing insensibly the sentiments at first inspired in him by the man's communications. He hesitated, and looked round doubtfully towards the lines of the camp.

There was a long silence, which was again interrupted by the stranger.

"Guard me, chain me, mock at me if you will!" he cried, with raised voice and flashing eyes, "but lead me to Alaric's tent! I swear to you, by the thunder pealing over our heads, that the words I would speak to him will be more precious in his eyes, than the brightest jewel he could ravish from the coffers of Rome."

Though visibly troubled and impressed, Hermanric still hesitated.

"Do you yet delay?" exclaimed the man, with contemptuous impatience. "Stand back! I will pass on by myself into the very heart of your camp! I entered on my project alone — I will work its fulfilment without help! Stand back!"

And he moved past Hermanric in the direction of the suburbs, with the same look of fierce energy on his withered features which had marked them so strikingly at the outset of his extraordinary interview with the young chieftain.

The daring devotion to his purpose, the reckless toiling after a dangerous and doubtful success, manifested in the words and actions of one so feeble and unaided as the stranger, aroused in the Goth that sentiment of irrepressible admiration, which the union of moral and physical courage inevitably awakens. In addition to the incentive to aid the man thus created, an ardent curiosity to discover his secret filled the mind of Hermanric, and further powerfully inclined him to conduct his determined companion into Alaric's presence — for by such proceeding only could he hope, after the man's firm declaration that he would communicate in the first instance to no one but the King, to penetrate ultimately the object of his mysterious errand. Animated, therefore, by such motives as these, he called to the stranger to stop; and briefly communicated to him his willingness to conduct him instantly to the presence of the leader of the Goths.

The man intimated by a sign his readiness to accept the offer. His physical powers were now evidently fast failing; but he still tottered painfully onward as they moved to the head-quarters of the camp, muttering and gesticulating to himself almost incessantly. Once only did he address his conductor during their progress; and then with a startling abruptness of manner, and in tones of vehement anxiety and suspicion, he demanded of the young Goth if he had ever examined the surface of the city wall before that night. Hermanric replied in the negative; and they then proceeded in perfect silence.

Their way lay through the line of encampment to the westward, and was imperfectly lighted by the flame of an occasional torch, or the glow of a distant watch-fire. The thunder had diminished in frequency, but had increased in volume; faint breaths of wind soared up fitfully from the west; and already a few raindrops fell slowly to the thirsty earth. The warriors not actually on duty at the different posts of observation, had retired to the shelter of their tents; none of the thousand idlers and attendants attached to the great army appeared at their usual haunts; even the few voices that were audible sounded distant and low. The night-scene here, among the ranks of the invaders of Italy, was as gloomy and repelling as on the solitary plains before the walls of Rome.

Ere long the stranger perceived that they had reached a part of the camp more thickly peopled, more carefully illuminated, more strongly fortified, than that through which they had already passed; and the liquid, rushing sound of the waters of the rapid Tiber now caught his suspicious and attentive ear. They still moved onward a few yards; and then paused suddenly before a tent, immediately surrounded by many others, and occupied at all its approaches by groups of richly-armed warriors. Here Hermanric stopped an instant to parley with the sentinel, who after a short delay raised the outer covering of the entrance to the tent, and the moment after the Roman adventurer beheld himself standing by his conductor's side in the presence of the Gothic King.

The interior of Alaric's tent was lined with skins, and illuminated by one small lamp, fastened to the centre pole that supported its roof. The only articles of furniture in the place were some bundles of furs flung down loosely on the ground, and a large, rudely-carved wooden chest, on which stood a polished human skull, hollowed into a sort of clumsy wine-cup. A thoroughly Gothic ruggedness of aspect, a stately northern simplicity prevailed over the spacious tent, and was indicated not merely in its thick shadows, its calm lights, and its freedom from pomp and glitter, but even in the appearance and employment of its remarkable occupant.

Alaric was seated alone on the wooden chest already described, contemplating with bent brow and abstracted gaze some old Runic characters, traced upon the carved surface of a brass and silver shield, full five feet high, which rested against the side of the tent. The light of the lamp falling upon the polished surface of the weapon — rendered doubly bright by the dark skins behind it — was reflected back upon the figure of the Goth chief. It glowed upon his ample cuirass; it revealed his firm lips, slightly curled by an expression of scornful triumph; it displayed the grand, muscular formation of his arm, which rested — clothed in tightly-fitting leather — upon his knee; it partly brightened over his short, light hair; and glittered steadily in his fixed, thoughtful, manly eyes, which were just perceptible beneath the partial shadow of his contracted brow, while it left the lower part of his body and his right hand, which was supported on the head of a huge, shaggy dog couching at his side, shadowed almost completely by the thick skins heaped confusedly against the sides of the wooden chest. He was so completely absorbed in the contemplation of the Runic characters, traced among the carved figures on his immense shield, that he did not notice the entry of Hermanric and the stranger until the growl of the watchful dog suddenly disturbed him in his occupation. He looked up instantly; his quick, penetrating glance dwelling for a moment on the young chieftain, and then resting steadily and inquiringly on his companion's feeble and mutilated form.

Accustomed to the military brevity and promptitude exacted by his commander in all communications addressed to him by his inferiors, Hermanic, without waiting to be interrogated or attempting to preface or excuse his narrative, shortly related the conversation that had taken place between the stranger and himself on the plain near the Pincian Gate; and then waited respectfully to receive the commendation, or incur the rebuke of the King, as the chance of the moment might happen to decide.

After again fixing his eyes in severe scrutiny on the person of the Roman, Alaric spoke to the young warrior in the Gothic language thus: —

"Leave the man with me — return to your post; and there await whatever commands it may be necessary that I should despatch to you to-night."

Hermanric immediately departed. Then, addressing the stranger for the first time, and speaking in the Latin language, the Gothic leader briefly and significantly intimated to his unknown visitant that they were now alone.

The man's parched lips moved, opened, quivered; his wild, hollow eyes brightened till they absolutely gleamed, but he seemed incapable of uttering a word; his features became horribly convulsed, the foam gathered about his lips, he staggered forward and would have fallen to the ground, had not the King instantly caught him in his strong grasp, and placed him on the wooden chest that he had hitherto occupied himself.

"Can a starving Roman have escaped from the beleaguered city?" muttered Alaric, as he took the skull cup, and poured some of the wine it contained down the stranger's throat.

The liquor was immediately successful in restoring composure to the man's features, and consciousness to his mind. He raised himself from the seat, dashed off the cold perspiration that overspread his forehead, and stood upright before the King — the solitary powerless old man before the vigorous lord of thousands, in the midst of his warriors — without a tremor in his steady eye, or a prayer for protection on his haughty lip.

"I, a Roman," he began, "come from Rome against which the invader wars with the weapon of famine, to deliver the city, her people, her palaces, and her treasures into the hands of Alaric the Goth."

The King started, looked on the speaker for a moment, and then turned from him in impatience and contempt.

"I lie not," pursued the enthusiast, with a calm dignity that affected even the hardy sensibilities of the Gothic hero. "Eye me again! Could I come starved, shrivelled, withered thus from any place but Rome? Since I quitted the city an hour has hardly past, and by the way that I left it the forces of the Goths may enter it to-night."

"The proof of the harvest is in the quantity of the grain, not in the tongue of the husbandman. Show me your open gates, and I will believe that you have spoken truth," retorted the King, with a rough laugh.

"I betray the city," resumed the man, sternly, "but on one condition; grant it me, and —"

"I will grant you *your life*," interrupted Alaric, haughtily.

"My life!" cried the Roman, and his shrunken form seemed to expand, and his tremulous voice to grow firm and steady in the very bitterness of his contempt, as he spoke. "My life! I ask it not of your power! The wreck of my body is scarce strong enough to preserve it to me a single day! I have no home, no loves, no friends, no possessions! I live in Rome a solitary in the midst of the multitude, a pagan in a city of apostates! What is my life to *me?* I cherish it but for the service of the gods, whose instruments of vengeance against the nation that has denied them I would make you and your hosts! If you slay me, it is a sign to me from them that I am worthless in their cause. I shall die content."

He ceased. The king's manner, as he listened to him, gradually lost the bluntness and carelessness that had hitherto characterised it, and assumed an attention and a seriousness more in accordance with his high station and important responsibilities. He began to regard the stranger as no common renegade, no ordinary spy, no shallow impostor, who might be driven from his tent with disdain; but as a man important enough to be heard, and ambitious enough to be distrusted. Accordingly, he resumed the seat from which he had risen during the interview, and calmly desired his new ally to explain the condition, on the granting of which depended the promised betrayal of the city of Rome.

The pain-worn and despondent features of Ulpius became animated by a glow of triumph, as he heard the sudden mildness and moderation of the king's demand; he raised his head proudly, and advanced a few steps, as he thus loudly and abruptly resumed:

"Assure to me the overthrow of the Christian churches, the extermination of the Christian priests, and the universal revival of the worship of the gods, and this night shall make you master of the chief city of the empire you are labouring to subvert!"

The boldness, the comprehensiveness, the insanity of wickedness displayed in such a proposition, and emanating from such a source, so astounded the mind of Alaric, as to deprive him for the moment of speech. The stranger, perceiving his temporary inability to answer him, broke the silence which ensued, and continued:

"Is my condition a hard one? A conqueror is all-powerful; he can overthrow the worship, as he can overthrow the government of a nation. What matters it to you, while empire, renown, and treasure are yours, what deities the people adore? Is it a great price to pay for an easy conquest, to make a change which threatens neither your power, your fame, nor your wealth? Do you marvel that I desire from you such a revolution as this? I was born for the gods, in their service I inherited rank and renown, for their cause I have suffered degradation and woe, for their restoration I will plot, combat, die! Assure me then, by oath, that with a new rule you will erect an ancient worship, and through my secret inlet to the city, I will introduce men enough of the Goths to murder with security the sentinels at the guard-houses, and open the gates of Rome to the numbers of your whole invading forces. Think not to despise the aid of a man unprotected and unknown! The citizens will never yield to your blockade; you shrink from risking the dangers of an assault; the legions of Ravenna are reported on their way hitherward — outcast as I am, I tell it to you here, in the midst of your camp — your speediest assurance of success rests on my discovery and on *me!*"

The king started suddenly from his seat: — "What fool or madman," he cried, fixing his eyes in furious scorn and indignation on the stranger's face, "prates to me about the legions of Ravenna and the dangers of an assault? Think you, renegade, that your city could have resisted me had I chosen to storm it on the first day when I encamped before its walls? Know you that your effeminate soldiery have laid aside the armour of their ancestors, because their puny bodies are too feeble to bear its weight; and that the half of my army here, trebles the whole number of the guards of Rome? Now, while you stand before me, I have but to command, and the city shall be annihilated with fire and sword, without the aid of one of the herd of traitors cowering beneath the shelter of its ill-defended walls!"

As Alaric spoke thus, some invisible agency seemed to crush, body and mind, the lost wretch whom he addressed. The shock of such an answer as he now heard seemed to strike him idiotic, as a flash of lightning strikes with blindness. He regarded the king with a bewildered stare, waving his hand tremulously backwards and forwards before his face, as if to clear some imaginary darkness off his eyes; then his arm fell helpless by his side, his head drooped upon his breast, and he moaned out in low, vacant tones, "The restoration of the gods — that is the condition of conquest — the restoration of the gods!"

"I come not hither to be the tool of a frantic and forgotten priesthood," cried Alaric disdainfully. "Wherever I meet with your accursed idols I will melt them down into armour for my warriors and shoes for my horses; I will turn your temples into granaries, and cut your images of wood into billets for the watchfires of my hosts!"

"Slay me, and be silent!" groaned the man, staggering back against the side of the tent, and shrinking under the merciless words of the Goth, like a slave under the lash.

"I leave the shedding of such blood as yours to your fellow Romans," answered the king; "they alone are worthy of the deed!"

No syllable of reply now escaped the stranger's lips, and after an interval of silence Alaric resumed, in tones divested of their former fiery irritation, and marked by a solemn earnestness that conferred irresistible dignity and force on every word that he uttered.

"Behold the characters engraven there!" said he, pointing to the shield; "they trace the curse denounced by Odin against the great oppressor, Rome! Once these words made part of the worship of our fathers; the worship has long since vanished, but the words remain; they seal the eternal hatred of the people of the north to the people of the south; they contain the spirit of the great destiny that has brought me to the walls of Rome. Citizen of a fallen empire, the measure of your crimes is full! The voice of a new nation calls through me for the freedom of the earth, which was made for man, and not for Romans! The rule that your ancestors won by strength, their posterity shall no longer keep by fraud. For two hundred years, hollow and unlasting truces have alternated with long and bloody wars between your people and mine. Remembering this, remembering the wrongs of the Goths in their settlements in Thrace, the murder of the Gothic youths in the towns of Asia, the massacre of the Gothic hostages in Aquileia, I come — chosen by the supernatural decrees of heaven — to assure the freedom and satisfy the wrath of my nation, by humbling at its feet the power of tyrannic Rome! It is not for battle and bloodshed that I am encamped before yonder walls. It is to crush to the earth, by famine and woe, the pride of your people and the spirit of your rulers; to tear from you your hidden wealth, and to strip you of your boasted honour; to overthrow by oppression the oppressors of the world; to deny you the glories of a resistance, and to impose on you the shame of a submission. It is for this that I now abstain from storming your city, to encircle it with an immovable blockade!"

As the declaration of his great mission burst thus from the lips of the Gothic king, the spirit of his lofty ambition seemed to diffuse itself over his outward form. His noble stature, his fine proportions, his commanding features, became invested with a simple, primeval grandeur. Contrasted as he now was with the shrunken figure of the spirit-broken stranger, he looked almost sublime.

A succession of protracted shudderings ran through the Pagan's frame, but he neither wept nor spoke. The unavailing defence of the Temple of Serapis, the defeated revolution at Alexandria, and the abortive intrigue with Vetranio, were now rising on his memory, to heighten the horror of his present and worst overthrow. Every circumstance connected with his desperate passage through the rifted wall revived, fearfully vivid on his mind. He remembered all the emotions of his first night's labour in the darkness, all the miseries of his second night's torture under the fallen brickwork, all the woe, danger, and despondency, that accompanied his subsequent toil — persevered in under the obstructions of a famine-weakened body, and a helpless arm — until he passed, in delusive triumph, the last of the hindrances in the long-laboured breach. One after another, these banished recollections returned to his memory, as he listened to Alaric's rebuking words, — reviving past infirmities, opening old wounds, inflicting new lacerations. But, saving the shudderings that still shook his body, no outward witness betrayed the inward torment that assailed him. It was too strong for human words; too terrible for human sympathy; — he suffered it in brute silence. Monstrous as was his plot, the moral punishment of its attempted consummation was severe enough to be worthy of the projected crime.

After watching the man for a few minutes more, with a glance of pitiless disdain, Alaric summoned one of the warriors in attendance; and having previously commanded him to pass the word to the sentinels, authorising the stranger's free passage through the encampment, he then turned; and, for the last time, addressed him as follows: —

"Return to Rome, through the hole whence, reptile-like, you emerged! — and feed your starving citizens with the words you have heard in the barbarian's tent!"

The guard approached, led him from the presence of the king, issued the necessary directions to the sentinels, and left him to himself. Once he raised his eyes in despairing appeal to the heaven frowning over his head; but still, no word, or tear, or groan, escaped him. He moved slowly on, through the thick darkness; and turning his back on the city, passed, careless whither he strayed, into the streets of the desolate and dispeopled suburbs.

CHAPTER III.
Love Meetings.

Who that has looked on a threatening and tempestuous sky, has not felt the pleasure of discovering unexpectedly a small spot of serene blue, still shining among the stormy clouds? The more unwilling the eye has wandered over the gloomy expanse of the rest of the firmament, the more gladly does it finally rest on the little oasis of light which meets at length its weary gaze, and which, when it was dispersed over the whole heaven, was perhaps only briefly regarded with a careless glance. Contrasted with the dark and mournful hues around it, even that small spot of blue gradually acquires the power of investing the wider and sadder prospect with a certain interest and animation that it did not before possess — until the mind recognises in the surrounding atmosphere of storm, an object adding variety to the view — a spectacle whose mournfulness may interest as well as repel.

Was it with sensations resembling these, (applied however, rather to the mind than to the eye) that the reader perused those pages devoted to Hermanric and Antonina? Does the happiness there described now appear to him to beam through the stormy progress of the narrative, as the spot of blue beams through the gathering clouds? Did that small prospect of brightness present itself, at the time, like a garden of repose amid the waste of fierce emotions which encompassed it? Did it encourage him, when contrasted with what had gone before, to enter on the field of gloomier interest which was to follow? If, indeed, it has thus affected him, if he can still remember the scene at the farm-house beyond the suburbs, with emotions such as these, he will not now be unwilling to turn again for a moment from the gathering clouds to the spot of blue, — he will not deny us an instant's digression from Ulpius and the city of famine, to Antonina and the lonely plains.

During the period that has elapsed since we left her, Antonina has remained secure in her solitude; happy in her well-chosen concealment. The few straggling Goths who at rare intervals appeared in the neighbourhood of her sanctuary, never intruded on its peaceful limits. The sight of the ravaged fields and emptied granaries of the deserted little property, sufficed invariably to turn their marauding steps in other directions. Day by day ran smoothly and swiftly onward for the gentle usurper of the abandoned farmhouse. In the narrow round of its gardens and protecting woods, was comprised for her the whole circle of the pleasures and occupations of her new life.

The simple stores left in the house, the fruits and vegetables to be gathered in the garden sufficed amply for her support. The pastoral solitude of the place had in it a quiet, dreamy fascination; a novelty; an unwearying charm; — after the austere loneliness to which her former existence had been subjected in Rome. And, when evening came, and the sun began to burnish the tops of the western trees, then after the

calm emotions of the solitary day, came the hour of
absorbing cares and happy expectations — ever the
same, yet ever delighting and ever new. Then the
rude shutters were carefully closed; the open door was
shut and barred; the small light — now invisible to
the world without — was joyfully kindled; and then,
the mistress and author of these preparations resigned
herself to await, with pleased anxiety, the approach
of the guest for whose welcome they were designed.

And never did she expect the arrival of that treasured
companion in vain. Hermanric remembered his
promise to repair constantly to the farm-house, and
performed it with all the constancy of love, and all
the enthusiasm of youth. When the sentinels under
his command were arranged in their order of watching
for the night, and the trust reposed in him by his
superiors exempted his actions from superintendence
during the hours of darkness that followed, he left the
camp, passed through the desolate suburbs, and gained
the dwelling where the young Roman awaited him —
returning before day-break to receive the communications
regularly addressed to him, at that hour, by his
inferior in the command.

Thus, false to his nation, yet true to the new
Egeria of his thoughts and actions — traitor to the
requirements of vengeance and war, yet faithful to the
interests of tranquillity and love — did he seek, night
after night, Antonina's presence. His passion, though
it denied him to his warrior duties, wrought no deteriorating
change in his disposition. All that it altered

in him, it altered nobly. It varied and exalted his rude emotions; for it was inspired, not alone by the beauty and youth that he *saw*, but by the pure thoughts, the artless eloquence that he *heard*. And *she* — the forsaken daughter, the source whence the northern warrior derived those new and higher sensations that had never animated him until now — regarded her protector, her first friend and companion as her first love, with a devotion which, in its mingled and exalted nature may be imagined by the mind, but can be but imperfectly depicted by the pen. It was a devotion created of innocence and gratitude, of joy and sorrow, of apprehension and hope. It was too fresh, too unworldly, to own any upbraidings of artificial shame, any self-reproaches of artificial propriety. It resembled in its essence, though not in its application, the devotion of the first daughters of the Fall to their brother-lords.

But it is now time that we return to the course of our narrative; although, ere we again enter on the stirring and rapid present, it will be necessary for a moment more, to look back in another direction, to the eventful past.

But it is not on peace, beauty, and pleasure, that our observation now fixes itself. It is to anger, disease, and crime — to the unappeasable and unwomanly Goisvintha, that we now revert.

Since the day when the violence of her conflicting emotions had deprived her of consciousness, at the moment of her decisive triumph over the scruples of Hermanric and the destiny of Antonina, a raging fever had visited on her some part of those bitter sufferings that she would fain have inflicted on others. Part of the time she lay in a raving delirium; part of the time in helpless exhaustion; but she never forgot, whatever the form assumed by her disease, the desperate purpose in the pursuit of which she had first incurred it. Slowly and doubtfully, her vigour at length returned to her, and with it strengthened and increased the fierce ambition of vengeance that absorbed her lightest thoughts, and governed her most careless actions.

Report informed her of the new position, on the line of blockade, on which Hermanric was posted; and only enumerated as the companions of his sojourn, the warriors sent thither under his command. But, though thus persuaded of the separation of Antonina and the Goth, her ignorance of the girl's fate rankled unintermittingly in her savage heart. Doubtful whether she had permanently reclaimed Hermanric to the interests of vengeance and bloodshed, vaguely suspecting that he might have informed himself in her absence of Antonina's place of refuge, or direction of flight; still resolutely bent on securing the death of her victim, wherever she might have strayed, she awaited with trembling eagerness that day of restoration to available activity and strength, which would enable her to resume her influence over the Goth, and her machinations against the safety of the fugitive girl. The time of her final and long expected recovery, was the very day preceding the stormy night we have already described, and her first employment of her renewed energy, was to send word to the young Goth of her intention of seeking him at his encampment ere the evening closed.

It was this intimation which caused the inquietude mentioned as characteristic of the manner of Hermanric, at the commencement of the preceding Chapter. The evening there described, was the first that saw him deprived, through the threatened visit of Goisvintha, of the anticipation of repairing to Antonina, as had been his wont, under cover of the night; for to slight his kinswoman's ominous message, was to risk the most fatal of discoveries. Trusting to the delusive security of her sickness, he had hitherto banished the unwelcome remembrance of her existence from his thoughts. But, now that she was once more capable of exertion and of crime, he felt that if he would preserve the secret of Antonina's hiding-place and the security of Antonina's life, he must remain to oppose force to force, and stratagem to stratagem, when Goisvintha sought him at his post, even at the risk of inflicting by his absence from the farm-house, all the pangs of anxiety and apprehension on the lonely girl.

Absorbed in such reflections as these; longing to depart, yet determined to remain, he impatiently awaited Goisvintha's approach, until the rising of the storm with its mysterious and all-engrossing train of events, forced his thoughts and actions into a new channel. When, however, his interviews with the stranger and the Gothic king were passed, and he had returned as he had been bidden to his appointed sojourn in the camp, his old anxieties, displaced but not destroyed, resumed their influence over him. He demanded eagerly of his comrades if Goisvintha had arrived in his absence; and received the same answer in the negative from each.

As he now listened to the melancholy rising of the wind; to the increasing loudness of the thunder; to the shrill cries of the distant night-birds hurrying to shelter, emotions of mournfulness and awe possessed themselves of his heart. He now wondered that any events, however startling, however appalling, should have had the power to turn his mind for a moment, from the dreary contemplations that had engaged it at the close of day. He thought of Antonina, solitary and helpless, listening to the tempest in affright, and watching vainly for his long-delayed approach. His fancy arrayed before him dangers, plots, and crimes, robed in all the horrible exaggerations of a dream. Even the quick monotonous dripping of the rain-drops outside, aroused within him dark and indefinable forebodings of ill. The passion that had hitherto created for him new pleasures, was now fulfilling the other half of its earthly mission, and causing him new pains.

As the storm strengthened, as the darkness lowered deeper and deeper, so did his inquietude increase, until at length it mastered the last feeble resistance of his wavering firmness. Persuading himself that after having delayed so long, Goisvintha would now refrain from seeking him until the morrow; and that all communications from Alaric, had they been despatched, would have reached him ere this; unable any longer to combat his anxiety for the safety of Antonina; determined to risk the worst possibilities, rather than be absent at such a time of tempest and peril from the farm-house, he made a last visit to the stations of the watchful sentinels, and quitted the camp for the night.

CHAPTER IV.
The Huns.

MORE than an hour after Hermanric had left the encampment, a man hurriedly entered the house set apart for the young chieftain's occupation. He made no attempt to kindle either light or fire, but sat down in the principal apartment, occasionally whispering to himself in a strange and barbarous tongue.

He had remained but a short time in possession of his comfortless solitude, when he was intruded on by a camp follower, bearing a small lamp, and followed closely by a woman, who, as he started up and confronted her, announced herself as Hermanric's kinswoman, and eagerly demanded an interview with the Goth.

Haggard and ghastly though it was from recent suffering and long agitation, the countenance of Goisvintha (for it was she) appeared absolutely attractive, as it was now opposed by the lamp-light to the face and figure of the individual she addressed. A flat nose, a swarthy complexion, long, coarse, tangled locks of deep black hair, a beardless retreating chin, and small, savage, sunken eyes, gave a character almost bestial to this man's physiognomy. His broad, brawny shoulders overhung a form that was as low in stature as it was athletic in build; you looked on him and saw the sinews of a giant strung in the body of a dwarf. And yet this deformed Hercules was no solitary error of Nature — no extraordinary exception to his fellow-beings; but the actual type of a whole race, stunted and repulsive as himself. He was a Hun.

This savage people, the terror even of their barbarous neighbours, living without government, laws, or religion, possessed but one feeling in common with the human race — the instinct of war. Their historical career may be said to have begun with their early conquests in China, and to have proceeded in their first victories over the Goths, who regarded them as demons, and fled their approach. The hostilities thus commenced between the two nations, were at length suspended by the temporary alliance of the conquered people with the empire, and subsequently ceased in the gradual fusion of the interests of each, in one animating spirit — detestation of Rome.

By this bond of brotherhood, the Goths and the Huns became publicly united, though still privately at enmity — for the one nation remembered its former defeats, as vividly as the other remembered its former victories. With various disasters, dissensions, and successes, they ran their career of battle and rapine — sometimes separate, sometimes together, until the period of our romance, when Alaric's besieging forces numbered among the ranks of their barbarian auxiliaries a body of Huns, who, unwillingly admitted to the title of Gothic allies, were dispersed about the army in subordinate stations, and of whom, the individual above described was one of those contemptuously favoured by promotion to an inferior command, under Hermanric, as a Gothic chief.

An expression of aversion, but not of terror, passed over Goisvintha's worn features as she approached the barbarian, and repeated her desire to be conducted to Hermanric's presence. For the second time, however, the man gave her no answer. He burst into a shrill, short laugh, and shook his huge shoulders in clumsy derision.

The woman's cheek reddened for an instant, and then turned again to livid paleness, as she thus resumed: —

"I came not hither to be mocked by a barbarian, but to be welcomed by a Goth! Again I ask you, where is my kinsman, Hermanric?"

"Gone!" — cried the Hun. And his laughter grew more wild and discordant as he spoke.

A sudden tremor ran through Goisvintha's frame, as she marked the manner of the barbarian and heard his reply. Repressing with difficulty her anger and agitation, she continued, with apprehension in her eyes and entreaty in her tones: —

"Whither has he gone? Wherefore has he departed? — I know that the hour I appointed for our meeting here has long passed; but I have suffered a sickness of many weeks; and when, at evening, I prepared to set forth, my banished infirmities seemed suddenly to return to me again. I was borne to my bed. But, though the women who succoured me bid me remain and repose, I found strength in the night to escape them, and through storm and darkness to come hither alone — for I was determined, though I should perish for it, to seek the presence of Hermanric, as I had promised by my messengers. You, that are the companion of his watch, must know whither he is gone. Go to him, and tell him what I have spoken. I will await his return!"

"His business is secret," sneered the Hun. "He has departed, but without telling me whither. How should I, that am a barbarian, know the whereabouts of an illustrious Goth? It is not for me to know his actions, but to obey his words!"

"Jeer not about your obedience" — returned Goisvintha, with breathless eagerness — "I say to you again, you know whither he is gone, and you must tell me for what he has departed. You obey *him* — there is money to make you obey *me!*"

"When I said his business was secret, I lied not," said the Hun, picking up with avidity the coins she flung to him — "but he has not kept it secret from *me!* The Huns are cunning! Aha, ugly and cunning!"

Suspicion, the only refined emotion in a criminal heart, half discovered to Goisvintha, at this moment, the intelligence that was yet to be communicated. No word, however, escaped her, while she signed the barbarian to proceed.

"He has gone to a farm-house on the plains beyond the suburbs behind us. He will not return till day-break," continued the Hun, tossing his money carelessly in his great, horny hands.

"Did you *see* him go?" gasped the woman.

"I tracked him to the house," returned the barbarian. "For many nights I watched and suspected him — to-night I saw him depart. It is but a short time since I returned from following him. The darkness did not delude me; the place is on the high road from the suburbs — the first bye-path to the westward leads to its garden gate. — I know it! I have discovered his secret! I am more cunning than he!"

"For what did he seek the farm-house at night?" demanded Goisvintha after an interval, during which she appeared to be silently fixing the man's last speech in her memory, "Are you cunning enough to tell me that?"

"For what do men venture their safety and their lives; their money and their renown?" laughed the barbarian. "They venture them for women! There is a girl at the farm-house; I saw her at the door when the chief went in!"

He paused; but Goisvintha made no answer. Remembering that she was descended from a race of women who slew their wounded husbands, brothers, and sons, with their own hands, when they sought them after battle, dishonoured by a defeat; remembering that the fire of the old ferocity of such ancestors as these still burnt at her heart; remembering all that she had hoped from Hermanric, and had plotted against Antonina; estimating in all its importance the shock of the intelligence she now received, we are alike unwilling and unable to describe her emotions at this moment. For some time, the stillness in the room was interrupted by no sounds but the rolling of the thunder without; the quick, convulsive respiration of Goisvintha; and the clinking of the money which the Hun still continued to toss mechanically from hand to hand.

"I shall reap good harvest of gold and silver after to-night's work," pursued the barbarian, suddenly breaking the silence. "*You* have given me money to speak — when the chief returns and hears that I have discovered him, *he* will give me money to be silent. I shall drink to-morrow with the best men in the army, Hun though I am!"

He returned to his seat as he ceased, and began beating in monotonous measure, with one of his pieces of money on the blade of his sword, some chorus of a favourite drinking song; while Goisvintha, standing pale and breathless near the door of the chamber, looked down on him with fixed vacant eyes. At length a deep sigh broke from her; her hands involuntarily clenched themselves at her side; her lips moved with a bitter smile; then, without addressing another word to the Hun, she turned, and softly and stealthily quitted the room.

The instant she was gone, a sudden change arose in the barbarian's manner. He started from his seat, a scowl of savage hatred and triumph appeared on his shaggy brows, and he paced to and fro through the chamber like a wild beast in his cage. "I shall tear him from the pinnacle of his power at last!" he whispered fiercely to himself. "For what I have told her this night, his kinswoman will hate him — I knew it while she spoke! For his desertion of his post, Alaric may dishonour him; may banish him; may hang him! His fate is at my mercy; I shall rid myself nobly of him and his command! More than all the rest of his nation I loathe this Goth! I will be by when they drag him to the tree, and taunt him with his shame as he has taunted me with my deformity." Here he paused to laugh in complacent approval of his project, quickening his steps and hugging himself joyfully in the barbarous exhilaration of his triumph.

His secret meditations had thus occupied him for some time longer, when the sound of a footstep was audible outside the door. He recognised it instantly, and called softly to the person without to approach. At the signal of his voice a man entered — less athletic in build, but in deformity the very counterpart of himself. The following discourse was then immediately held between the two Huns, the new-comer beginning it thus: —

"Have you tracked him to the door?"

"To the very threshold."

"Then his downfall is assured! I have seen Alaric."

"We shall trample him under our feet! — this boy, who has been set over us that are his elders, because he is a Goth and we are Huns! But what of Alaric? How did you gain his ear!"

"The Goths round his tent, scoffed at me as a savage, and swore that I was begotten between a demon and a witch. But I remembered the time when these boasters fled from their settlements; when our tribes mounted their black steeds and hunted them like beasts! Aha, their very lips were pale with fear in those days."

"Speak of Alaric — our time is short;" interrupted the other fiercely.

"I answered not a word to their taunts," resumed his companion, "but I called out loudly that I was a Gothic ally; that I brought messages to Alaric; and that I had the privilege of audience like the rest. My voice reached the ears of the king: he looked forth from his tent, and beckoned me in. I saw his hatred of my nation lowering in his eye as we looked on one another, but I spoke with submission and in a soft voice. I told him how his chieftain whom he had set over us, secretly deserted his post; I told him how we had seen his favoured warrior for many nights, journeying towards the suburbs; how on this night, as on others before, he had stolen from the encampment, and how you had gone forth to track him to his lurking-place."

"Was the tyrant angered?"

"His cheeks reddened, and his eyes flashed, and his fingers trembled round the hilt of his sword while I spoke! When I ceased, he answered me that I lied. He cursed me for an infidel Hun, who had slandered a Christian chieftain. He threatened me with hanging! I cried to him to send messengers to our quarters to prove the truth, ere he slew me. He commanded a warrior to return hither with me. When we arrived, the most Christian chieftain was nowhere to be beheld — none knew whither he had gone! We turned back again to the tent of the king; his warrior whom he honoured, spoke the same words to him as the Hun whom he despised. Then the wrath of Alaric rose. 'This very night,' he cried, 'did I with my own lips direct him to await my commands with vigilance at his appointed post! I would visit such disobedience with punishment on my own son! Go, take with you others of your troop — your comrade who has tracked him will guide you to his hiding-place — bring him prisoner into my tent!' Such were his words! Our companions wait us without — lest he should escape let us depart without delay."

"And if he should resist us," cried the other, leading the way eagerly towards the door; "what said the king, if he should resist us?"

"Slay him with your own hands."

4*

CHAPTER V.

The Farm House.

As the night still advanced, so did the storm increase. On the plains in the open country its violence was most apparent. Here no living voices jarred with the dreary music of the elements; no flaming torches opposed the murky darkness, or imitated the glaring lightning. The thunder pursued uninterruptedly its tempest symphony, and the fierce wind joined it, swelling into wild harmony, when it rushed through the trees, as if in their waving branches it struck the chords of a mighty harp.

In the small chamber of the farm-house sat together Hermanric and Antonina, listening in speechless attention to the increasing tumult of the storm.

The room and its occupants were imperfectly illuminated by the flame of a smouldering wood fire. The little earthenware lamp hung from its usual place in the ceiling, but its oil was exhausted, and its light was extinct. An alabaster vase of fruit lay broken by the side of the table, from which it had fallen unnoticed to the floor. No other articles of ornament appeared in the apartment. Hermanric's downcast eyes and melancholy unchanging expression, betrayed the gloomy abstraction in which he was absorbed. With one hand clasped in his, and the other resting with her head on his shoulder, Antonina listened attentively to the alternate rising and falling of the wind. Her beauty had grown fresher and more woman-like during her sojourn at the farm-house. Cheerfulness and hope seemed to have gained, at length, all the share in her being assigned to them by nature at her birth. Even at this moment of tempest and darkness, there was more of wonder and awe than of agitation and affright in her expression, as she sat hearkening, with flushed cheek and brightened eye, to the progress of the nocturnal storm.

Thus engrossed by their thoughts, Hermanric and Antonina remained silent in their little retreat, until the reveries of both were suddenly interrupted by the snapping asunder of the bar of wood which secured the door of the room, the stress of which, as it bent under the repeated shocks of the wind, the rotten spar was too weak to sustain any longer. There was something inexpressibly desolate in the flood of rain, wind, and darkness that seemed instantly to pour into the chamber, through the open door, as it flew back violently on its frail hinges. Antonina changed colour, and shuddered involuntarily, as Hermanric hastily rose and closed the door again, by detaching its rude latch from the sling which held it when not wanted for use. He looked round the room as he did so, for some substitute for the broken bar, but nothing that was fit for the purpose immediately met his eye, and he muttered to himself as he returned impatiently to his seat, "While we are here to watch it, the latch is enough: it is new and strong."

He seemed on the point of again relapsing into his former gloom, when the voice of Antonina arrested his attention, and aroused him for the moment from his thoughts.

"Is it in the power of the tempest to make *you*, a warrior of a race of heroes, thus sorrowful and sad?" she asked, in accents of gentle reproach. "Even I, as I look on these walls that are so eloquent of my happiness, and sit by you whose presence makes that happiness, can listen to the raging storm, and feel no heaviness over my heart! What is there to either of us in the tempest, that should oppress us with gloom? Does not the thunder of the winter night come from the same heaven as the sunshine of the summer day? You are so young, so generous, so brave, — you have loved, and pitied, and succoured *me*, — why should the night language of the sky cast such sorrow and such silence over you?"

"It is not from sorrow that I am silent," replied Hermanric, with a constrained smile, "but from weariness with much toil in the camp."

He stifled a sigh as he spoke. His head returned to its old downcast position. The struggle between his assumed carelessness and his real inquietude was evidently unequal. As she looked fixedly on him, with the vigilant eye of affection, the girl's countenance saddened with his. She nestled closer to his side and resumed the discourse in anxious and entreating tones.

"It is haply the strife between our two nations which has separated us already, and may separate us again, that thus oppresses you," said she, "but think, as I do, of the peace that must come, and not of the warfare that now is. Think of the pleasures of our past days, and of the happiness of our present moments, — thus united, thus living, loving, hoping for each other; and, like me, you will doubt not of the future that is in preparation for us both! The season of tranquillity may return with the season of spring. The serene heaven will then be reflected on a serene country and a happy people; and in those days of sunshine and peace, will any hearts among all the glad population be more joyful than ours?"

She paused a moment. Some sudden thought or recollection heightened her colour and caused her to hesitate ere she proceeded. She was about at length to continue, when a peal of thunder, louder than any which had preceded it, burst threateningly over the house and drowned the first accents of her voice. The wind moaned loudly; the rain splashed against the door; the latch rattled long and sharply in its socket. Once more Hermanric rose from his seat, and approaching the fire, placed a fresh log of wood upon the dying embers. His dejection seemed now to communicate itself to Antonina, and as he reseated himself by her side, she did not address him again.

Thoughts dreary and appalling beyond any that had occupied it before, were rising in the mind of the Goth. His inquietude at the encampment in the suburbs was tranquillity itself, compared to the gloom which now oppressed him. All the evaded dues of his nation, his family, and his calling; all the suppressed recollections of the martial occupations he had slighted, and the martial enmities he had disowned, now revived avengingly in his memory. Yet, vivid as these remembrances were, they weakened none of those feelings of passionate devotion to Antonina, by which their influence within him had hitherto been overcome. They existed with them — the old recollections with the new emotions — the stern rebukings of the warrior's nature with the anxious forebodings of the lover's heart. And now, his mysterious meeting with Ulpius; Goisvintha's unexpected restoration to health; the dreary rising and furious progress of the night tempest, began to impress his superstitious mind as a train of unwonted and meaning incidents, destined to mark the fatal return of his kinswoman's influence over his own actions and Antonina's fate.

One by one, his memory revived with laborious minuteness every incident that had attended his different interviews with the Roman girl, from the first night when she had strayed into his tent, to the last happy evening that he had spent with her at the deserted farm-house. Then tracing further backwards the course of his existence, he figured to himself his meeting with Goisvintha among the Italian Alps; his presence at the death of her last child, and his solemn engagement, on hearing her recital of the massacre at Aquileia, to avenge her on the Romans with his own hands. Roused by these opposite pictures of the past, his imagination peopled the future with images of Antonina again endangered, afflicted, and forsaken;

with visions of the impatient army, spurred at length into ferocious action, making universal havoc among the people of Rome, and forcing him back for ever into their avenging ranks. No decision for resistance or resignation to flight presented itself to his judgment. Doubt, despair, and apprehension held unimpeded sway over his impressible, but inactive faculties. The night itself, as he looked forth on it, was not more dark; the wild thunder, as he listened to it, not more gloomy; the name of Goisvintha, as he thought on it, not more ominous of evil, than the sinister visions that now startled his imagination, and oppressed his weary mind.

There was something indescribably simple, touching, and eloquent in the very positions of Hermanric and Antonina as they now sat together, — the only members of their respective nations who were united in affection and peace, — in the lonely farm-house. Both the girl's hands were clasped over Hermanric's shoulder, and her head rested on them, turned from the door towards the interior of the room, and so displaying her rich, black hair in all its luxuriance. The head of the Goth was still sunk on his breast, as though he were wrapped in a deep sleep, and his hands hung listlessly side by side over the scabbard of his sheathed sword, which lay across his knees. The fire flamed only at intervals, the fresh log that had been placed on it not having been thoroughly kindled as yet. Sometimes the light played on the white folds of Antonina's dress; sometimes over the bright surface of Hermanric's cuirass, which he had removed and laid by his side on the ground; sometimes over his sword, and his hands, as they rested on it; but it was not sufficiently powerful or lasting to illuminate the room, the walls and corners of which it left in almost complete darkness.

The thunder still pealed from without, but the rain and wind had partially lulled. The night hours had moved on more swiftly than our narrative of the events that marked them. It was now midnight.

No sound within the room reached Antonina's ear but the quick rattling of the door-latch, shaken in its socket by the wind. As one by one the moments journeyed slowly onward, it made its harsh music with as monotonous a regularity as though it were moved by their progress, and kept pace with their eternal march. Gradually the girl found herself listening to this sharp, discordant sound, with all the attention she could have bestowed at other times on the ripple of a distant rivulet, or the soothing harmony of a lute, when, just as it seemed adapting itself most easily to her senses, it suddenly ceased, and the next instant a gust of wind, like that which had rushed through the open door on the breaking of its rotten bar, waved her hair about her face, and fluttered the folds of her light, loose dress. She raised her head and whispered tremulously to Hermanric; —

"The door is again open — the latch has given way!"

The Goth started from his reverie, and looked up

hastily. At that instant the rattling of the latch recommenced as suddenly as it had ceased, and the air of the room recovered its former tranquillity.

"Calm yourself, beloved one," said Hermanric gently; "your fancy has misled you — the door is safe."

He parted back her dishevelled hair caressingly as he spoke. Incapable of doubting the lightest word that fell from his lips, and hearing no suspicious or unwonted sound in the room, she never attempted to justify her suspicions. As she again rested her head on his shoulder, a vague misgiving oppressed her heart, and drew from her an irrepressible sigh; but she gave her apprehensions no expression in words. After listening for a moment more to assure himself of the security of the latch, the Goth resumed insensibly the contemplations from which he had been disturbed; once more his head drooped, and again his hands returned mechanically to their old listless position, side by side, on the scabbard of his sword.

The faint, fickle flames still rose and fell, gleaming here and sinking there, the latch sounded sharply in its socket, the thunder yet uttered its surly peal, but the wind was now subsiding into fainter moans, and the rain began to splash faintly and more faintly against the shutters without. To the watchers in the farmhouse nothing was altered to the eye, and little to the ear. Fatal security! The last few minutes had darkly determined their future destinies — in their loved and cherished retreat they were now no longer alone.

They heard no stealthy footstep pacing round their dwelling, they saw no fierce eyes peering into the interior of the farm-house through a chink in the shutters, they marked no dusky figure passing through the softly and quickly opened door, and gliding into the darkest corner of the room. Yet, now as they sat together, communing in silence with their young, sad hearts, the threatening figure of Goisvintha stood, shrouded in congenial darkness, under their protecting roof, and in their beloved chamber, rising still and silent almost at their very sides.

Though the fire of her past fever had raged again through her veins, though startling visions of the murders at Aquileia had flashed before her mind as the wild lightning before her eyes, she had traced her way through the suburbs and along the high road, and down the little path to the farm-house gate, without straying, without hesitating. Regardless of the darkness and the storm, she had prowled about the house, had raised the latch, had waited for a loud peal of thunder ere she passed the door, and had stolen shadow-like into the darkest corner of the room, with a patience and a determination that nothing could disturb. And now, when she stood at the goal of her worst wishes, even now, when she looked down upon the two beings by whom she had been thwarted and deceived, her fierce self-possession did not desert her; her lips quivered over her locked teeth, her bosom heaved beneath her drenched garments, but neither sighs nor curses, not even a smile of triumph or a movement of anger escaped her.

She never looked at Antonina; her eyes wandered not for a moment from Hermanric's form. The quickest, faintest gleam of firelight that gleamed over it, was followed through its fitful course by her eager glance, rapid and momentary as itself. Soon her attention fixed wholly upon his hands, as they lay over the scabbard of his sword; and then, slowly and obscurely, a new and fatal resolution sprung up within her. The various emotions pictured in her face became resolved into one sinister expression, and, without removing her eyes from the Goth, she slowly drew from the bosom-folds of her garment a long sharp knife.

The flames alternately trembled into light and subsided into darkness as at first; Hermanric and Antonina yet continued in their old positions, absorbed in their thoughts and in themselves; and still Goisvintha remained unmoved as ever, knife in hand, watchful, steady, silent as before.

But beneath the concealment of her outward tranquillity, raged a contention under which her mind darkened and her heart writhed. Twice she returned the knife to its former hiding-place, and twice she drew it forth again; her cheeks grew paler and paler, she pressed her clenched hand convulsively over her bosom, and leant back languidly against the wall behind her. No thought of Antonina had part in this great strife of secret emotions; her wrath had too much of anguish in it to be wrath against a stranger and an enemy.

After the lapse of a few moments more, her strength returned — her firmness was aroused. The last traces of grief and despair that had hitherto appeared in her eyes vanished from them in an instant. Rage, vengeance, ferocity, lowered over them as she crept stealthily forward to the very side of the Goth; and when the next gleam of fire played upon him — drew the knife fiercely across the back of his hands. The cut was true, strong, and rapid — it divided the tendons from first to last — he was crippled for life.

At that instant the fire touched the very heart of the log that had been laid on it. It crackled gaily; it blazed out brilliantly. The whole room was as brightly illuminated as if a Christmas festival of ancient England had been preparing within its walls!

The warm, cheerful light, showed the Goth the figure of his assassin, ere the first cry of anguish had died away on his lips, or the first start of irrepressible horror ceased to vibrate through his frame. The cries of his hapless companion, as the whole scene of vengeance, treachery, and mutilation, flashed in one terrible instant, before her eyes, seemed not even to reach his ears. Once he looked down upon his helpless hands, when the sword rolled heavily from them to the floor. Then his gaze directed itself immovably upon Goisvintha, as she stood at a little distance from him, with her blood-stained knife, silent as himself.

There was no fury — no defiance — not even the

passing distortion of physical suffering in his features, as he now looked on her. Blank, rigid horror — tearless, voiceless, helpless despair, seemed to have petrified the expression of his face into an everlasting form, unyouthful and unhopeful — as if he had been imprisoned from his childhood, and a voice was now taunting him with the pleasures of liberty, from a grating in his dungeon walls. Not even when Antonina, recovering from her first agony of terror, pressed her convulsive kisses on his cold cheek, entreating him to look on her, did he turn his head, or remove his eyes from Goisvintha's form.

At length, the deep, steady accents of the woman's voice were heard through the desolate silence.

"Traitor in word and thought you may be yet — but traitor in deed you never more shall be!" — she began, pointing to his hands with her knife. "Those hands that have protected a Roman life, shall never grasp a Roman sword, shall never pollute again by their touch a Gothic weapon! — I remembered, as I watched you in the darkness, how the women of my race once punished their recreant warriors, when they fled to them from a defeat. — So have I punished *you!* The arm that served not the cause of sister and sister's children — of king and king's nation — shall serve no other! I am half avenged of the murders at Aquileia, now that I am avenged on *you!* Go, fly with the Roman you have chosen, to the city of her people! Your life as a warrior is at an end!"

He made her no answer. There are emotions the

last of a life — which tear back from nature the strongest barriers that custom raises to repress her, which betray the lurking existence of the first rude social feeling of the primeval days of a great nation in the breasts of their most distant descendants, however widely their acquirements, their prosperities, and their changes may seem to have morally separated them from their ancestors of old. Such were the emotions now awakened in the heart of the Goth. His Christianity, his love, his knowledge of high aims, and his experience of new ideas, sank and deserted him, as though he had never known them. He thought on his mutilated hands, and no other spirit moved within him, but the ancient Gothic spirit of centuries back; the inspiration of his nation's early northern songs, and early northern achievements — the renown of courage, and the supremacy of strength.

Vainly did Antonina, in the midst of the despair that still possessed her, yearn for a word from his lips, or a glance from his eyes; vainly did her trembling fingers — tearing the bandages from her robe — stanch the blood on his wounded hands; vainly did her voice call on him to fly and summon help from his companions in the camp! His mind was far away, brooding over the legends of the battle-fields of his ancestors, remembering how, even in the day of victory, they slew themselves if they were crippled in the fray, how they scorned to exist for other interests than the interests of strife, how they mutilated traitors as Goisvintha had mutilated *him!* Such were the objects that enchained his inward faculties, while his outward senses were still enthralled by the horrible fascination that existed for him, in the presence of the assassin by his side. His very consciousness of his existence, though he moved and breathed, seemed to have ceased.

"You thought to deceive me in my sickness, you hoped to profit by my death" — resumed Goisvintha, returning contemptuously her victim's glance. — "You trusted in the night, and the darkness, and the storm — you were secure in your boldness, in your strength, in the secrecy of this lurking-place that you have chosen for your treachery; but your stratagems and your expectations have failed you! At Aquileia I learnt to be wily and watchful as you! I discovered your desertion of the warriors and the camp; I penetrated the paths to your hiding place; I entered it as softly as I once departed from the dwelling where my children were slain! In my just vengeance I have treated *you* as treacherously as you would have treated *me!* Remember your murdered brother; remember the child I put into your arms wounded, and received from them dead; remember your broken oaths and forgotten promises, and make to your nation, to your duties, and to me, the atonement — the last and the only one — that in my mercy I have left in your power — the atonement of death."

Again she paused, and again no reply awaited her. Still the Goth neither moved nor spoke, and still Antonina — kneeling unconsciously upon the sword, now useless to him for ever — continued to stanch the blood on his hands with a mechanical earnestness, that seemed to shut out the contemplation of every other object from her eyes. The tears streamed incessantly down her cheeks, but she never turned towards Goisvintha, never suspended her occupation.

Meanwhile, the fire still blazed noisily on the cheerful hearth; but the storm, as if disdaining the office of heightening the human horror of the farm-house scene, was rapidly subsiding. The thunder pealed less frequently and less loudly, the wind fell into intervals of noiseless calm, and occasionally the moonlight streamed, in momentary brightness, through the ragged edges of the fast-breaking clouds. The breath of the still morning was already moving upon the firmament of the stormy night.

"Has life its old magic for you yet?" continued Goisvintha, in tones of pitiless reproach. "Have you forgotten, with the spirit of your people, the end for which your ancestors lived? Is not your sword at your feet? Is not the knife in my hand? Do not the waters of the Tiber, rolling yonder to the sea, offer to you the grave of oblivion that all may seek? Die then! In your last hour be a Goth; even to the Romans you are worthless now! Already your comrades have discovered your desertion; will you wait till you are hung for a rebel? Will you live to implore the mercy of your enemies; or, dishonoured and defenceless, will you endeavour to escape? You are of the blood of my family, but again I say it to you — die!"

His pale lips trembled; he looked round for the first time at Antonina, but his utterance struggled ineffectually, even yet, against unyielding despair. He was still silent.

Goisvintha turned from him disdainfully, and approaching the fire sat down before it, bending her haggard features over the brilliant flames. For a few minutes, she remained absorbed in her evil thoughts, but no articulate word escaped her; and when at length she again abruptly broke the silence, it was not to address the Goth, or to fix her eyes on him, as before.

Still cowering over the fire, apparently as regardless of the presence of the two beings whose happiness she had just crushed for ever, as if they had never existed, she began to recite, in solemn, measured, chanting tones, a legend of the darkest and earliest age of Gothic history, keeping time to herself with the knife that she still held in her hand. The malignity in her expression, as she pursued her employment, betrayed the heartless motive that animated it, almost as palpably as the words of the composition she was repeating: thus she now spoke: —

> "The tempest-god's pinions o'ershadow the sky,
> The waves leap to welcome the storm that is nigh,
> Through the hall of old Odin re-echo the shocks
> That the fierce ocean hurls at his rampart of rocks,
> As, alone on the crags that soar up from the sands,
> With his virgin SIONA the young AGNAR stands;
> Tears sprinkle their dew on the sad maiden's cheeks,
> And the voice of the chieftain sinks low while he speaks: —

"'Crippled in the fight for ever;
Number'd with the worse than slain;
Weak, deform'd, disabled! — never
Can I join the hosts again! —
With the battle that is won
AGNAR's earthly course is run!

'When thy shatter'd frame must yield,
If thou seek'st a future field;
When thy arm that sway'd the strife,
Fails to shield thy worthless life;
When thy hands no more afford,
Full employment to the sword;
Then, preserve — respect thy name;
Meet thy death — to live is shame!
Such is Odin's mighty will;
Such commands I now fulfil!'"

At this point in the legend, she paused and turned suddenly to observe its effect on Hermanric. All its horrible application to himself thrilled through his heart. His head drooped, and a low groan burst from his lips. But even this evidence of the suffering she was inflicting failed to melt the iron malignity of Goisvintha's determination.

"Do you remember the death of Agnar?" she cried. "When you were a child, I sung it to you ere you slept, and you vowed as you heard it, that when you were a man, if you suffered his wounds you would die his death! *He* was crippled in a victory, yet he slew himself on the day of his triumph; *you* are crippled in your treachery, and have forgotten your boy's honour, and will live in the darkness of your shame! Have you lost remembrance of that ancient song? You heard it from me in the morning of your years; listen, and you shall hear it to the end, it is the dirge for your approaching death!"

She continued —

"'SIONA, mourn not! — where I go
The warriors feel nor pain nor woe;
They raise aloft the gleaming steel,
Their wounds yet warm, untended heal;
Their arrows bellow through the air
In showers, as they battle there;
In mighty cups their wine is pour'd,
Bright virgins throng their midnight board!

'Yet think not that I die unmov'd;
I mourn the doom that sets me free,
As I think, betroth'd — belov'd,
On all the joys I lose in thee!
To form my boys to meet the fray,
Where'er the Gothic banner streams;
To guard thy night, to glad thy day,
Made all the bliss of AGNAR's dreams —
Dreams that must now be all forgot,
Earth's joys have passed from AGNAR's lot!

'See, athwart the face of light,
Float the clouds of sullen Night!
Odin's warriors watch for me
By the earth-encircling sea!
The waters' dirges howl my knell;
'Tis time I die — Farewell — Farewell!'

"He rose with a smile to prepare for the spring,
He flew from the rock like a bird on the wing;
The sea met her prey with a leap and a roar,
And the maid stood alone by the wave-riven shore!
The winds mutter'd deep with a woe-boding sound,
As she wept o'er the footsteps he'd left on the ground;
And the wild vultures shriek'd, for the chieftain who spread
Their battle-field banquets, was laid with the dead;"

As, with a slow and measured emphasis, Goisvintha pronounced the last lines of the poem she again approached Hermanric. But the eyes of the Goth sought her no longer. She had calmed the emotions that she had hoped to irritate. Of the latter divisions of her legend, those only which were pathetic had arrested the lost chieftain's attention, and the blunted faculties of his heart recovered their old refinement as he listened to them. A solemn composure of love, grief, and pity, appeared in the glance of affection that he now directed on the girl's despairing countenance. Years of good thoughts, an existence of tender cares, an eternity of youthful devotion, spoke in that rapt, momentary, eloquent gaze, and imprinted on his expression a character ineffably beautiful and calm — a nobleness above the human, and approaching the angelic and divine.

Intuitively Goisvintha followed the direction of his eyes, and looked, like him, on the Roman girl's face. A lowering expression of hatred replaced the scorn that had hitherto distorted her passionate features. Mechanically her hand again half raised the knife, and the accents of her wrathful voice once more disturbed the sacred silence of affection and grief.

"Is it for the girl there that you would still live?" she cried, sternly. "I foreboded it, coward, when I first looked on you! I prepared for it, when I wounded you! I made sure, that when my anger again threatened this new ruler of your thoughts and mover of your actions, you should have lost the power to divert it from her again! Think you that, because my disdain has delayed it, my vengeance on her is abandoned? Long since I swore to you that she should die, and I will hold to my purpose! I have punished *you*, I will slay *her!* Can you shield her from the blow to-night, as you shielded her in your tent? You are weaker before me than a child!"

She ceased abruptly, for at this moment a noise of hurrying footsteps and contending voices became suddenly audible from without. As she heard it, a ghastly paleness chased the flush of anger from her cheeks. With the promptitude of apprehension she snatched the sword of Hermanric from under Antonina, and ran it through the staples intended to hold the rude bar of the door. The next instant the footsteps sounded on the garden path, and the next the door was assailed.

The good sword held firm, but the frail barrier that it sustained yielded at the second shock, and fell inwards, shattered, to the floor. Instantly the gap was darkened by human forms, and the fire-light glowed over the repulsive countenances of two Huns who headed the intruders, habited in complete armour and furnished with naked swords.

"Yield yourself prisoner by Alaric's command!" cried one of the barbarians: "or you shall be slain as a deserter where you now stand!"

The Goth had risen to his feet as the door was burst in. The arrival of his pursuers seemed to restore his lost energies, to deliver him at once from an all-powerful thraldom. An expression of triumph and defiance shone over his steady features, when he heard the summons of the Hun. For a moment he stooped towards Antonina, as she clung fainting round him. His mouth quivered and his eye glistened, as he kissed her cold cheek. In that moment all the hopelessness of his position, all the worthlessness of his marred existence, all the ignominy preparing for him when he returned to the camp, rushed over his mind. In that moment the worst horrors of departure and death, the fiercest rackings of love and despair assailed, but did not overcome him. In that moment he paid his final tribute to the dues of affection, and braced for the last time the fibres of manly dauntlessness and Spartan resolve!

The next instant he tore himself from the girl's arms, the old hero-spirit of his conquering nation possessed every nerve in his frame, his eye brightened again gloriously with its lost warrior-light, his limbs grew firm, his face was calm, he confronted the Huns with a mien of authority and a smile of disdain, and, as he presented to them his defenceless breast, not the faintest tremor was audible in his voice, while he cried in accents of steady command —

"Strike! I yield not!"

The Huns rushed forward with fierce cries, and buried their swords in his body. His warm young blood gushed out upon the floor of the dwelling which had been the love-shrine of the heart that shed it. Without a sigh from his lips, or a convulsion on his features, he fell dead at the feet of his enemies; all the valour of his disposition, all the gentleness of his heart, all the vigour of his form, resolved in one humble instant into a senseless and burdensome mass!

Antonina beheld the assassination, but was spared the sight of the death that followed it. She fell insensible by the side of her young warrior — her dress was spotted with his blood, her form was motionless as his own.

"Leave him there to rot! His pride in his superiority will not serve him now — even to a grave!" cried the Hun leader to his companions, as he dried on the garments of the corpse his reeking sword.

"And this woman," demanded one of his comrades, "is she to be liberated or secured?"

He pointed as he spoke to Goisvintha. During the brief scene of the assassination, the very exercise of her faculties seemed to have been suspended. She had never stirred a limb, or uttered a word.

The Hun recognised her as the woman who had questioned and bribed him at the camp. "She is the traitor's kinswoman, and is absent from the tents without leave," he answered. "Take her prisoner to Alaric, she will bear us witness that we have done as he commanded us. As for the girl," he continued, glancing at the blood on Antonina's dress, and stirring her figure carelessly with his foot, "she may be dead too, for she neither moves nor speaks, and may be left like her protector to lie graveless where she is. For us, it is time that we depart — the King is impatient of delay."

As they led her roughly from the house, Goisvintha

shuddered, and attempted to pause for a moment, when she passed the corpse of the Goth. Death, that can extinguish enmities as well as sunder loves, rose awful and appealing, as she looked her last at her murdered brother, and remembered her murdered husband. No tears flowed from her eyes, no groans broke from her bosom; but there was a pang, a last momentary pang of grief and pity at her heart, as she murmured while they forced her away — "Aquileia! Aquileia! have I outlived thee for this!"

The troops retired. For a few minutes silence ruled uninterruptedly over the room where the senseless girl still lay by the side of all that was left to her of the object of her first youthful love. But ere long footsteps again approached the farm-house door, and two Goths, who had formed part of the escort allotted to the Hun, approached the young chieftain's corpse. Quickly and silently they raised it in their arms and bore it into the garden. There they scooped a shallow hole with their swords in the fresh, flower-laden turf, and having laid the body there, they hastily covered it, and rapidly departed without returning to the house.

These men had served among the warriors committed to Hermanric's command. By many acts of frank generosity and encouragement, the young chieftain had won their rough attachment. They mourned his fate, but dared not obstruct the sentence, or oppose the act that determined it. At their own risk they had secretly quitted the advancing ranks of their comrades, to use the last privilege and obey the last dictate of human kindness — and they thought not of the lonely girl, as they now left her desolate, and hurried away to re-assume their appointed stations ere it was too late.

The turf lay caressingly round the young warrior's form; its crushed flowers pressed' softly against his cold cheek; the fragrance of the new morning wafted its pure incense gently about his simple grave! Around him flowered the delicate plants that the hand of Antonina had raised to please his eye. Near him stood the dwelling, sacred to the first and last kiss that he had impressed upon her lips; and about him, on all sides, rose the plains and woodlands that had engrossed, with her image, the devotion of all her dearest thoughts. He lay, in his death, in the midst of the magic circle of the best joys of his life! It was a fitter burial-place for the earthly relics of that bright and generous spirit, than the pit in the carnage-laden battle field, or the desolate sepulchres of a northern land!

CHAPTER VI.
The Guardian Restored.

Not long is the new-made grave left unwatched to the solemn guardianship of Solitude and Night. More than a few minutes have scarcely elapsed since it was dug, yet already human footsteps press its yielding surface, and a human glance scans attentively its small and homely mound.

But it is not Antonina, whom he loved; it is not

Goisvintha, through whose vengeance he was lost, who now looks upon the earth above the young warrior's corpse. It is a stranger, an outcast; a man lost, dishonoured, abandoned — it is the solitary and ruined Ulpius who now gazes with indifferent eyes upon the peaceful garden and the eloquent grave.

In the destinies of woe committed to the keeping of the night, the Pagan had been fatally included. The destruction that had gone forth against the body of the young man who lay beneath the earth, had overtaken the mind of the old man who stood over his simple grave. The frame of Ulpius, with all its infirmities, was still there; but the soul of ferocious patience and unconquerable daring that had lighted it grandly in its ruin, was gone. Over the long anguish of that woful life, the veil of self-oblivion had closed for ever!

He had been dismissed by Alaric, but he had not returned to the city whither he was bidden. Throughout the night he had wandered about the lonely suburbs, striving in secret and horrible suffering for the mastery of his mind. There, did the overthrow of all his hopes from the Goths expand rapidly into the overthrow of the whole intellect that had created his aspirations. There, had reason burst the bonds that had so long chained, perverted, degraded it! At length, wandering hither and thither, he had dragged the helpless body, possessed no longer by the perilous mind, to the farmhouse garden in which he now stood, gazing alternately at the upturned sods of the chieftain's grave, and the red gleam of the fire as it glowed from the dreary room, through the gap of the shattered door.

His faculties were fatally disordered, rather than utterly destroyed. His penetration, his firmness, and his cunning were gone; but a wreck of memory, useless and unmanageable, — a certain capacity for momentary observation, still remained to him. The shameful miscarriage in the tent of Alaric, which had overthrown his faculties, had passed from him as an event that never happened; but he remembered fragments of his past existence; he still retained a vague consciousness of the ruling purpose of his whole life.

These embryo reflections, disconnected and unsustained, flitted to and fro over his dark mind, as luminous exhalations over a marsh, — rising and sinking, harmless and delusive, fitful and irregular. What he remembered of the past he remembered carelessly, viewing it with as vacant a curiosity as if it were the visionary spectacle of another man's struggles, and misfortunes, and hopes; — acting under it as under a mysterious influence, neither the end nor the reason of which he cared to discover. For the *future*, it was to his thoughts a perfect blank. For the *present*, it was a jarring combination of bodily weariness and mental repose.

He shuddered as he stood shelterless under the open heaven. The cold that he had defied in the vaults of the rifted wall, pierced him in the farm-house garden; his limbs, which had resisted repose on the hard journey from Rome to the camp of the Goths, now trembled so that he was fain to rest them on the ground. For a short time he sat glaring with vacant and affrighted eyes upon the open dwelling before him, as though he longed to enter it but dared not. At length the temptation of the ruddy firelight seemed to vanquish his irresolution; he rose with difficulty, and slowly and hesitatingly entered the house.

He had advanced, thief-like, but a few steps, he had felt but for a moment the welcome warmth of the fire, when the figure of Antonina, still extended insensible upon the floor, caught his eye; he approached it with eager curiosity, and, raising the girl on his arm, looked at her with a long and rigid scrutiny.

For some moments no expression of recognition passed his lips or appeared on his countenance, as, with a mechanical, doting gesture of fondness he smoothed her dishevelled hair over her forehead. While he was thus engaged, while the remains of the gentleness of his childhood were thus awfully revived in the insanity of his age, a musical string wound round a small piece of gilt wood, fell from its concealment in her bosom; he snatched it from the ground — it was the fragment of her broken lute, which had never quitted her since the night when, in her innocent grief, she had wept over it in her maiden bedchamber.

Small, obscure, insignificant as it was, this little token touched the fibre in the Pagan's shattered mind which the all-eloquent form and presence of its hapless mistress had failed to reach; his memory flew back instantly to the garden on the Pincian Mount and to his past duties in Numerian's household, but spoke not to him of the calamities he had wreaked since that period on his confiding master. His imagination presented to him at this moment but one image — his servitude in the Christian's abode; and as he now looked on the girl he could regard himself but in one light — as "the guardian restored."

"What does she with her music here?" he whispered apprehensively. "This is not her father's house, and the garden yonder looks not from the summit of the hill!"

As he curiously examined the room, the red spots on the floor suddenly attracted his attention. A panic, a frantic terror seemed instantly to overwhelm him. He rose with a cry of horror, and, still holding the girl on his arm hurried out into the garden trembling and breathless, as if the weapon of an assassin had scared him from the house.

The shock of her rough removal, the sudden influence of the fresh, cold air, restored Antonina to the consciousness of life at the moment when Ulpius, unable to support her longer, laid her against the little heap of turf which marked the position of the young chieftain's grave; her eyes opened wildly; their first glance fixed upon the shattered door and the empty room. She rose from the ground, advanced a few steps towards the house, then paused, rigid, breathless, silent, and, turning slowly, faced the upturned turf.

The grave was all-eloquent of its tenant. His

cuirass, which the soldiers had thought to bury with the body that it had defended in former days, had been overlooked in the haste of the secret interment, and lay partly imbedded in the broken earth, partly exposed to view — a simple monument over a simple grave! Her tearless, dilated eyes looked down on it as though they would number each blade of grass, each morsel of earth by which it was surrounded! Her hair waved idly about her cheeks, as the light wind fluttered it; but no expression passed over her face, no gestures escaped her limbs. Her mind toiled and quivered, as if crushed by a fiery burden; but her heart was voiceless, and her body was still.

Ulpius had stood unnoticed by her side. At this moment he moved so as to confront her, and she suddenly looked up at him. A momentary expression of bewilderment and suspicion lightened the heavy vacancy of despair which had chased their natural and feminine tenderness from her eyes, but it disappeared rapidly. She turned from the Pagan, knelt down by the grave, and pressed her face and bosom against the little mound of turf beneath her.

No voice comforted her, no arm caressed her, as her mind now began to penetrate the mysteries, to probe the darkest depths of the long night's calamities! Unaided and unsolaced, while the few and waning stars glimmered from their places in the sky, while the sublime stillness of tranquillised Nature stretched around her, she knelt at the altar of death, and raised her soul upward to the great heaven above her, charged with its sacred offering of human grief!

Long did she thus remain; and when at length she arose from the ground, when approaching the Pagan she fixed on him her tearless, dreary eyes, he quailed before her glance, as his dull faculties struggled vainly to resume the old, informing power that they had now for ever lost. Nothing but the remembrance aroused by his first sight of the fragment of the lute lived within him even yet, as he whispered to her in low, entreating tones: —

"Come home — come home! Your father may return before us — come home!"

As the words "home" and "father" — those household gods of the heart's earliest existence — struck upon her ear, a change flashed with electric suddenness over the girl's whole aspect. She raised her wan hands to the sky; all her woman's tenderness repossessed itself of her heart; and as she again knelt down over the grave, her sobs rose audibly through the calmed and fragrant air.

With Hermanric's corpse beneath her, with the blood-sprinkled room behind her, with a hostile army and a famine-wasted city beyond her, it was only through that flood of tears, that healing passion of gentle emotions, that she rose superior to the multiplied horrors of her situation at the very moment when her faculties and her life seemed sinking under them alike. Fully, freely, bitterly she wept, on the kindly and parent earth — the patient, friendly ground that once bore the light footsteps of the first of a race not created for death; that now holds in its sheltering arms the loved ones whom, in mourning, we lay there to sleep; that shall yet be bound to the farthermost of its depths, when the sun-bright presence of returning spirits shines over its renovated frame, and love is resumed in angel perfection at the point where death suspended it in mortal frailness!

"Come home — your father is awaiting you — come home!" repeated the Pagan vacantly, moving slowly away as he spoke.

At the sound of his voice she started up; and clasping his arm with her trembling fingers, to arrest his progress, looked affrightedly into his seared and listless countenance. As she thus gazed on him she appeared for the first time to recognise him. Fear and astonishment mingled in her expression with grief and despair, as she sunk at his feet, moaning in tones of piercing entreaty: —

"Oh, Ulpius! — if Ulpius you are — have pity on me and take me to my father! My father! my father! In all the lonely world there is nothing left to me but my father!"

"Why do you weep to *me* about your broken lute?" answered Ulpius, with a dull, unmeaning smile, "It was not *I* that destroyed it!"

"They have slain him!" she shrieked distractedly, heedless of the Pagan's reply. "I saw them draw their swords on him! See, his blood is on me — *me!* — Antonina whom he protected and loved! Look there, that is a grave — *his* grave — I know it! I have never seen him since; he is down — down there! under the flowers I grew to gather for him! They slew him; and when I knew it not, they have buried him! — or *you* — you have buried him! You have hidden him under the cold garden earth! He is gone! — Ah, gone, gone — for ever gone!"

And she flung herself again with reckless violence on the grave. After looking stedfastly on her for a moment, Ulpius approached and raised her from the earth.

"Come!" he cried angrily, "the night grows on — your father waits!"

"The walls of Rome shut me from my father! I shall never see my father, nor Hermanric again!" she cried, in tones of bitter anguish, remembering more perfectly all the miseries of her position, and struggling to release herself from the Pagan's grasp.

The walls of Rome! At those words the mind of Ulpius opened to a flow of dark remembrances, and lost the visions that had occupied it until that moment. He laughed triumphantly.

"The walls of Rome bow to *my* arm!" he cried, in exulting tones; "I pierced them with my good bar of iron! I wound through them with my bright lantern! Spirits roared on me, and struck me down, and grinned upon me in the thick darkness, but I passed the wall! The thunder pealed around me as I crawled along the winding rifts; but I won my way through them! I came out conquering on the other side! Come, come,

come, come! We will return! I know the track, even in the darkness! I can outwatch the sentinels! You shall walk in the pathway that I have broken through the bricks!"

The girl's features lost for a moment their expression of grief, and grew rigid with horror, as she glanced at his fiery eyes, and felt the fearful suspicion of his insanity darkening over her mind. She stood powerless, trembling, unresisting, in his grasp, without attempting to delude him into departure, or to appease him into delay.

"Why did I make my passage through the wall?" muttered the Pagan in a low, awe-struck voice, suddenly checking himself, as he was about to step forward. "Why did I tear down the strong brickwork, and go forth into the dark suburbs?"

He paused, and for a few moments struggled with his purposeless and disconnected thoughts; but a blank, a darkness, an annihilation overwhelmed Alaric and the Gothic camp, which he vainly endeavoured to disperse. He sighed bitterly to himself — "It is gone!" and still grasping Antonina by the hand, drew her after him to the garden gate.

"Leave me!" she shrieked, as he passed onward into the pathway that led to the high road. "Oh, be merciful, and leave me to die where *he* has died!"

"Peace! or I will rend you limb by limb, as I rent the stones from the wall when I passed through' it!" he whispered to her in fierce accents, as she struggled to escape him. "You shall return with me to Rome!

You shall walk in the track that I have made in the rifted brickwork!"

Terror, anguish, exhaustion, overpowered her weak efforts. Her lips moved, partly in prayer, and partly in ejaculation; but she spoke in murmurs only, as she mechanically suffered the Pagan to lead her onward by the hand.

They paced on under the waning starlight, over the cold, lonely road, and through the dreary and deserted suburbs, — a fearful and discordant pair! Coldly, obediently, impassively, as if she were walking in a dream, the spirit-broken girl moved by the side of her scarce-human leader! Disjointed exclamations, alternating horribly between infantine simplicity and fierce wickedness, poured incessantly from the Pagan's lips, but he never addressed himself further to his terror-stricken companion. So, wending rapidly onward, they gained the Gothic lines; and here the madman slackened his pace, and paused, beast-like, to glare around him, as he approached the habitations of men.

Still not opposed by Antonina, whose faculties of observation were petrified by her terror into perfect inaction, even here, within reach of the doubtful aid of the enemies of her people, the Pagan crept forward through the loneliest places of the encampment, and guided by the mysterious cunning of his miserable race, eluded successfully the observation of the drowsy sentinels. Never bewildered by the darkness — for the moon had gone down — always led by the animal instinct co-existent with his disease, he passed over the waste ground between the hostile encampment and the city, and arrived triumphant at the heap of stones that marked his entrance to the rifted wall.

For one moment he stopped, and turning towards the girl, pointed proudly to the dark, low breach he was about to penetrate. Then, drawing her half-fainting form closer to his side, looking up attentively to the ramparts, and stepping as noiselessly as though turf were beneath his feet, he entered the dusky rift with his helpless charge.

As they disappeared in the recesses of the wall, Night, the stormy, the eventful, the fatal! — reached its last limit; and the famished sentinel on the fortifications of the besieged city roused himself from his dreary and absorbing thoughts, for he saw that the new day was dawning in the East.

CHAPTER VII.
The Breach Repassed.

SLOWLY and mournfully the sentinel at the rifted wall raised his eyes towards the eastern clouds, as they brightened before the advancing dawn. Desolate as was the appearance of the dull, misty daybreak, it was yet the most welcome of all the objects surrounding the starving soldier, on which he could fix his languid gaze. To look back on the city behind him, was to look back on the dreary charnel-house of famine and death: to look down on the waste ground, without the walls, was to look down on the dead body of the comrade of his watch, who, maddened by the pangs of hunger which he had suffered during the night, had cast himself from the rampart to meet a welcome death on the earth beneath. Famished and despairing, the sentinel crouched on the fortifications, which he had now neither strength to pace nor care to defend; yearning for the food that he had no hope to obtain, as he watched the grey daybreak from his solitary post.

While he was thus occupied, the gloomy silence of the scene was suddenly broken by the sound of falling brickwork at the inner base of the wall, followed by faint entreaties for mercy and deliverance, which rose on his ear, strangely mingled with disjointed expressions of defiance and exultation from a second voice. He slowly turned his head, and looking down, saw on the ground beneath, a young girl struggling in the grasp of an old man, who was hurrying her onward in the direction of the Pincian Gate.

For one moment the girl's eye met the sentinel's vacant glance, and she renewed, with a last affort of strength, and a greater vehemence of supplication, her cries for help; but the soldier neither moved nor answered. Exhausted as he was, no sight could affect him now but the sight of food. Like the rest of the citizens, he was sunk in the heavy stupor of starvation, — selfish, reckless, brutalised. No disasters could depress, no atrocities arouse him. Famine had torn asunder every social tie, had withered every human sympathy, among his besieged fellow-citizens, and he was famishing like them.

So, as the girl's entreaties for protection now grew fainter and fainter on his ear, he made no effort to move his languid limbs; he watched her with a dull, mechanical gaze, as she was dragged away, until a turn in the pathway at the foot of the Pincian Hill hid her from sight; then his eyes slowly reverted to the cloudy heaven which had been the object of their former contemplation, and his mind resumed its old painful, purposeless abstraction, as if no event had happened to challenge its failing faculties but the instant before.

At the moment when the dawn had first appeared, could he have looked down by some mysterious agency to the interior foundations of the wall, from the rampart on which he kept his weary watch, such a sight must then have presented itself as would have aroused even *his* sluggish observation to rigid attention and involuntary surprise.

Winding upward and downward among jagged masses of ruined brickwork, now lost amid the shadows of dreary chasms, now prominent over the elevations of rising arches, the dark irregular passages broken by Ulpius in the rotten wall would then have presented themselves to his eyes, — not stretching forth in dismal solitude, not peopled only by the reptiles native to the place, but traced in all their mazes by human forms. Then he would have perceived the fierce, resolute Pagan, moving through darkness and obstacles with a sure, solemn progress, drawing after him, like a dog devoted to his will, the young girl whose hapless fate had doomed her to fall into his power. Her half-fainting figure might have been seen, sometimes prostrate on the higher places of the breach, while her fearful guide descended before her into a chasm beyond, and then turned to drag her after him to a darker and a lower depth yet, — sometimes bent in supplication, when her lips moved once more with a last despairing entreaty, and her limbs trembled with a final effort to escape from her captor's relentless grasp. While still, through all that opposed him, the same fierce tenacity of purpose would have been invariably visible in every action of Ulpius, constantly confirming him in his mad resolution to make his victim the follower of his progress through the wall, ever guiding him with a strange instinct through every hindrance, and preserving him from every danger in his path, until it brought him forth triumphant, with his prisoner still in his power, again free to tread the desolated streets, and mingle with the famine-stricken citizens of Rome.

And now, when after peril and anguish she once more stood within the city of her home, what hope remained to Antonina of obtaining her last refuge under her father's roof, and deriving her solitary consolation from the effort to regain her father's love? With the termination of his passage through the breach in the wall, had ended every recollection associated with it in the Pagan's shattered memory. A new blank

now pervaded his lost faculties, desolate as that which
had overwhelmed them in the night when he first stood
in the farm-house garden by the young chieftain's
grave. He moved onward, unobservant, unthinking,
without aim or hope, driven by a mysterious restlessness, forgetting the very presence of Antonina as she
followed him, but still mechanically grasping her hand,
and dragging her after him he knew not whither.

And she, on her part, made no effort more for deliverance. She had seen the sentinel unmoved by her
entreaties, she had seen the walls of her father's house
receding from her longing eyes, as Ulpius pitilessly
hurried her further and further from its distant door;
and she lost the last faint hope of restoration, the last
lingering desire of life, as the sense of her helplessness
now weighed heaviest on her mind. Her heart was
full of her young warrior who had been slain, and of
her father from whom she had parted in the hour of
his wrath, as she now feebly followed the Pagan's
steps, and resigned herself to a speedy exhaustion and
death, in her utter despair.

They turned from the Pincian Gate and gained the
Campus Martius; and here the aspect of the besieged
city and the condition of its doomed inhabitants were
fully and fearfully disclosed to view. On the surface
of the noble area, once thronged with bustling crowds
passing to and fro in every direction as their various
destinations or caprices might lead them, not twenty
moving figures were now discernible. These few, who
still retained their strength or the resolution to pace

the greatest thoroughfare of Rome, stalked backwards and forwards incessantly, their hollow eyes fixed on vacancy, their wan hands pressed over their mouths; each separate, distrustful, silent; fierce as imprisoned madmen; restless as spectres disturbed in a place of tombs.

Such were the citizens who still moved over the Campus Martius; and, besetting their path wherever they turned, lay the gloomy numbers of the dying and the dead — the victims already stricken by the pestilence which had now arisen in the infected city, and joined the famine in its work of desolation and death. Around the public fountains, where the water still bubbled up as freshly as in the summer time of prosperity and peace, the poorer population of beleaguered Rome had chiefly congregated to expire. Some still retained strength enough to drink greedily at the margin of the stone basins, across which others lay dead — their heads and shoulders immersed in the water — drowned from lack of strength to draw back after their first draught. Children mounted over the dead bodies of their parents, to raise themselves to the fountain's brim — parents stared vacantly at the corpses of their children, alternately floating and sinking in the water, into which they had fallen unsuccoured and unmourned.

In other parts of the place, at the open gates of the theatres and hippodromes, in the unguarded porticos of the palaces and the baths, lay the discoloured bodies of those who had died ere they could reach the fountains — of women and children, especially — surrounded, in frightful contrast, by the abandoned furniture of luxury and the discarded inventions of vice — by gilded couches — by inlaid tables — by jewelled cornices — by obscene pictures and statues — by brilliantly-framed, gaudily-tinted manuscripts of licentious songs, still hanging at their accustomed places on the lofty marble walls. Further on, in the by-streets and the retired courts, where the corpse of the tradesman was stretched on his empty counter; where the soldier of the city guard dropped down overpowered ere he reached the limit of his rounds; where the wealthy merchant lay pestilence-stricken upon the last hoards of repulsive food which his gold had procured; the assassin and the robber might be seen — now greedily devouring the offal that lay around them, now falling dead upon the bodies which they had rifled but the moment before.

Over the whole prospect, far and near, wherever it might extend, whatever the horrors by which it might be occupied, was spread a blank, supernatural stillness. Not a sound arose; the living were as silent as the dead; crime, suffering, despair, were all voiceless alike; the trumpet was unheard in the guard-house; the bell never rang from the church — even the thick, misty rain, that now descended from the black and unmoving clouds, and obscured in cold shadows the outlines of distant buildings and the pinnacle-tops of mighty palaces, fell noiseless to the ground. The sky had no wind; the earth no echoes — the pervading desolation appalled the eye; the vast stillness weighed dull on the ear — it was a scene, as of the last-left city of an exhausted world, decaying noiselessly into primeval chaos.

Through this atmosphere of darkness and death; along these paths of pestilence and famine; unregarding and unregarded, the Pagan and his prisoner passed slowly onward, towards the quarter of the city opposite the Pincian Mount. No ray of thought, even yet, brightened the dull faculties of Ulpius; still he walked forward vacantly, and still he was followed wearily by the fast-failing girl.

Sunk in her mingled stupor of bodily weakness and mental despair, she never spoke, never raised her head, never looked forth on the one side or the other. She had now ceased even to feel the strong, cold grasp of the Pagan's hand. Shadowy visions of spheres beyond the world, arrayed in enchanting beauty, and peopled with happy spirits in their old earthly forms; where a long deathless existence moved smoothly and dreamily onward, without mark of time or taint of woe, were opening before her mind. She lost all memory of afflictions and wrongs, all apprehension of danger from the madman at whose mercy she remained. And thus, she still moved feebly onward as the will of Ulpius guided her, with no observation of her present peril, and no anxiety for her impending fate.

They passed the grand circular structure of the Pantheon, entered the long narrow streets leading to the banks of the river, and finally gained the margin of the Tiber — hard by the little island that still rises in the midst of its waters. Here, for the first time, the Pagan paused mechanically in his course, and vacantly directed his dull dreamy eyes on the prospect before him, where the walls, stretching abruptly outward from their ordinary direction, inclosed the Janiculum Hill, as it rose with its irregular mass of buildings on the opposite bank of the river.

At this sudden change from action to repose, the overtasked energies which had hitherto gifted the limbs of Antonina with an unnatural power of endurance, abruptly relaxed. She sank down helpless and silent; her head drooped towards the hard ground, as towards a welcome pillow, but found no support; for the Pagan's iron grasp of her hand remained unyielding as ever. Infirm though he was, he appeared at this moment to be unconscious that his prisoner was now hanging at his side. Every association connected with her, every recollection of his position with her in her father's house, had vanished from his memory. A darker blindness seemed to have sunk over his bodily perceptions; his eyes rolled slowly to and fro over the prospect before him, but regarded nothing; his panting breaths came thick and fast; his shrunk chest heaved as if some deep, dread agony were pent within it — it was evident that a new crisis in his insanity was at hand.

At this moment one of the bands of marauders — the desperate criminals of famine and plague — who still prowled through the city, appeared in the street. Their trembling hands sought their weapons, and their haggard faces brightened when they first discerned the Pagan and the girl; but as they approached nearer they saw enough in the figures of the two, at a glance, to destroy their hopes of seizing on them either for plunder or food. For an instant they stood by their intended victims, as if debating whether to murder them only for murder's sake, when the appearance of two women, stealthily quitting a house further on in the street, carrying a basket covered by some tattered garments, attracted their attention. They turned instantly to follow the bearers of the basket, and again Ulpius and Antonina were left alone on the river's bank.

The appearance of the assassins had been powerless, as every other sight or event in the city, in arousing the faculties of Ulpius. He had neither looked on them nor fled from them when they surrounded him; but now when they were gone, he slowly turned his head in the direction by which they had departed. His gaze wandered over the wet flagstones of the street, over two corpses stretched on them at a little distance, over the figure of a female slave, who lay forsaken near the wall of one of the houses, exerting her last energies to drink from the turbid rain-water which ran down the kennel by her side; and still his eyes remained unregardful of all that they encountered. The next object which by chance attracted his vacant attention, was a deserted temple. This solitary building fixed him immediately in contemplation, — it was destined to open a new and a warning scene in the dark tragedy of his closing life.

In his course through the city he had passed unheeded many temples far more prominent in situation, far more imposing in structure, than this. It was a building of no remarkable extent or extraordinary beauty. Its narrow porticos and dark doorway were more fitted to repel, than to invite the eye; but it had one attraction, powerful above all glories of architecture, and all grandeur of situation, to arrest in *him* those wandering faculties, whose sterner and loftier aims were now suspended for ever: it was dedicated to Serapis, — to the idol which had been the deity of his first worship, and the inspiration of his last struggle for the restoration of his faith. The image of the god, with the three-headed monster encircled by a serpent, obedient beneath his hand, was carved over the portico.

What flood of emotions rushed into the vacant mind of Ulpius, at the instant when he discerned the long-loved, well-known image of the Egyptian god, there was nothing, for some moments, outwardly visible in him to betray. His moral insensibility appeared but to be deepened, as his gaze was now fixed with rigid intensity on the temple portico. Thus he continued to remain motionless, as if what he saw had petrified him where he stood, when the clouds, which had been closing in deeper and deeper blackness as the morning advanced, and which, still charged with electricity, were gathering to revive the storm of the past night, burst abruptly into a loud peal of thunder over his head.

At that warning sound, as if it had been the supernatural signal awaited to arouse him, — as if in one brief moment it awakened every recollection of all that he had resolutely attempted during the night of thunder that was past, he started into instant animation. His countenance brightened, his form expanded, he dropped the hand of Antonina, raised his arm aloft towards the wrathful heaven in frantic triumph, then staggering forwards, fell on his knees at the base of the temple steps.

Whatever the remembrances of his passage through the wall at the Pincian Hill, and of the toil and peril succeeding it, which had revived when the thunder first sounded in his ear, they had now vanished as rapidly as they had arisen, and had left his wandering memory free to revert to the scenes which the image of Serapis was most fitted to recal. Recollections of his boyish enjoyments in the Temple at Alexandria, of his youth's enthusiasm, of the triumphs of his early manhood, — all disjointed and wayward, yet all bright, glorious, intoxicating, — flashed before his shattered mind. Tears, the first that he had shed since his happy youth, flowed quick down his withered cheeks. He pressed his hot forehead, he beat his parched hand in ecstasy, on the cold, wet steps beneath him. He muttered breathless ejaculations, he breathed strange murmurs of endearment, he humbled himself in his rapturous delight beneath the walls of the temple,

like a dog that has discovered his lost master, and
fawns affectionately at his feet. Criminal as he was,
his joy in his abasement, his glory in his miserable
isolation from humanity, was a doom of degradation
pitiable to be beheld.

After an interval his mood changed. He rose to
his feet; his trembling limbs strengthened with a youthful vigour, as he ascended the temple steps, and gained
its doorway. He turned for a moment, and looked
forth over the street, ere he entered the hallowed
domain of his distempered imagination. To *him* the
cloudy sky above was now shining with the radiance
of the sun-bright East. The death-laden highways of
Rome, as they stretched before him, were beautiful
with lofty trees, and populous with happy figures; and
along the dark flagstones beneath, where still lay the
corpses which he had no eye to see, he beheld already
the priests of Serapis, with his revered guardian, his
beloved Macrinus of former days, at their head, advancing to meet and welcome him in the hall of the
Egyptian god. Visions such as these passed gloriously
before the Pagan's eyes, as he stood triumphant on
the steps of the temple, and brightened to him with a
noonday light its dusky recesses, when after his brief
delay he turned from the street, and disappeared
through the doorway of the sacred place.

The rain poured down more thickly than before;
the thunder, once aroused, now sounded in deep and
frequent peals, as Antonina raised herself from the
ground, and looked around her, in momentary expecta-

tion that the dreaded form of Ulpius must meet her eyes. No living creature was visible in the street. The forsaken slave still reclined near the wall of the house where she had first appeared, when the Pagan gained the approaches to the temple; but she now lay there dead. No fresh bands of robbers appeared in sight. An uninterrupted solitude prevailed in all directions, as far as the eye could reach.

At the moment when Ulpius had relinquished his grasp of her hand, Antonina had sunk to the ground, helpless and resigned, but not exhausted beyond all power of sensation, or all capacity for thought. While she lay on the cold pavement of the street, her mind still pursued its visions of a speedy death, and a tranquil life-in-death to succeed it in a future state. But, as minute after minute elapsed, and no harsh voice sounded in her ear, no pitiless hand dragged her from the ground, no ominous footsteps were audible around her, a change passed gradually over her thoughts; the instinct of self-preservation slowly revived within her; and, as she raised herself to look forth on the gloomy prospect, the chances of uninterrupted flight and present safety presented by the solitude of the street, aroused her like a voice of encouragement, like an unexpected promise of help.

Her perception of outer influences returned, she felt the rain that drenched her garments, she shuddered at the thunder sounding over her head, she marked with horror the dead bodies lying before her on the stones. An overpowering desire animated her to fly from the place, to escape from the desolate scene around, even though she should sink exhausted by the effort in the next street. Slowly she arose, — her limbs trembled with a premature infirmity; but she gained her feet. She tottered onward, turning her back on the river, passed bewildered between long rows of deserted houses, and arrived opposite a public garden, surrounding a little summer-house, whose deserted portico offered both concealment and shelter. Here, therefore, she took refuge, crouching in the darkest corner of the building, and hiding her face in her hands, as if to shut out all view of the dreary though altered scenes which spread before her eyes.

Woful thoughts and recollections now moved within her in bewildering confusion. All that she had suffered since Ulpius had dragged her from the farm-house in the suburbs — the night-pilgrimage over the plain — the fearful passage through the wall — revived in her memory, mingled with vague ideas, now for the first time aroused, of the plague and famine that were desolating the city; and, with sudden apprehensions that Goisvintha might still be following her, knife in hand, through the lonely streets: while passively prominent over all these varying sources of anguish and dread, the scene of the young chieftain's death lay like a cold weight on her heavy heart. The damp turf of his grave seemed still to press against her breast; his last kiss yet trembled on her lips; she knew, though she dared not look down on them, that the spots of his blood yet stained her garments.

Whether she strove to rise and continue her flight; whether she crouched down again under the portico, resigned for one bitter moment to perish by the knife of Goisvintha, — if Goisvintha were near; to fall once more into the hands of Ulpius, — if Ulpius were tracking her to her retreat, the crushing sense that she was utterly bereaved of her beloved protector, — that the friend of her brief days of happiness was lost to her for ever, — that Hermauric, who had preserved her from death, had been murdered in his youth and his strength by her side, never deserted her. Since the assassination in the farm-house, she was now for the first time alone; and now for the first time she felt the full severity of her affliction, and knew how dark was the blank which was spread before every aspiration of her future life.

Enduring, almost eternal, as the burden of her desolation seemed now to have become, it was yet to be removed, ere long, by feelings of a tenderer mournfulness, and a more resigned woe. The innate and innocent fortitude of disposition, which had made her patient under the rigour of her youthful education, and hopeful under the trials that assailed her on her banishment from her father's house; which had never deserted her until the awful scenes of the past night of assassination and death rose in triumphant horror before her eyes; and which, even then, had been suspended but not destroyed, was now destined to regain its healing influence over her heart. As she still cowered in her lonely refuge, the final hope, the yearning dependence on a restoration to her father's presence and her father's love, that had moved her over the young chieftain's grave, and had prompted her last effort for freedom when Ulpius had dragged her through the passage in the rifted wall, suddenly revived.

Once more she arose, and looked forth on the desolate city and the stormy sky, but now with mild and unshrinking eyes. Her recollections of the past grew tender in their youthful grief; her thoughts for the future became patient, solemn, and serene. Images of her first and her last-left protector, of her old familiar home, of her garden solitude on the Pincian Mount, spread beautiful before her imagination, as resting-places to her weary heart. She descended the steps of the summer-house, with no apprehension of her enemies, no doubt of her resolution; for she knew the beacon that was now to direct her onward course. The tears gathered full in her eyes, as she passed into the garden; but her step never faltered, her features never lost their combined expression of tranquil sorrow and subdued hope. So she once more entered the perilous streets; and, murmuring to herself — "My father! my father!" as if in those simple words lay the hand that was to guide, and the providence that was to preserve her, she began to trace her solitary way in the direction of the Pincian Mount.

It was a spectacle — touching, beautiful, even sublime — to see this young girl, but a few hours freed, by perilous paths and by criminal hands, from scenes which had begun in treachery, only to end in death, now passing resolute and alone, through the streets of a mighty city, overwhelmed by all that is poignant in human anguish and hideous in human crime. It was a noble evidence of the strong power over the world and the world's perils, with which the simplest affection may arm the frailest being — to behold her thus pursuing her way, superior to every horror of desolation and death that clogged her path, unconsciously discovering in the softly-murmured name of "father," which still fell at intervals from her lips, the pure purpose that sustained her — the steady heroism that ever held her in her doubtful course. The storms of heaven poured over her head — the crimes and sufferings of Rome darkened the paths of her pilgrimage; but she passed firmly onward through all, like a ministering spirit, journeying along earthly shores in the bright inviolability of its merciful mission and its holy thoughts — like a ray of light living in the strength of its own beauty, amid the tempest and obscurity of a stranger sphere.

Once more she entered the Campus Martius. Again she passed the public fountains, still unnaturally devoted to serve as beds for the dying and as sepulchres for the dead; again she trod the dreary highways, where the stronger among the famished populace yet paced hither and thither in ferocious silence and unsocial separation. No word was addressed, hardly a look was directed to her, as she pursued her solitary course. She was desolate among the desolate; forsaken among others abandoned like herself.

The robber, when he passed her by, saw that she was worthless for the interests of plunder as the poorest of the dying citizens around him. The patrician, loitering feebly onward to the shelter of his palace halls, avoided her as a new suppliant among the people for the charity which he had not to bestow, and quickened his pace as she approached him in the street. Unprotected, yet unmolested, hurrying from her loneliness and her bitter recollections to the refuge of her father's love, as she would have hurried when a child from her first apprehension of ill to the refuge of her father's arms, she gained at length the foot of the Pincian Hill — at length ascended the streets so often trodden in the tranquil days of old!

The portals and outer buildings of Vetranio's palace, as she passed them, presented a striking and ominous spectacle. Within the lofty steel railings which protected the building the famine-wasted slaves of the senator appeared reeling and tottering beneath full vases of wine, which they were feebly endeavouring to carry into the interior apartments. Gaudy hangings drooped from the balconies, garlands of ivy were wreathed round the statues of the marble front. In the midst of the besieged city, and in impious mockery of the famine and pestilence which were wasting it — hut and palace — to its remotest confines, were proceeding in this devoted dwelling the preparations for a triumphant feast!

Unheedful of the startling prospect presented by Vetranio's abode, her eyes bent but in one absorbing direction, her steps hurrying faster and faster with each succeeding instant, Antonina approached the home from which she had been exiled in fear, and to which she was returning in woe. Yet a moment more of stong exertion, of overpowering anticipation, and she reached the garden gate!

She dashed back the heavy hair, matted over her brows by the rain; she glanced rapidly around her; she beheld the window of her bedchamber with the old simple curtain still hanging at its accustomed place; she saw the well-remembered trees, the carefully-tended flower-beds, now drooping mournfully beneath the gloomy sky. Her heart swelled within her, her breath seemed suddenly arrested in her bosom, as she trod the garden path, and ascended the steps beyond. The door at the top was ajar. With a last effort she thrust it open, and stood once more — unaided and unwelcomed, yet hopeful of consolation, of pardon, of love — within her first and last sanctuary, the walls of her home!

CHAPTER VIII.
Father and Child.

FORSAKEN as it appears on an outward view during the morning of which we now write, the house of Numerian is yet not tenantless. In one of the sleeping apartments, stretched on his couch, with none to watch by its side, lies the master of the little dwelling. We last beheld him on the scene mingled with the famishing congregation in the Basilica of St. John Lateran, still searching for his child amid the confusion of the public distribution of food during the earlier stages of the misfortunes of besieged Rome. Since that time he has toiled and suffered much; and now the day of exhaustion long deferred, the hours of helpless solitude, constantly dreaded, have at length arrived.

From the first periods of the siege, while all around him in the city moved gloomily onward through darker and darker changes; while famine rapidly merged into pestilence and death; while human hopes and purposes gradually diminished and declined with each succeeding day, he alone remained ever devoted to the same labour, ever animated by the same object — the only one among all his fellow-citizens whom no outward event could influence for good or evil, for hope or fear.

In every street of Rome, at all hours, among all ranks of people, he was still to be seen constantly pursuing the same hopeless search. When the mob burst furiously into the public granaries to seize the last supplies of corn hoarded for the rich, he was ready at the doors watching them as they came out. When rows of houses were deserted by all but the dead, he was beheld within, passing from window to window, as he sought through each room for the treasure that he had lost. When some few among the populace, in the first days of the pestilence, united in the vain attempt to cast over the lofty walls the corpses that strewed the street, he mingled with them to look on the rigid faces of the dead. In solitary places, where the parent not yet lost to affection strove to carry his dying child from the desert roadway to the shelter of a roof; where the wife, still faithful to her duties, received her husband's last breath in silent despair; he was seen gliding by their sides, and for one brief instant looking on them with attentive and mournful eyes. Wherever he went, whatever he beheld, he asked no sympathy and sought no aid. He went his way, a pilgrim on a solitary path; an unregarded expectant for a boon that no others could care to partake.

When the famine first began to be felt in the city, he seemed unconscious of its approach — he made no effort to procure beforehand the provision of a few days' sustenance; if he attended the first public distributions of food, it was only to prosecute his search for his child amid the throng around him. He must have perished with the first feeble victims of starvation, had he not been met, during his solitary wanderings, by some of the members of the congregation whom his piety and eloquence had collected in former days.

By these persons, whose entreaties that he would suspend his hopeless search he always answered with the same firm and patient denial, his course was carefully watched, and his wants anxiously provided for. Out of every supply of food which they were enabled to collect, his share was invariably carried to his abode. They remembered their teacher in the hour of his dejection, as they had formerly reverenced him in the day of his vigour; they toiled to preserve his life as anxiously as they had laboured to profit by his instructions; they listened as his disciples once, they served him as his children now.

But over these, as over all other offices of human kindness, the famine was destined gradually and surely to prevail. The provision of food garnered up by the congregation, ominously lessened with each succeeding day. When the pestilence began darkly to appear, the numbers of those who sought their afflicted teacher at his abode, or followed him through the dreary streets, fatally decreased.

Then, as the nourishment which had supported and the vigilance which had watched him thus diminished, so did the hard-tasked energies of the unhappy father fail him faster and faster. Each morning as he arose, his steps were more feeble, his heart grew heavier within him, his wanderings through the city were less and less resolute and prolonged. At length his powers totally deserted him; the last-left members of his congregation, as they approached his abode with the last-left provision of food which they possessed, found him prostrate with exhaustion at his garden gate. They bore him to his couch, placed their charitable offering by his side, and leaving one of their numbers to protect him from the robber and the assassin, they quitted the house in despair.

For some days the guardian remained faithful to his post, until his sufferings from lack of food overpowered his vigilance. Dreading that, in his extremity, he might be tempted to take from the old man's small store of provision what little remained, he fled from the house, to seek sustenance, however loathsome, in the public streets; and thenceforth Numerian was left defenceless in his solitary abode.

He was first beheld on the scenes which these pages present, a man of austere purpose, of unwearied energy; a valiant reformer, who defied all difficulties that beset him in his progress; a triumphant teacher, leading at his will whoever listened to his words; a father, proudly contemplating the future position which he destined for his child. Far different did he now appear. Lost to his ambition, broken in spirit, helpless in body, separated from his daughter by his own act, he lay on his untended couch in a death-like lethargy. The cold wind blowing through his opened window awakened no sensations in his torpid frame, — the cup of water and the small relics of coarse food stood near his hand, but he had no vigilance to discern them. His open eyes looked stedfastly upward, and yet he reposed as one in a deep sleep, or as one already devoted to the tomb; save when, at intervals, his lips moved slowly with a long and painfully-drawn breath, or a fever flush tinged his hollow cheek with changing and momentary hues.

While thus in outward aspect appearing to linger between life and death, his faculties yet remained feebly vital within him. Aroused by no external influence and governed by no mental restraint, they now created before him a strange waking vision, palpable as an actual event.

It seemed to him that he was reposing, not in his own chamber, but in some mysterious world, filled with a twilight atmosphere, inexpressibly soothing and gentle to his aching sight. Through this mild radiance he could trace, at long intervals, shadowy representations of the scenes through which he had passed in search of his lost child. The gloomy streets, the lonely houses abandoned to the unburied dead, which he had explored, alternately appeared and vanished before him in solemn succession; and ever and anon, as one vision disappeared ere another rose, he heard afar off a sound as of gentle, womanly voices, murmuring in solemn accents, "The search has been made in penitence, in patience, in prayer, and has not been pursued in vain. The lost shall return — the beloved shall yet be restored!"

Thus, as it had begun, the vision long continued. Now the scenes through which he had wandered passed slowly before his eyes, now the soft voices murmured pityingly in his ear. At length the first disappeared, and the last became silent; then ensued a long vacant interval, and then the grey, tranquil light brightened slowly at one spot, out of which he beheld advancing towards him the form of his lost child.

She came to his side, she bent lovingly over him; he saw her eyes, with their old patient, childlike expression, looking sorrowfully down upon him. His heart revived to a sense of unspeakable awe and contrition, to emotions of yearning love and mournful hope; his speech returned; he whispered tremulously, "Child! child! I repented in bitter woe the wrong that I did to thee; I sought thee, in my loneliness on earth, through the long day and the gloomy night! And now the merciful God has sent thee to pardon me! I loved thee; I wept for thee."

His voice died within him, for now his outward sensations quickened. He felt warm tears falling on his cheeks, he felt embracing arms clasped round him; he heard tenderly repeated, "Father! speak to me as you were wont: love me, father, and forgive me, as you loved and forgave me when I was a little child!"

The sound of that well-remembered voice — which had ever spoken kindly and reverently to him; which had last addressed him in tones of despairing supplication; which he had hardly hoped to hear again on earth — penetrated his whole being, like awakening music in the dead silence of night. His eyes lost their vacant expression; he raised himself suddenly on the couch; he saw that what had begun as a vision had ended as a reality; that his dream had proved the immediate forerunner of its own fulfilment; that his daughter in her bodily presence was indeed restored; and his head drooped forward, and he trembled and wept upon her bosom, in the overpowering fulness of his gratitude and delight.

For some moments Antonina, calming with the resolute heroism of affection her own thronging emotions of awe and affright, endeavoured to soothe and support her fast-failing parent. Her horror almost overwhelmed her, as she thought that now, when through grief and peril she was at last restored to him, he might expire in her arms; but even yet her resolution did not fail her. The last hope of her brief and bitter life was now the hope of reviving her father; and she clung to it with the tenacity of despair.

She calmed her voice while she spoke to him; she entreated him to remember that his daughter had returned to watch over him, to be his obedient pupil as in days of old. Vain effort! Even while the words passed her lips, his arms, which had been pressed over her, relaxed; his head grew heavier on her bosom. In the despair of the moment, she tore herself from him, and looked round to seek the help that none were near to afford. The cup of water, the last provision of food, attracted her eye. With quick instinct she caught them up. Hope, success, salvation, lay in those miserable relics. She pressed the food into his mouth; she moistened his parched lips, his dry brow, with the water. During one moment of horrible suspense she saw him still insensible; then the vital functions revived; his eyes opened again, and fixed famine-struck on the wretched nourishment before him. He devoured it ravenously; he drained the cup of water to its last drop; he sank back again on the couch. But now the torpid blood moved once more in his veins; his heart beat less and less feebly: he was saved. She saw it as she bent over him, — saved by the lost child in the hour of her return! It was a sensation of ecstatic triumph and gratitude, which no woful remembrances had power to embitter in its bright, sudden birth! She knelt down by the side of the couch, almost crushed by her own emotions. Over the grave of the young warrior she had raised her heart to Heaven in agony and grief, and now by her father's side she poured forth her whole soul to her Creator, in trembling ejaculations of thankfulness and hope!

Thus — the one slowly recovering whatever of life and vigour yet continued in his weakened frame, the other still filled with her all-absorbing emotions of gratitude — the father and daughter long remained. And now, as morning waned towards noon, the storm began to subside. Gradually and solemnly the vast thunder-clouds rolled asunder, and the bright blue heaven beyond, appeared through their fantastic rifts. The lessening rain-drops fell light and silvery to the earth, and breeze and sunshine were wafted at fitful intervals over the plague-tainted atmosphere of Rome. As yet, subdued by the shadows of the floating clouds, the dawning sunbeams glittered softly through the windows of Numerian's chamber. They played, warm and reviving, over his worn features, like messengers of resurrection and hope from their native heaven. Life seemed to expand within him under their fresh and gentle ministering. Once more he raised himself, and turned towards his child: and now his heart throbbed with a healthful joy, and his arms closed round her, not in the helplessness of infirmity, but in the welcome of love.

His words, when he spoke to her, fell at first almost inarticulately from his lips — they were mingled together in confused phrases of tenderness, contrition, thanksgiving. All the native enthusiasm of his disposition, all the latent love for his child, which had for years been suppressed by his austerity, or diverted by his ambition, now at last burst forth.

Trembling and silent in his arms, Antonina vainly endeavoured to return his caresses, and to answer his words of welcome. Now for the first time she knew how deep was her father's affection for her; she felt how foreign to his real nature had been his assumed severity in their intercourse of former days; and in the quick flow of new feelings and old recollections produced by the delighting surprise of the discovery, she found herself speechless. She could only listen eagerly, breathlessly, while he spoke. His words, faltering and confused though they were, were words of endearment which she had never heard from him before; they were words which no mother had ever pronounced beside her infant bed; and they sank divinely consoling over her heart, as messages of pardon from angel's lips.

Gradually Numerian's voice grew calmer. He raised his daughter in his arms, and bent wistfully on her face his attentive and pitying eyes. "Returned, returned!" he murmured, while he gazed on her, "never again to depart! Returned, beautiful and patient, kinder and more tender than ever! Love me and pardon me, Antonina. I sought for you in bitter loneliness and despair. Think not of me as what I was, but as what I am! There were days when you were yet an infant, when I had no thought but how to cherish and delight you, and now those days have come again. You shall read no gloomy task-books; you shall never be separated from me more; you shall play sweet music on the lute; you shall be all garlanded with flowers which I will provide for you! We will find friends and glad companions; we will bring happiness with us wherever we are seen. God's blessing goes forth from children like you, — it has fallen upon me, — it has raised me from the dead! My Antonina shall teach me to worship, as I once taught her. She shall pray for me in the morning, and pray for me at night; and when she thinks not of it, when she sleeps, I shall come softly to her bedside, and wait and watch over her, so that when she opens her eyes, they shall open on me, — they are the eyes of my child who has been restored to me, — there is nothing on earth that can speak to me like them of happiness and peace!"

He paused for a moment, and looked rapturously on her face as it was turned towards him. His features partially saddened while he gazed; and taking her long hair — still wet and dishevelled from the rain — in his hands, he pressed it over his lips, over his face, over his neck. Then, when he saw that she was endeavouring to speak, when he beheld the tears that were now filling her eyes, he drew her closer to him, and hurriedly continued in lower tones: —

"Hush! hush! No more grief — no more tears! Tell me not whither you have wandered — speak not of what you have suffered; for would not every word be a reproach to me? And you have come to pardon, and not to reproach! Let not the recollection that it was I who cast you off be forced on me from your lips! let us remember only that we are restored to each other; let us think that God has accepted my penitence and forgiven me my sin, in suffering my child to return! Or, if we must speak of the days of separation that are past, speak to me of the days that found you tranquil and secure; rejoice me, by telling me that it was not all danger and woe in the bitter destiny which my guilty anger prepared for my own child! Say to me that you met protectors as well as enemies, in the hour of your flight, — that all were not harsh to you, as I was, — that those of whom you asked shelter and safety, looked on your face as on a petition for charity and kindness from friends whom they loved! Tell me only of your protectors, Antonina, for in that there will be consolation: and you have come to console!"

As he waited for her reply, he felt her tremble on his bosom; he saw the shudder that ran over her frame. The despair in her voice, though she only pronounced in answer to him the simple words, "There was one" — and then ceased, unable to proceed — penetrated coldly to his heart. "Is he not at hand?" he hurriedly resumed. "Why is he not here? Let us seek him without delay. I must humble myself before him, in my gratitude. I must show him that I was worthy that my Antonina should be restored."

"He is dead!" she gasped, sinking down in the arms that embraced her, as the recollections of the past night again crowded in all their horror on her memory. "They murdered him by my side. — Oh, father! father! he loved *me*; he would have reverenced and protected *you!*"

"May the merciful God receive him among the blessed angels, and honour him among the holy martyrs!" cried the father, raising his tearful eyes in supplication. "May his spirit, if it can still be observant of the things of earth, know that his name shall be written on my heart with the name of my child; that I will think on him as on a beloved companion, and mourn for him as for a son that has been taken from me!"

He ceased, and looked down on Antonina, whose features were still hidden from him. Each felt that a new bond of mutual affection had been created between them by what each had spoken; but both now remained silent.

During this interval, the thoughts of Numerian wandered from the reflections which had hitherto occupied him. The few mournful words which his daughter had spoken had been sufficient to banish its fulness of joy from his heart, and to turn him from the happy contemplation of the present to the dark recollections of the past. Vague doubts and fears now mingled with his gratitude and hope; and involuntarily his thoughts reverted to what he would fain have forgotten for ever, — to the morning when he had driven Antonina from her home.

Baseless apprehensions of the return of the treacherous Pagan and his profligate employer, with the return of their victim, — despairing convictions of his own helplessness and infirmity rose startlingly in his mind. His eyes wandered vacantly round the room, his hands closed trembling over his daughter's form; then, suddenly releasing her, he arose as one panic-stricken, and exclaiming, "The doors must be secured — Ulpius may be near — the senator may return!" endeavoured to cross the room. But his strength was unequal to the effort; he leaned back for support against the wall, and breathlessly repeating, "Secure the doors — Ulpius, Ulpius!" he motioned to Antonina to descend.

She trembled as she obeyed him. Remembering her passage through the breach in the wall, and her fearful journey through the streets of Rome, she more than shared her father's apprehensions as she descended the stairs.

The door remained half-open, as she had left it when she entered the house. Ere she hurriedly closed and barred it, she cast a momentary glance on the street beyond. The gaunt figures of the slaves still moved wearily to and fro, amid the mockery of festal preparation in Vetranio's palace; and here and there a few ghastly figures lay on the ground contemplating them in languid amazement. Over all other parts of the street the deadly tranquillity of plague and famine still prevailed.

Hurriedly ascending the steps, Antonina hastened to assure her father that she had obeyed his commands, and that they were now secure from all intrusion from without. But, during her brief absence, a new and more ominous prospect of calamity had presented itself before the old man's mind.

As she entered the room, she saw that he had returned to his couch, and that he was holding before him the little wooden bowl, which had contained his last supply of food, and which was now empty. He addressed not a word to her when he heard her enter; his features were rigid with horror and despair as he looked down on the empty bowl: he muttered vacantly, "It was the last provision that remained, and it was I that exhausted it! The beasts of the forest carry food to their young, and I have taken the last morsel from my child!".

In an instant the utter desolateness of their situation — forgotten in the first joy of their meeting — forced itself with appalling vividness upon Antonina's mind. She endeavoured to speak of comfort and hope to her father; but the fearful realities of the famine in the city now rose palpably before her, and suspended the vain words of solace on her lips. In the midst of still populous Rome, within sight of those surrounding plains where the creative sun ripened hour by hour the vegetation of the teeming earth, where field and granary displayed profusely their abundant stores, the father and daughter now looked on each other, as helpless to replace their exhausted provision of food, as if they had been abandoned on the raft of the shipwrecked in an unexplored sea, or banished to a lonely island, whose inland products were withered by infected winds, and around whose arid shores ran such destroying waters as seethe over the "Cities of the Plain."

The silence which had long prevailed in the room; the bitter reflections which still held the despairing father and the patient daughter speechless alike, were at length interrupted by a hollow and melancholy voice from the street, pronouncing, in the form of a public notice, these words: —

"I, Publius Dalmatius, messenger of the Roman Senate, proclaim, that in order to clear the streets from the dead, three thousand sestertii will be given by the Prefect for every ten bodies that are cast over the walls. This is the true decree of the Senate."

The voice ceased; but no sound of applause, no murmur of popular tumult was heard in answer. Then, after an interval, it was once more faintly audible as the messenger passed on and repeated the decree in another street; and then the silence again sank down over all things more awfully pervading than before.

Every word of the proclamation, when repeated in the distance as when spoken under his window, had reached Numerian's ears. His mind, already sinking in despair, was riveted on what he had heard from the woe-boding voice of the herald, with a fascination as absorbing as that which rivets the eye of the traveller, already giddy on the summit of a precipice, upon the spectacle of the yawning gulphs beneath. When all sound of the proclamation had finally died away, the unhappy father dropped the empty bowl which he had hitherto mechanically continued to hold before him, and glancing affrightedly at his daughter, groaned to himself: "The corpses are to be cast over the walls; the dead are to be flung forth to the winds of heaven!— there is no help for us in the city — Oh God, God!— *she* may die! — *her* body may be cast away like the rest, and I may live to see it!"

He rose suddenly from the couch, his reason seemed for a moment to be shaken as he tottered to the window, crying "Food! food! — I will give my house and all it contains for a morsel of food — I have nothing to support my own child — she will starve before me by to-morrow if I have no food! I am a citizen of Rome— I demand help from the Senate! Food! food!"

In tones declining lower and lower he continued to cry thus from the window, but no voice answered him either in sympathy or derision. Of all the people — now increased in numbers — collected in the street before Vetranio's palace, not one turned even to look on him. For days and days past, such fruitless appeals as his had been heard, and heard unconcernedly, at every hour and in every street of Rome — now ringing through the heavy air in the shrieks of delirium; now faintly audible in the last faltering murmurs of exhaustion and despair.

Thus vainly entreating help and pity from a populace who had ceased to give the one, or to feel the other, Numerian might long have remained; but now his daughter approached his side, and drawing him gently towards his couch, said in tender and solemn accents: — "Remember, father, that God sent the ravens to feed Elijah, and replenished the widow's cruse! He will not desert us, for He has restored us to each other; and has sent me hither not to perish in the famine, but to watch over you!"

"God has deserted the city and all that it contains!" he answered distractedly. "The angel of destruction has gone forth into our streets, and death walks in his shadow! On this day, when hope and happiness seemed opening before us both, our little household has been doomed! The young and the old; the weary and the watchful — they strew the streets alike — the famine has mastered them all — the famine will master us — there is no help; no escape! I, who would have died patiently for my daughter's safety, must now die despairing, leaving her friendless in the wide, dreary, perilous world; in the dismal city of anguish, of horror, of death — where the enemy threatens without, and hunger and pestilence waste within! Oh, Antonina! you have returned to me but for a little time; the day of our second separation draws near!"

For a few moments his head drooped and his sobs choked his utterance; then he once more rose painfully to his feet. Heedless of Antonina's entreaties, he again endeavoured to cross the room, only again to find his feeble powers unequal to sustain him. As he fell back panting upon a seat, his eyes assumed a wild, unnatural expression — despair of mind and weakness of body had together partially unhinged his faculties. When his daughter affrightedly approached to soothe and succour him, he impatiently waved her back; and began to speak in a dull, hoarse, monotonous voice, pressing his hand firmly over his brow, and directing his eyes backwards and forwards incessantly, on object after object, in every part of the room.

"Listen, child, listen!" he hastily began; "I tell you there is no food in the house, and no food in Rome! — we are besieged — they have taken from us our granaries in the suburbs, and our fields on the plains — there is a great famine in the city — those who still eat, eat strange food which men sicken at when it is named. I would seek even this, but I have no strength to go forth into the by-ways and force it from others at the point of the sword! I am old and feeble, and heart-broken: — I shall die first, and leave fatherless my good, kind daughter, whom I sought for so long, and whom I loved as my only child!"

He paused for an instant — not to listen to the words of encouragement and hope which Antonina mechanically addressed to him while he spoke — but to collect his wandering thoughts; to rally his failing strength. His voice acquired a quicker tone, and his features presented a sudden energy and earnestness of expression, as if some new project had flashed across his mind, when, after an interval, he continued thus:—

"But though my child shall be bereaved of me; though I shall die in the hour when I most longed to live for her, I must not leave her helpless; I will send her among my congregation who have deserted *me*, but who will repent when they hear that I am dead, and will receive Antonina among them for my sake! Listen to this — listen, listen! You must tell them to remember all that I once revealed to them of my brother, from whom I parted in my boyhood; my brother, whom I have never seen since; he may yet be alive, he may be found; they must search for him — for to you he would be father to the fatherless, and guardian to the unguarded — he may now be in Rome, he may be rich and powerful — he may have food to spare, and shelter that is good against all enemies and strangers! Attend, child, to my words: in these latter days I have thought of him much; I have seen him in dreams as I saw him for the last time in my father's house; he was happier and more beloved than I was; and in envy and hatred I quitted my parents and parted from him. You have heard nothing of this; but you must hear it now; that when I am dead you may know you have a protector to seek! So I received in anger my brother's farewell, and fled from my home — (those days were well remembered by me once, but all things grow dull on my memory now) — long years of turmoil and change passed on, and I never met him; and men of many nations were my companions, but he was not among them; then much affliction fell upon me, and I repented and learnt the fear of God, and went back to my father's house. Since that, years have passed; I know not how many; I could have told them when I spoke of my former life to *him;* to my friend, when we stood near St. Peter's, ere the city was besieged, looking on the sunset, and speaking of the early days of our companionship; but now my very remembrance fails me; the famine that threatens us with separation and death, casts darkness over my thoughts — yet hear me, hear me patiently — for your sake I must continue!"

"Not now, father — not now! At another time, on a happier day!" murmured Antonina in tremulous entreating tones.

"My home, when I arrived to look on it, was gone," pursued the old man, sadly, neither heeding nor hearing her. "Other houses were built where my father's house had stood; no man could tell me of my parents and my brother; then I returned, and my former companions grew hateful in my eyes; I left them, and they followed me with persecution and scorn. — Listen, listen! — I set forth secretly in the night, with you, to escape them; and to make perfect my reformation where they should not be near to hinder it; and we travelled onward many days until we came to Rome; and I made my abode there. But I feared that my companions whom I abhorred might discover and persecute me again; and in the new city of my dwelling I called myself by another name than the name that I bore; thus I knew that all trace of me would be lost, and that I should be kept secure from men whom I thought on only as enemies now. Go, child! — go quickly! — bring your tablets and write down the names that I shall tell you; for so you will discover your protector when I am gone! Say not to him that you are the child of Numerian — he knows not the name; say that you are the daughter of Cleander, his brother, who died longing to be restored to him — write! write carefully, Cleander! — that was the name my father gave to me, that was the name I bore until I fled from my evil companions and changed it, dreading their pursuit! Cleander! write and remember, Cleander! I have seen in visions that my brother shall be discovered: he will not be discovered to *me*, but he will be discovered to *you!* Your tablets — your tablets! write his name with mine — it is —"

He stopped abruptly. His mental powers, fluctuating between torpor and animation — shaken, but not overpowered by the trials which had assailed them — suddenly rallied, and, resuming somewhat of their accustomed balance, became awakened to a sense of their own aberration. His vague revelations of his past life (which the reader will recognise as resembling his communications on the same subject to the fugitive landowner, previously related) now appeared before him in all their incongruity and uselessness. His countenance fell — he sighed bitterly to himself: — "My reason begins to desert me! — my judgment, which should guide my child — my resolution, which should uphold her, both fail me! — how should my brother, since boyhood lost to *me*, be found by *her?*

Against the famine that threatens us, I offer but vain words! — already her strength declines; her face, that I loved to look on, grows wan before my eyes! — God have mercy upon us! — God have mercy upon us!"

He returned feebly to his couch; his head declined on his bosom; sometimes a low groan burst from his lips; but he spoke no more.

Deep as was the prostration under which he had now fallen, it was yet less painful to Antonina to behold it than to listen to the incoherent revelations which had fallen from his lips but the moment before, and which, in her astonishment and affright, she had dreaded might be the awful indications of the overthrow of her father's reason. As she again placed herself by his side, she trembled to feel that her own weariness was fast overpowering her; but she still struggled with her rising despair — still strove to think only of capacity for endurance and chances of relief.

The silence in the room was deep and dismal, while they now sat together. The faint breezes, at long intervals, drowsily rose and fell, as they floated through the open window; the fitful sunbeams alternately appeared and vanished, as the clouds rolled upward in airy succession over the face of heaven; — Time moved sternly in its destined progress, and Nature varied tranquilly through its appointed limits of change, and still no hopes, no saving projects, nothing but dark recollections and woful anticipations occupied Antonina's mind — when, just as her weary head was drooping towards the ground — just as sensation and fortitude and grief itself seemed declining into a dreamless and deadly sleep — a last thought, void of discernible connection or cause, rose suddenly within her — animating, awakening, inspiring. She started up. "The garden, father — the garden!" — she cried, breathlessly — "Remember the food that grows in our garden below! — be comforted, we have provision left yet — God has not deserted us!"

He raised his face while she spoke; his features assumed a deeper mournfulness and hopelessness of expression; he looked upon her in ominous silence, and laid his trembling fingers on her arm to detain her, when she hurriedly attempted to quit the room.

"Do not forbid me to depart," she anxiously pleaded. "To me every corner in the garden is known; for it was my possession in our happier days — our last hopes rest on the garden; and I must search through it without delay! Bear with me," she added, in low and melancholy tones, "bear with me, dear father, in all that I would now do! I have suffered, since we parted, a bitter affliction, which clings dark and heavy to all my thoughts — there is no consolation for me but the privilege of caring for *your* welfare — my only hope of comfort is in the employment of aiding *you!*"

The old man's hand had pressed heavier on her arm, while she addressed him; but when she ceased, it dropped from her, and he bent his head in speechless submission to her entreaty. For one moment she lingered, looking on him silent as himself; the next, she left the apartment with hasty and uncertain steps.

On reaching the garden, she unconsciously took the path leading to the bank where she had once loved to play secretly upon her lute, and to look on the distant mountains reposing in the warm atmosphere which summer evenings shed over their blue expanse. How eloquent was this little plot of ground of the quiet events now for ever gone by! — of the joys, the hopes, the happy occupations, which rise with the day that chronicles them, and pass like that day, never to return the same! — which the memory alone can preserve as they were; and the heart can never resume but in a changed form, divested of the presence of the companion, of the incident of the departed moment, which formed the charm of the past and makes the imperfection of the present.

Tender and thronging were the remembrances which the surrounding prospect called up, as the sad mistress of the garden looked again on her little domain! She saw the bank where she could never more sit to sing with a renewal of the same feelings which had once inspired her music — she saw the drooping flowers that she could never restore with the same child-like enjoyment of the task which had animated her in former hours! Young though she still was, the emotions of the youthful days that were gone could never be revived as they had once existed! As waters they had welled up, and as waters they had flowed forth, never to return to their source! Thoughts of these former years — of the young warrior who lay cold beneath the heavy earth — of the desponding father who mourned hopeless in the room above — gathered thick at her heart, as she turned from her flower-beds — not, as in other days, to pour forth her happiness to the music of her lute — but to search laboriously for the sustenance of life.

At first, as she stooped over those places in the garden where she knew that fruits and vegetables had been planted by her own hand, her tears blinded her — she hastily dashed them away, and looked eagerly around.

Alas, others had reaped the field from which she had hoped abundance! In the early days of the famine, Numerian's congregation had entered the garden, and gathered for him whatever it contained; its choicest and its homeliest products were alike exhausted; withered leaves lay on the barren earth, and naked branches waved over them in the air. She wandered from path to path, searching amid the briars and thistles, which already cast an aspect of ruin over the deserted place; she explored its most hidden corners with the painful perseverance of despair; but the same barrenness spread around her wherever she turned. On this once fertile spot, which she had entered with such joyful faith in its resources, there remained but a few decayed roots, dropped and forgotten amid tangled weeds and faded flowers.

She saw that they were barely sufficient for one

scanty meal, as she collected them, and returned slowly to the house. No words escaped her, no tears flowed over her cheeks, when she re-ascended the steps — hope, fear, thought, sensation itself, had been stunned within her, from the first moment when she had discovered that, in the garden as in the house, the inexorable famine had anticipated the last chances of relief.

She entered the room; and still holding the withered roots, advanced mechanically to her father's side. During her absence, his mental and bodily faculties had both yielded to wearied nature — he lay in a deep heavy sleep.

Her mind experienced a faint relief, when she saw that the fatal necessity of confessing the futility of the hopes she had herself awakened, was spared her for awhile. She knelt down by Numerian, and gently smoothed the hair over his brow — then she drew the curtain across the window, for she feared even that the breeze blowing through it might arouse him. A strange, secret satisfaction, at the idea of devoting to her father every moment of the time and every particle of the strength that might yet be reserved for her; a ready resignation to death, in dying for *him*, overspread her heart, and took the place of all other aspirations and all other thoughts.

She now moved to and fro through the room, with a cautious tranquillity which nothing could startle; she prepared her decayed roots for food, with a patient attention which nothing could divert. Lost, through the aggravated miseries of her position, to recent grief and present apprehension, she could still instinctively perform the simple offices of the woman and the daughter, as she might have performed them amid a peaceful nation and a prosperous home. Thus do the first-born affections outlast the exhaustion of all the stormy emotions, all the aspiring thoughts of after years, which may occupy, but which cannot absorb, the spirit within us; thus does their friendly and familiar voice, when the clamour of contending passions has died away in its own fury, speak again, serene and sustaining as in the early time, when the mind moved secure within the limits of its native simplicity, and the heart yet lay happy in the pure tranquillity of its first repose!

The last scanty measure of food was soon prepared; it was bitter and unpalatable when she tasted it — life could barely be preserved, even in the most vigorous, by provision so wretched — but she set it aside as carefully as if it had been the most precious luxury of the most abundant feast.

Nothing had changed during the interval of her solitary employment — her father yet slept; the gloomy silence yet prevailed in the street. She placed herself at the window, and partially drew aside the curtain to let the warm breezes from without blow over her cold brow. The same ineffable resignation, the same unnatural quietude, which had sunk down over her faculties since she had entered the room, overspread them still. Surrounding objects failed to impress her attention; recollections and forebodings stagnated in her mind. A marble composure prevailed over her features; sometimes her eyes wandered mechanically from the morsels of food by her side to her sleeping father, as her one vacant idea of watching for his service, till the feeble pulses of life had throbbed their last, alternately revived and declined — but no other evidences of bodily existence or mental activity appeared in her. As she now sat in the half-darkened room, by the couch on which her father reposed, — her features pale, calm and rigid, her form enveloped in cold white drapery, — there were moments when she looked like one of the penitential devotees of the primitive Church, appointed to watch in the house of mourning, and surprised on her saintly vigil by the advent of death.

Time flowed on — the monotonous hours of the day waned again towards night; and plague and famine told their lapse in the fated highways of Rome. For father and child the *sand in the glass* was fast running out; and neither marked it as it diminished. The sleeper still reposed, and the guardian by his side still watched — but now her weary gaze was directed on the street; unconsciously attracted by the sound of voices, which at length rose from it at intervals, and by the light of torches and lamps, which appeared in the great palace of the senator Vetranio, as the sun gradually declined in the horizon and the fiery clouds around were quenched in the vapours of the advancing night. Steadily she looked upon the sight beneath and before her; but, even yet, her limbs never moved; no expression relieved the blank solemn peacefulness of her features.

Meanwhile, the soft, brief twilight glimmered over the earth, and showed the cold moon, poised solitary in the starless heaven — then, the stealthy darkness arose at her pale signal, and closed slowly round the City of Death!

CHAPTER IX.
The Banquet of Famine.

Of all prophecies none are, perhaps, so frequently erroneous as those on which we are most apt to venture, in endeavouring to foretell the effect of outward events on the characters of men. In no form of our anticipations are we more frequently baffled than in such attempts to estimate beforehand the influence of circumstance over conduct, not only in others, but also even in ourselves. Let the event but happen, and men, whom we view by the light of our previous observation of them, act under it as the living contradictions of their own characters. The friend of our daily social intercourse, in the progress of life, and the favourite hero of our historic studies, in the progress of the page, astonish, exceed, or disappoint our expectations alike. We find it as vain to foresee a cause, as to fix a limit, for the arbitrary inconsistencies in the dispositions of mankind.

But though to speculate upon the future conduct

of others under impending circumstances, be but too often to expose the fallacy of our wisest anticipations, to contemplate the nature of that conduct after it has been displayed, is an useful subject of curiosity, and may, perhaps, be made a fruitful source of instruction. Similar events which succeed each other at different periods are relieved from monotony, and derive new importance, from the ever-varying effects which they produce on the human character. Thus in the great occurrence which forms the foundation of our narrative, we may find little in the siege of Rome, looking at it as a mere event, to distinguish it remarkably from any former siege of the city — the same desire for glory and vengeance, wealth and dominion, which brought Alaric to her walls, brought other invaders before him. But if we observe the effect of the Gothic descent upon Italy on the inhabitants of her capital, we shall find ample matter for novel contemplation and unbounded surprise.

We shall perceive, as an astonishing instance of the inconsistencies of the human character, the spectacle of a whole people resolutely defying an overwhelming foreign invasion at their very doors, just at the period when they had fallen most irremediably from the highest position of national glory to the lowest depths of national degradation; resisting an allpowerful enemy with inflexible obstinacy, for the honour of the Roman name, which they had basely dishonoured, or carelessly forgotten for ages past. We shall behold men, who have hitherto laughed at the

very name of patriotism, now starving resolutely in
their country's cause; who stopped at no villany to
obtain wealth, now hesitating to employ their ill-gotten
gains in the purchase of the most important of all
gratifications — their own security and peace. In-
stances of the unimaginable effect produced by the
event of the siege of Rome on the characters of her
inhabitants, might be drawn from all classes, from the
lowest to the highest, from patrician to plebeian; but
to produce them here would be to admit too long an
interruption in the progress of the present narrative.
If we are to enter at all into detail on such a subject,
it must be only in a case clearly connected with the
actual requirements of our story; and such a case may
be found, at this juncture, in the conduct of the senator
Vetranio, under the influence of the worst calamities
attending the blockade of Rome by the Goths.

Who, it may be asked, knowing the previous character of this man, his frivolity of disposition, his volup-
tuous anxiety for unremitting enjoyment and ease, his
horror of the slightest approaches of affliction or pain,
would have imagined him capable of rejecting in disdain all the minor chances of present security and
future prosperity, which his unbounded power and
wealth might have procured for him, even in a famine-
stricken city, and rising suddenly to the sublime of
criminal desperation, in the resolution to abandon life
as worthless the moment it had ceased to run in the
easy current of all former years? Yet to this determination had he now arrived; and, still more extra-

ordinary, in this determination had he found others, of his own patrician order, to join him.

The reader will remember his wild announcement of his intended orgy to the Prefect Pompeianus, during the earlier periods of the siege: that announcement was now to be fulfilled. Vetranio had bidden his guests to the Banquet of Famine. A chosen number of the senators of the great city were to vindicate their daring by dying the revellers that they had lived; by resigning in contempt all prospect of starving, like the common herd, on a lessening daily pittance of loathsome food; by making their triumphant exit from a fettered and ungrateful life, drowned in floods of wine, and lighted by the fires of the wealthiest palace of Rome!

It had been intended to keep this frantic determination a profound secret, to let the mighty catastrophe burst upon the remaining inhabitants of the city like a prodigy from heaven; but the slaves entrusted with the organisation of the suicide banquet had been bribed to their tasks with wine, and in the carelessness of intoxication had revealed to others whatever they heard within the palace walls. The news passed from mouth to mouth. There was enough in the prospect of beholding the burning palace and the drunken suicide of its desperate guests, to animate even the stagnant curiosity of a famishing mob.

On the appointed evening the people dragged their weary limbs from all quarters of the city towards the Pincian Hill. Many of them died on the way; many lost their resolution to proceed to the end of their journey, and took shelter sullenly in the empty houses on the road; many found opportunities for plunder and crime as they proceeded, which tempted them from their destination, — but many persevered in their purpose, the living dragging the dying along with them, the desperate driving the cowardly before them in malignant sport, until they gained the palace gates. It was by their voices, as they reached her ear from the street, that the fast-sinking faculties of Antonina had been startled, though not revived; and there, on the broad pavement, lay these citizens of a falling city; a congregation of pestilence and crime; a starving and an awful band!

The moon, brightened by the increasing darkness, now clearly illuminated the street, and revealed, in a narrow space, a various and impressive scene.

One side of the roadway in which stood Vetranio's palace, was occupied along each extremity, as far as the eye could reach at night, by the groves and outbuildings attached to the senator's mansion. The palace-grounds, at the higher and further end of the street — looking *from* the Pincian Gate — crossed it by a wide archway, and then stretched backward, until they joined the trees of the little garden of Numerian's abode. In a line with this house, but separated from it by a short space, stood a long row of buildings, let out floor by floor to separate occupants, and towering to an unwieldy altitude — for in Ancient Rome, as in Modern London, in consequence of the high price of land in an overpopulated city, builders could only secure space in a dwelling by adding inconveniently to its height. Beyond these habitations rose the trees surrounding another patrician abode, and beyond that the houses took a sudden turn, and nothing more was visible in a straight line, but the dusky indefinite objects of the distant view.

The whole appearance of the street before Vetranio's mansion, had it been unoccupied by the repulsive groups now formed in it, would have been eminently beautiful, at the hour of which we now write. The nobly symmetrical frontage of the palace itself, with its graceful succession of long porticos and colossal statues, contrasted by the picturesquely irregular appearance of the opposite dwelling of Numerian, and the lofty houses by its side; the soft, indistinct masses of foliage, running parallel along the upper ends of the street, terminated and connected by the archway garden across the road, on which were planted a group of tall pine-trees, rising in gigantic relief against the transparent sky; the brilliant light streaming across the pavement from Vetranio's gaily-curtained windows, immediately opposed by the tranquil moonlight which lit the more distant view — formed altogether a prospect in which the natural and the artificial were mingled together in the most exquisite proportions — a prospect whose ineffable poetry and beauty might, on any other night, have charmed the most careless eye and exalted the most frivolous mind. But now, overspread as it was by groups of people, gaunt with famine and hideous with disease; startled as it was, at gloomy intervals, by contending cries of supplication, defiance, and despair, its brightest beauties of Nature and Art appeared but to shine with an aspect of bitter mockery around the human misery which their splendour disclosed.

Upwards of a hundred people — mostly of the lowest orders — were congregated before the senator's devoted dwelling. Some few among them passed slowly to and fro in the street, their figures gliding shadowy and solemn through the light around them; but the greater number lay on the pavement before the wall of Numerian's dwelling and the doorways of the lofty houses by its side. Illuminated by the full glare of the light from the palace windows, these groups, huddled together in the distorted attitudes of suffering and despair, assumed a fearful and unearthly appearance. Their shrivelled faces, their tattered clothing, their wan forms, here prostrate, there half-raised, were bathed in a steady red glow. High above them, at the windows of the tall houses, now tenanted in every floor by the dead, appeared a few figures (the mercenary guardians of the dying within) bending forward to look out upon the palace opposite — their haggard faces showing pale in the clear moonlight. Sometimes their voices were heard, calling in mockery to the mass of people below, to break down the strong steel gates of the palace, and tear the full wine-cup from its master's lips. Sometimes those beneath replied with execrations, which rose wildly mingled with the wailing of women and children, the moans of the plaguestricken, and the supplications of the famished to the slaves passing backwards and forwards behind the palace railings, for charity and help.

In the intervals, when the tumult of weak voices was partially lulled, there was heard a dull, regular, beating sound, produced by those who had found dry bones on their road to the palace, and were pounding them on the pavement, in sheltered places, for food. The wind, which had been refreshing during the day, had changed at sunset, and now swept up slowly over the street, in hot, faint gusts, plague-laden from the East. Particles of the ragged clothing on some prostrate forms lying most exposed in its course, waved slowly to and fro, as it passed, like banners planted by Death on the yielding defences of the citadel of Life. It wound through the open windows of the palace, hot and mephitic, as if tainted with the breath of the foul and furious words which it bore onward into the banqueting-hall of the senator's reckless guests. Driven over such scenes as now spread beneath it, it derived from them a portentous significance, — it seemed to blow like an atmosphere exuded from the furnace-depths of centre earth, breathing sinister warnings of some deadly convulsion in the whole fabric of Nature over the thronged and dismal street.

Such was the prospect before the palace, and such the spectators assembled in ferocious anxiety to behold the destruction of the senator's abode. Meanwhile, within the walls of the building, the beginning of the fatal orgy was at hand.

It had been covenanted by the slaves (who, during the calamities in the besieged city, had relaxed in their accustomed implicit obedience to their master with perfect impunity), that as soon as the last labours of preparation were completed, they should be free to consult their own safety by quitting the devoted palace. Already some of the weakest and most timid of their numbers might be seen passing out hastily into the gardens, by the back gates, like engineers who had fired a train, and were escaping ere the explosion burst forth. Those among the menials who still remained in the palace, were for the greater part occupied in drinking from the vases of wine which had been placed before them, to preserve to the last moment their failing strength.

The mockery of festivity had been extended even to their dresses, — green liveries girt with cherry-coloured girdles arrayed their wasted forms. They drank in utter silence. Not the slightest appearance of revelry or intoxication prevailed among their ranks. Confusedly huddled together, as if for mutual protection, they ever and anon cast quick glances of suspicion and apprehension upon some six or eight of the superior attendants of the palace, who walked backwards and forwards at the outer extremity of the hall occupied by their comrades, and occasionally advancing along the straight passages before them to the front gates of the building, appeared to be exchanging furtive signals with some of the people in the street. Reports had been vaguely spread of a secret conspiracy between some of the principal slaves and certain chosen ruffians of the populace, to murder all the inmates of the palace, seize on its treasures, and, opening the city gates to the Goths, escape with their booty during the confusion of the pillage of Rome. Nothing had as yet been positively discovered; but the few attendants who kept ominously apart from the rest, were unanimously suspected by their fellows, who now watched them over their wine-cups with anxious eyes. Different as was the scene among the slaves still left in the palace, from the scene among the people dispersed in the street, the one was nevertheless in its own degree as gloomily suggestive of some great impending calamity as the other.

The grand banqueting-hall of the palace, prepared though it now was for festivity, wore a changed and melancholy aspect.

The massive tables still ran down the whole length of the noble room, surrounded by luxurious couches, as in former days; but not a vestige of food appeared upon their glittering surfaces. Rich vases, flasks, and drinking-cups, all filled with wine, alone occupied the festal board. Above, hanging low from the ceiling, burnt ten large lamps, corresponding to the number of guests assembled, as the only procurable representatives of the hundreds of revellers who had feasted at Vetranio's expense, during the brilliant nights that were now passed for ever. At the lower end of the room, beyond the grand door of entrance, hung a thick, black curtain, apparently intended to conceal, mysteriously, some object behind it. Before the curtain burnt a small lamp of yellow glass, raised upon a high gilt pole, and around and beneath it, heaped against the side walls, and over part of the table, lay a various and confused mass of rich objects, all of a nature more or less inflammable, and all besprinkled with scented oils. Hundreds of yards of gorgeously variegated hangings, rolls upon rolls of manuscripts, gaudy dresses of all colours, toys, utensils, innumerable articles of furniture, formed in rare and beautifully inlaid woods, were carelessly flung together against the walls of the apartment, and rose high towards its ceiling.

On every part of the tables not occupied by the vases of wine, were laid gold and jewelled ornaments, which dazzled the eye by their brilliancy; while in extraordinary contrast to the magnificence thus profusely displayed, there appeared in one of the upper corners of the hall an old wooden stand, covered by a coarse cloth, on which were placed one or two common earthenware bowls, containing what may be termed a "mash" of boiled bran and salted horseflesh. Any repulsive odour which might have arisen from this strange compound was overpowered by the various perfumes sprinkled about the room, which mingling with the hot breezes wafted through the windows from the street, produced an atmosphere as oppressive and debilitating, in spite of its artificial allurements to the sense of smell, as the air of a dungeon, or the vapours of a marsh.

Remarkable as was the change in the present appearance of the banqueting-hall, it was but the feeble reflection of the alteration for the worse in the aspect of the host and his guests. Vetranio reclined at the head of the table, dressed in a scarlet mantle. An embroidered towel, with purple tassels and fringes, connected with rings of gold fell over his breast, and silver and ivory bracelets were clasped round his arms. But of the former man, the habiliments were all that remained. His head was bent forward, as if with the weakness of age; his emaciated arms seemed barely able to support the weight of the ornaments which glittered on them; his eyes had contracted a wild, unsettled expression; and a deadly paleness overspread the once plump and jovial cheeks which so many mistresses had kissed, in mercenary rapture, in other days. Both in countenance and manner the elegant voluptuary of our former acquaintance at the Court of Ravenna was entirely and fatally changed. Of the other eight patricians who lay on the couches around their altered host, — some wild and reckless, some gloomy and imbecile, — all had suffered in the ordeal of the siege, the famine and the pestilence, like him.

Such were the members of the assemblage, represented from the ceiling by nine of the burning lamps. The tenth and last lamp indicated the presence of one more guest, who reclined a little apart from the rest.

This man was hump-backed; his gaunt bony features were repulsively disproportioned in size to his puny frame, which looked doubly contemptible, enveloped as it was in an ample tawdry robe. Sprung from the lowest ranks of the populace, he had gradually forced himself into the favour of his superiors by his skill in coarse mimicry, and his readiness in ministering to the worst vices of all who would employ him. Having lost the greater part of his patrons during the siege, finding himself abandoned to starvation on all sides, he had now, as a last resource; obtained permission to participate in the banquet of famine, to enliven it by a final exhibition of his buffoonery, and to die with his masters, as he had lived with them, — the slave, the parasite, and the imitator of the lowest of their vices and the worst of their crimes.

At the commencement of the orgy, little was audible beyond the clash of the wine-cups, the low occasional whispering of the revellers, and the confused voices of the people without, floating through the window from the street. The desperate compact of the guests, now that its execution had actually begun, awed them at first, in spite of themselves. At length, when there was a lull of all sounds — when a temporary calm prevailed over the noises outside — when the wine-cups were emptied, and left for a moment ere they were filled again — Vetranio feebly rose, and, announcing with a mocking smile that he was about to speak a funeral oration over his friends and himself, pointed to the wall immediately behind him, as to an object fitted to awaken the astonishment or the hilarity of his moody guests.

Against the upper part of the wall were fixed various small statues in bronze and marble, all representing the owner of the palace, and all hung with golden plates. Beneath these appeared the rent-roll of his estates, written in various colours, on white vellum! and beneath that, scratched on the marble in faint irregular characters, was no less an object than his own epitaph, composed by himself. It may be translated thus: —

Stop, Spectator!
If thou hast reverently cultivated the pleasures of the taste,
pause amid these illustrious ruins of what was once
a palace;
and peruse with respect, on this stone,
the epitaph of
VETRANIO, a senator.
he was the first man who invented a successful
nightingale sauce;
his bold and creative genius added much, and would have
added more, to
THE ART OF COOKERY —
but, alas for the interests of science!
he lived in the days when the Gothic barbarians besieged
THE IMPERIAL CITY;
famine left him no matter for gustatory experiment;
and pestilence deprived him of cooks to enlighten!
opposed at all points by the force of adverse circumstances,
finding his life of no further use to the culinary
interests of Rome,
he called his chosen friends together to assist him,
conscientiously drank up every drop of wine remaining
in his cellars,
lit the funeral pile of himself and his guests
in the banqueting-hall of his own palace,
and died, as he had lived,
the patriotic CATO
of his country's gastronomy!

"Behold!" — cried Vetranio pointing triumphantly to the epitaph — "behold in every line of those eloquent letters at once the seal of my resolute adherence to the engagement that unites us here, and the foundation of my just claim to the reverence of posterity on the most useful of the arts which I exercised for the benefit of my species! Read — friends, brethren, fellow martyrs of glory — and, as you read, rejoice with me over the hour of our departure from the desecrated arena, no longer worthy the celebration of the Games of Life! Yet, ere the feast proceeds, hear me while I speak — I make my last oration, as the arbiter of our funeral sports, as the host of the Banquet of Famine!

"Who would sink ignobly beneath the slow superiority of starvation, or perish under the quickly-glancing steel of the barbarian conqueror's sword, when such a death as ours is offered to the choice? — when wine flows bright, to drown sensation in oblivion, and a palace and its treasures furnish alike the scene of the revel and the radiant funeral-pile? The mighty philosophers of India — the inspired Gymnosophists — died as we shall die! Calanus before Alexander, Zamarus in the presence of Augustus, lit the fires that consumed them! Let us follow their glorious example! No worms will prey upon our bodies, no hired mourners will howl discordant at our funerals! Purified in the radiance of primeval fire, we shall vanish triumphant from enemies and friends — a marvel to the earth, a vision of glory to the gods themselves!

"Is it a day more or a day less of life that is now of importance to us? No; it is only towards the easiest and the noblest death that our aspirations can turn! Among our number, there is now not one whom the care of existence can further occupy!

"Here, at my right hand, reclines my estimable comrade of a thousand former feasts, Furius-Balburius-Placidus, who, when we sailed on the Lucrine Lake, was wont to complain of intolerable hardship if a fly settled on the gilded folds of his umbrella; who languished for a land of Cimmerian darkness if a sunbeam penetrated the silken awnings of his garden-terrace; and who now wrangles for a mouthful of horse-flesh with the meanest of his slaves, and would exchange the richest of his country villas for a basket of dirty bread! Oh, Furius-Balburius-Placidus, of what further use is life to thee?

"There, at my left, I discern the changed though still expressive, countenance of the resolute Thascius — he who chastised a slave with a hundred lashes if his warm water was not brought immediately at his command; he whose serene contempt for every member of the human species but himself once ranked him among the greatest of human philosophers; even *he* now wanders through his palace unserved, and fawns upon the plebeian who will sell him a measure of wretched bran! Oh, admired friend, oh, rightly-reasoning Thascius, say, is there anything in Rome which should delay thee on thy journey to the Elysian Fields?

"Further onward at the table, drinking largely while I speak, I behold, oh, Marcus-Mœcius-Mœmmius, thy once plump and jovial form! — thou, in former days accustomed to rejoice in the length of thy name, because it enabled thy friends to drink the more, in drinking a cup to each letter of it, tell me what banqueting-hall is now open to thee but this? — and thus desolate in the city of thy social triumphs, what should disincline thee to make of our festal solemnity thy last revel on earth?

"Thou, too, facetious hunchback, prince of parasites, unscrupulous Reburrus, where, but at this banquet of famine, will thy buffoonery now procure for thee a draught of reviving wine? Thy masters have abandoned thee to thy native dung-hill! No more shalt thou wheedle for them when they borrow, or bully for them when they pay! No more charges of poisoning or magic shalt thou forge to imprison their troublesome creditors! Oh, officious sycophant, thy occupations are no more! Drink while thou canst, and then resign thy carcase to congenial mire!

"And you, my five remaining friends, whom — little desirous of further delay — I will collectively address, think on the days when the suspicion of an infectious malady in any one of your companions was sufficient to separate you from the dearest of them; when the slaves who came to you from their palaces underwent long ceremonies of ablution before they approached your presence; and remembering this, reflect that most, perhaps all of us, now meet here plague-tainted already; and then say, of what advantage is it to languish for a life which is yours no longer?

"No, my friends, my brethren of the banquet; feeling that when life is worthless, it is folly to live, you cannot shrink from the lofty resolution by which we are bound, you cannot pause on our joyful journey of departure from the scenes of earth — I wrong you even by a doubt! Let me now, rather, ask your attention for a worthier subject — the enumeration of the festal ceremonies by which the progress of the banquet will be marked. That task concluded, that last ceremony of my last welcome to you in these halls duly performed, I join you once more in your final homage to the deity of our social lives — the God of Wine!

"It is not unknown to you — learned as you are in the jovial antiquities of the table — that it was, among some of the ancients, a custom for a master-spirit of philosophy to preside — the teacher as well as the guest — at their feasts. This usage it has been my care to revive; and, as this our meeting is unparalleled in its heroic design, so it was my ambition to bid to it one unparalleled, either as a teacher or a guest. Fired by an original idea, unobserved of my slaves, aided only by my singing-boy, the faithful Glyco, I have succeeded in placing behind that black curtain, such an associate of our revels as you have never feasted with before — whose appearance at the fitting moment must strike you irresistibly with astonishment; and whose discourse — not of human wisdom only — will be inspired by the midnight secrets of the tomb. By my side, on this parchment, lies the formulary of questions to be addressed by Reburrus, when the curtain is withdrawn, to the Oracle of the Mysteries of other Spheres.

"Before you, behold in those vases all that remains of my once well-stocked cellars; and all that is provided for the palates of my guests! We sit at the Banquet of Famine, and no coarser sustenance than inspiring wine finds admittance at the Bacchanalian board. Yet, should any among us, in his last moments, be feeble enough to pollute his lips with nourishment alone worthy of the vermin of the earth, let him seek the wretched and scanty table, type of the wretched and scanty food that covers it, placed yonder, in obscurity, behind me. There will he find (in all barely sufficient for one man's poorest meal) the last morsels of the vilest nourishment left in the palace. For me, my resolution is fixed — it is only the generous wine-cup that shall now approach my lips!

"Above me are the ten lamps, answering to the number of my friends here assembled. One after another, as the wine overpowers us, those burning images of life will be extinguished in succession by the guests who remain proof against our draughts; and the last of these, lighting his torch at the last lamp, will consummate the banquet, and celebrate its glorious close, by firing the funeral pile of my treasures, heaped yonder against my palace walls! If *my* powers fail me before *yours* swear to me, that whoever among you is able to lift the cup to his lips, after it has dropped from the hands of the rest, will fire the pile! Swear it by your lost mistresses, your lost friends, your lost treasures! — by your own lives, devoted to the pleasures of wine and the purification of fire!"

As, with flashing eyes and flushed countenance, Vetranio sank back on his couch, his companions, inflamed with the wine they had already drunk, arose cup in hand, and turned towards him. Their voices, discordantly mingled, pronounced the oath together — then, as they resumed their former positions, their eyes all turned towards the black curtain in ardent expectation.

They had observed the sinister and sarcastic expression of Vetranio's eye, as he spoke of his concealed guest; they knew that the hunchback Reburrus possessed, among his other powers of buffoonery, the art of ventriloquism; and they suspected the presence of some hideous or grotesque image of a heathen god or demon in the hidden recess, which the jugglery of the parasite was to gift with the capacity of speech. Blasphemous comments upon life, death, and immortality were eagerly awaited. The general impatience for the withdrawal of the curtain was perceived by Vetranio, who, waving his hand for silence, authoritatively exclaimed — "The hour has not yet arrived — more draughts must be drunk, more libations poured out, ere the mystery of the curtain is revealed! Ho! Glyco!" — he continued, turning towards the singing-boy, who had silently entered the room —

"the moment is yours! Tune your lyre, and recite my last ode, which I have addressed to *you!* Let the charms of Poetry preside over the feast of Death!"

The boy advanced trembling, his once ruddy face was colourless and haggard; his eyes were fixed with a look of rigid terror on the black curtain; his features palpably expressed the presence within him of some secret and overwhelming recollection, which had crushed all his other faculties and perceptions. Steadily, almost guiltily, averting his face from his master's countenance, he stood by Vetranio's couch, a frail and fallen being, a mournful spectacle of perverted docility and degraded youth.

Still true, however, to the duties of his vocation, he ran his thin, trembling fingers over the lyre, and mechanically preluded the commencement of the ode. But during the silence of attention which now prevailed, the confused noises from the people in the street penetrated more distinctly into the banqueting-room; and, at this moment, high above them all — hoarse, raving, terrible — rose the voice of one man.

"Tell me not," it cried, "of perfumes wafted from the palace! — foul vapours flow from it! — see, they sink, suffocating over me! — they bathe sky and earth, and men who move around us, in fierce, green light!"

Then other voices of men and women, shrill and savage, broke forth in interruption together: — "Peace,

Davus! you awake the dead about you!" "Hide in the darkness; you are plague-struck; your skin is shrivelled; your gums are toothless!" "When the palace is fired, you shall be flung into the flames to purify your rotten carcase!"

"Sing!" cried Vetranio, furiously, observing the shudders that ran over the boy's frame and held him speechless, "Strike the lyre, as Timotheus struck it before Alexander! Drown, in melody, the barking of the curs who wait for our offal in the street!"

Feebly and interruptedly the terrified boy began, the wild, continuous noises of the moaning voices from without sounding their awful accompaniment to the infidel philosophy of his song, as he breathed it forth in faint and faltering accents. It ran thus: —

TO GLYCO.

Ah, Glyco! why in flow'rs array'd?
Those festive wreaths less quickly fade
  Than briefly-blooming joy!
Those high-prized friends who share your mirth
Are counterfeits of brittle earth,
  False coin'd in Death's alloy!

The bliss your notes could once inspire,
When lightly o'er the god-like lyre
  Your nimble fingers pass'd,
Shall spring the same from others' skill —
When you're forgot, the music still
  The player shall outlast!

The sun-touch'd cloud that mounts the sky,
That brightly glows to warm the eye,
  Then fades we know not where,

>   Is image of the little breath
> Of life — and then, the doom of Death
>   That you and I must share!
>
> Helpless to make or mar our birth,
> We blindly grope the ways of earth,
>   And live our paltry hour;
> Sure, that when life has ceased to please,
> To die at will, in Stoic ease,
>   Is yielded to our pow'r!
>
> Who, timely wise, would meanly wait
> The dull delay of tardy Fate,
>   When Life's delights are shorn?
> No! When its outer gloss has flown,
> Let's fling the tarnish'd bauble down
>   As lightly as 'twas worn!

"A health to Glyco! A deep draught to a singer from heaven come down upon earth!" cried the guests, seizing their winecups, as the ode was concluded, and draining them to the last drop. But their drunken applause fell noiseless upon the ear to which it was addressed. The boy's voice, as he sang the final stanza of the ode, had suddenly changed to a shrill, almost an unearthly tone, then suddenly sank again as he breathed forth the last few notes; and now, as his dissolute audience turned towards him with approving glances, they saw him standing before them cold, rigid, and voiceless. The next instant his fixed features were suddenly distorted; his whole frame collapsed, as if torn by an internal spasm — he fell back heavily to the floor. Those around approached him with unsteady feet, and raised him in their arms. His soul had burst the bonds of vice in which others had entangled it; the voice of Death had whispered to the slave of the great despot, Crime — "Be free!"

"We have heard the note of the swan singing its own funeral hymn!" said the patrician Placidus, looking in maudlin pity from the corpse of the boy to the face of Vetranio, which presented, for the moment, an involuntary expression of grief and remorse.

"Our miracle of beauty, and boy-god of melody, has departed before us to the Elysian fields!" muttered the hunchbank Reburrus in harsh, sarcastic accents.

Then, during the short silence that ensued, the voices from the street — joined on this occasion to a noise of approaching footsteps on the pavement — became again distinctly audible in the banqueting-hall. "News! news!" cried these fresh auxiliaries of the horde already assembled before the palace. "Keep together, you who still care for your lives! Solitary citizens have been lured by strange men into desolate streets, and never seen again! Jars of newly-salted flesh, which there were no beasts left in the city to supply, have been found in a butcher's shop! Keep together! Keep together!"

"No cannibals among the mob shall pollute the body of my poor boy!" cried Vetranio, rousing himself from his short lethargy of grief. "Ho! Thascius! Marcus! you who can yet stand! let us bear him to the funeral pile! He has died first — his ashes shall be first consumed!"

The two patricians arose as the senator spoke, and

aided him in carrying the body to the lower end of the room, where it was laid across the table, beneath the black curtain, and between the heaps of drapery and furniture piled up against each of the walls. Then, as his guests reeled back to their places, Vetranio remaining by the side of the corpse, and seizing in his unsteady hands a small vase of wine, exclaimed in tones of fierce exultation — "The hour has come — the banquet of Famine has ended — the banquet of Death has begun! A health to the guest behind the curtain! Fill — drink — behold!"

He drank deeply from the vase as he ceased, and drew aside the black drapery above him. A cry of terror and astonishment burst from the intoxicated guests, as they beheld in the recess now disclosed to view the corpse of an aged woman, clothed in white, and propped up on a high black throne, with the face turned towards them, and the arms (artificially supported) stretched out as if in denunciation over the banqueting table. The lamp of yellow glass which burnt high above the body threw over it a lurid and flickering light — the eyes were open, the jaw had fallen, the long, grey tresses drooped heavily on either side of the white, hollow cheeks.

"Behold!" — cried Vetranio, pointing to the corpse — "Behold my secret guest! Who so fit as the dead to preside at the banquet of death? Compelling the aid of Glyco, shrouded by congenial night, seizing on the first corpse exposed before me in the street, I have set up there, unsuspected by all, the proper idol of our worship, and philosopher at our feast! Another health to the queen of the fatal revels — to the teacher of the mysteries of worlds unseen; rescued from rotting unburied, to perish in the consecrated flames with the senators of Rome! A health! — a health to the mighty mother, ere she begin the mystic revelations! Fill — drink!"

Fired by their host's example, recovered from their momentary awe, already inflamed by the mad recklessness of debauchery, the guests started from their couches, and with Bacchanalian shouts answered Vetranio's challenge. The scene at this moment approached the supernatural. The wild disorder of the richly-laden tables; the wine flowing over the floor from overthrown vases; the great lamps burning bright and steady over the confusion beneath; the fierce gestures, the disordered countenances of the revellers, as they waved their jewelled cups over their heads in frantic triumph; and then the gloomy and terrific prospect at the lower end of the hall — the black curtain, the light burning solitary on its high pole, the dead boy lying across the festal table, the living master standing by his side, and, like an evil spirit, pointing upward in mockery to the white-robed corpse of the woman, as it towered above all in its unnatural position, with its skinny arms stretched forth, with its ghastly features appearing to move as the faint and flickering light played over them — produced together such a combination of scarce-earthly objects as might be painted, but cannot be described. It was an embodiment of a sorcerer's vision — an apocalypse of sin triumphing over the world's last relics of mortality in the vaults of death.

"To your task, Reburrus!" cried Vetranio, when the tumult was lulled; "to your questions without delay! Behold the teacher with whom you are to hold commune! Peruse carefully the parchment in your hand — question, and question loudly — you speak to the apathetic dead!"

For some time before the disclosure of the corpse, the hunchback had been seated apart at the end of the banqueting-hall opposite the black-curtained recess, conning over the manuscript containing the list of questions and answers which formed the impious dialogue he was to hold, by the aid of his powers of ventriloquism, with the violated dead. When the curtain was withdrawn he had looked up for a moment, and had greeted the appearance of the sight behind it, with a laugh of brutal derision, returning immediately to the study of his blasphemous formulary which had been confided to his care. At the moment when Vetranio's commands were addressed to him, he arose, reeled down the apartment towards the corpse, and opening the dialogue as he approached it, began in loud jeering tones: — "Speak, miserable relict of decrepit mortality!"

He paused as he uttered the last word; and, gaining a point of view from which the light of the lamp fell full upon the solemn and stony features of the corpse, looked up defiantly at it. In an instant a frightful change passed over him, the manuscript dropped from his hand, his deformed frame shrank and tottered, a shrill cry of recognition burst from his lips, more like the yell of a wild beast than the voice of a man.

The next moment — when the guests started up to question or deride him — he turned slowly and faced them. Desperate and drunken as they were, his look awed them into utter silence. His face was death-like in hue, as the face of the corpse above him — thick drops of perspiration trickled down it like rain — his dry, glaring eyes, wandered fiercely over the startled countenances before him; and as he extended towards them his clenched hands, he muttered in a deep gasping whisper: — "Who has done this? MY MOTHER! MY MOTHER!"

As these few words — of awful import, though of simple form — fell upon the ears of those whom he addressed, such of them as were not already sunk in insensibility, looked round on each other almost sobered for the moment, and all speechless alike. Not even the clash of the wine-cups was now heard at the banqueting table — nothing was audible but the sound, still fitfully rising and falling, of the voices of terror, ribaldry, and anguish, from the street; and the hoarse convulsive accents of the hunchback, still uttering at intervals his fearful identification of the dead body above him — "MY MOTHER! MY MOTHER!"

At length Vetranio, who was the first to recover himself, addressed the terrified and degraded wretch before him, in tones which, in spite of himself, betrayed as he began an unwonted tremulousness and restraint. "What, Reburrus!" he cried, "are you already drunken to insanity, that you call the first dead body which by chance I encountered in the street, and by chance brought hither — your mother? Was it to talk of your mother, whom dead or alive we neither know nor care for, that you were admitted here? Son of obscurity and inheritor of rags, what are your plebeian parents to us!" he continued, refilling his cup, and lashing himself into assumed anger as he spoke — "To your dialogue without delay! or you shall be flung from the windows to mingle with your rabble-equals in the street!"

Neither by word nor look did the hunchback answer the senator's menaces. For *him*, the voice of the living was stifled in the presence of the dead. The retribution that had gone forth against him had struck his moral, as a thunderbolt might have stricken his physical, being. His soul strove in agony within him, as he thought on the awful fatality which had set the dead mother in judgment on the degraded son — which had directed the hand of the senator, unwittingly to select the corpse of the outraged parent, as the object for the infidel buffoonery of the reckless child, at the very close of his impious career. His past life rose before him, for the first time, like a foul vision; like a nightmare of horror, impurity, and crime. He staggered up the room, groping his way along the wall, as if the darkness of midnight had closed round his eyes, and crouched down by the open window.

Beneath him, rose the evil and ominous voices from the street; around him, spread the pitiless array of his masters; before him, appeared the denouncing vision of the corpse.

He would have remained but a short time unmolested in his place of refuge, but for an event which now diverted from him the attention of Vetranio and his guests. Drinking furiously to drown all recollection of the catastrophe they had just witnessed, three of the revellers had already suffered the worst consequences of an excess which their weakened frames were ill-fitted to bear. One after another, at short intervals, they fell back senseless on their couches; and one after another, as they succumbed, the three lamps burning nearest to them were extinguished. The same speedy termination to the debauch seemed to be in reserve for the rest of their companions, with the exception of Vetranio and the two patricians who reclined at his right hand and his left. These three still preserved the appearance of self-possession; but an ominous change had already overspread their countenances. The expression of wild joviality, of fierce recklessness, had departed from their wild features — they silently watched each other with vigilant and suspicious eyes — each, in turn, as he filled his wine-cup, significantly handled the torch with which the last drinker was to fire the funeral pile. As the numbers of their rivals decreased, and the flame of lamp after lamp was extinguished, the fatal contest for a suicide supremacy assumed a present and powerful interest, in which all other purposes and objects were forgotten. The corpse at the foot of the banqueting table, and the wretch cowering in his misery at the window, were now alike unheeded. In the bewildered and brutalised minds of the guests, one sensation alone remained — the intensity of expectation which precedes the result of a deadly strife.

But ere long — awakening the attention which might otherwise never have been aroused — the voice of the hunchback was heard, as the spirit of repentance now moved within him, uttering, in wild moaning tones, a strange confession of degradation and sin — addressed to none; proceeding, independent of consciousness or will, from the depths of his stricken soul. He half raised himself; and fixed his sunken eyes upon the dead body, as these words dropped from his lips: — "It was the last time that I beheld her alive, when she approached me — lonely, and feeble, and poor — in the street; beseeching me to return to her in the days of her old age and her solitude; and to remember how she had loved me in my childhood for my very deformity, how she had watched me throughout the highways of Rome, that none should oppress or deride me! the tears ran down her cheeks; she knelt to me on the hard pavement! and I, who had deserted her for her poverty, to make myself a slave in palaces among the accursed rich, flung down money to her, as to a beggar who wearied me; and passed on! She died desolate! her body lay unburied, and I knew it not! The son who had abandoned the mother never saw her more, until she rose before him there — avenging, horrible, lifeless! a sight of death never to leave him! Woe, woe to the accursed in his deformity, and the accursed of his mother's corpse!"

He paused, and fell back again to the ground, grovelling and speechless. The tyrannic Thascius, regarding him with a scowl of drunken wrath, seized an empty vase, and poising it in his unsteady hand, prepared to hurl it at the hunchback's prostrate form, when again a single cry — a woman's — rising above the increasing uproar in the street, rang shrill and startling through the banqueting hall. The patrician suspended his purpose as he heard it, mechanically listening with the half-stupid, half-cunning attention of intoxication. "Help! help!" shrieked the voice beneath the palace windows, "he follows me still — he attacked my dead child in my arms! As I flung myself down upon it on the ground, I saw him watching his opportunity to drag it by the limbs from under me — famine and madness were in his eyes — I drove him back — I fled — he follows me still! — save us, save us!"

At this instant her voice was suddenly stifled in the sound of fierce cries and rushing footsteps, followed by an appalling noise of heavy blows, directed at several points, against the steel railings before the palace doors. Between the blows, which fell slowly and together at regular intervals, the infuriated wretches, whose last exertions of strength were strained to the utmost to deal them, could be heard shouting breathlessly to each other, "Strike harder, strike longer! the back gates are guarded against us by our comrades admitted to the pillage of the palace instead of us. You who would share the booty, strike firm! the stones are at your feet, the gates of entrance yield before you."

Meanwhile a confused sound of trampling footsteps and contending voices became audible from the lower apartments of the palace. Doors were violently shut and opened — shouts and execrations echoed and re-echoed along the lofty stone passages leading from the slaves' waiting rooms to the grand staircase; treachery betrayed itself as openly within the building, as violence still proclaimed itself in the assault on the gates outside. The chief slaves had not been suspected by their fellows without a cause; the bands of pillage and murder had been organised in the house of debauchery and death; the chosen adherents from the street had been secretly admitted through the garden gates, and had barred and guarded them against further intrusion — another doom than the doom they had impiously prepared for themselves was approaching the devoted senators, at the hands of the slaves whom they had oppressed, and the plebeians whom they had despised.

At the first sound of the assault without and the first intimation of the treachery within, Vetranio, Thascius, and Marcus started from their couches — the remainder of the guests, incapable either of thought or action, lay, in stupid insensibility, awaiting their fate. These three men alone comprehended the peril that threatened them; and, maddened with drink, defied, in their ferocious desperation, the death that was in store for them. "Hark! they approach, the rabble revolted from our rule," cried Vetranio scornfully, "to take the lives that we despise, and the treasures that we have resigned! The hour has come; I go to fire the pile that involves in one common destruction our assassins and ourselves!"

"Hold!" exclaimed Thascius, snatching the torch from his hand, "the entrance must first be defended, or, ere the flames are kindled, the slaves will be here! Whatever is moveable; couches, tables, corpses; let us hurl them all against the door!"

As he spoke he rushed towards the black-curtained recess, to set the example to his companions by seizing the corpse of the woman; but he had not passed more than half the length of the apartment, when the hunchback, who had followed him unheeded, sprang upon him from behind, and, with a shrill cry, fastening his fingers on his throat, hurled him torn and senseless to the floor. "Who touches the body that is mine!" shrieked the deformed wretch, rising from his victim, and threatening with his blood-stained hands Vetranio and Marcus, as they stood bewildered, and uncertain for the moment whether first to avenge their comrade, or to barricade the door — "The son shall rescue the mother! I go to bury her! Atonement! Atonement!"

He leaped upon the table as he spoke, tore asunder with resistless strength the cords which fastened the corpse to the throne, seized it in his arms, and the next instant gained the door. Uttering fierce, inarticulate cries, partly of anguish and partly of defiance, he threw it open, and stepped forward to descend, when he was met at the head of the stairs by the band of assassins hurrying up, with drawn swords and blazing torches, to their work of pillage and death. He stood before them — his deformed limbs set as firmly on the ground as if he were preparing to descend the stairs at one leap — with the corpse raised high on his breast; its unearthly features were turned towards them, its bare arms were still stretched forth as they had been extended over the banqueting table, its grey hair streamed back and mingled with his own: under the fitful illumination of the torches, which played red and wild over him and his fearful burden, the dead and the living looked joined to each other in one monstrous from.

Huddled together, motionless, on the stairs, their shouts of vengeance and fury frozen on their lips, the assassins stood for one moment, staring mechanically, with fixed, spell-bound eyes, upon the hideous bulwark opposing their advance on the victims whom they had expected so easily to surprise — the next instant, a superstitious panic seized them; as the hunchback suddenly moved towards them to descend, the corpse seemed to their terror-stricken eyes to be on the eve of bursting its way through their ranks. Ignorant of its introduction into the palace, imagining it, in the revival of their slavish fears, to be the spectral offspring of the magic incantations of the senators above, they turned with one accord and fled down the stairs. The sound of their cries of fear grew fainter and fainter in the direction of the garden, as they hurried through the secret gates at the back of the building. Then the heavy, regular tramp of the hunchback's footsteps, as he paced the solitary corridors after them, bearing his burden of death, became audible in awful distinctness; then that sound also died away and was lost, and nothing more was heard in the banqueting room save the sharp clang of the blows still dealt against the steel railings from the street.

But now these grew rare and more rare in their recurrence; the strong metal resisted triumphantly the utmost efforts of the exhausted rabble who assailed it; as the minutes moved on, the blows grew rapidly fainter and fewer; soon they diminished to three, struck at long intervals; soon to one, followed by deep execrations of despair; and after that, a great silence sank down over the palace and the street, where such strife and confusion had startled the night-echoes but a few moments before.

In the banqueting hall this rapid succession of events — the marvels of a few minutes — passed before Vetranio and Marcus as visions beheld by their eyes, but neither contained nor comprehended by their minds. Stolid in their obstinate recklessness, stupefied by the spectacle of the startling perils — menacing yet harmless, terrifying though transitory — which surrounded them, neither of the senators moved a muscle, or uttered a word, from the period when Thascius had fallen beneath the hunchback's attack, to the period when the last blow against the palace railings, and the last sound of voices from the street, had ceased in silence. Then the wild current of drunken exultation, suspended within them during this brief interval, flowed once more, doubly fierce, in its old course. Insensible, the moment after they had passed away, to the warning and terrific scenes they had beheld, each now looked round on the other with a glance of triumphant levity. "Hark!" cried Vetranio, "the mob without, feeble and cowardly to the last, abandon their puny efforts to force my palace gates! Behold our banqueting tables still sacred from the intrusion of the revolted menials, driven before my guest from the dead, like a flock of sheep before a single dog! Say, oh Marcus! did I not well to set the corpse at the foot of our banqueting table? What marvels has it not effected, borne before us by the frantic Reburrus, as a banner of the hosts of death, against the cowardly slaves whose fit inheritance is oppression, and whose sole sensation is fear! See, we are free to continue and conclude the banquet as we had designed! The gods themselves have interfered to raise us in security above our fellow-mortals, whom we despise! Another health, in gratitude to our departed guest, the instrument of our deliverance, under the auspices of omnipotent Jove!"

As Vetranio spoke, Marcus alone, out of all the revellers, answered his challenge. These two — the last-remaining combatants of the strife — having drained their cups to the health proposed, passed slowly down each side of the room, looking contemptuously on their prostrate companions, and extinguishing every lamp but the two which burnt over their own couches. Then, returning to the upper end of the tables, they resumed their places, not to leave them again until the fatal rivalry was finally decided, and the moment of firing the pile had actually arrived.

The torch lay between them; the last vases of wine stood at their sides. Not a word escaped the lips of either, to break the deep stillness prevailing over the palace. Each fixed his eyes on the other, in stern and searching scrutiny, and, cup for cup, drank in slow and regular alternation. The debauch, which had hitherto presented a spectacle of brutal degradation and violence, now that it was restricted to two men only — each equally unimpressed by the scenes of horror he had beheld, each vying with the other for the attainment of the supreme of depravity — assumed an appearance of hardly human iniquity; it became a contest for a satanic superiority of sin.

For some time, little alteration appeared in the countenances of either of the suicide-rivals; but they had now drunk to that final point of excess at which wine either acts as its own antidote, or overwhelms in fatal suffocation the pulses of life. The crisis in the strife was approaching for both, and the first to experience it was Marcus. Vetranio, as he watched him, observed a dark purple flush overspreading his face, hitherto pale, almost colourless. His eyes suddenly dilated; he panted for breath. The vase of wine, when he strove with a last effort to fill his cup from it, rolled from his hand to the floor. The stare of death was in his face as he half-raised himself, and for one instant looked steadily on his companion; the moment after, without word or groan, he dropped backward over his couch.

The contest of the night was decided! The host of the banquet and the master of the palace, had been reserved to end the one, and to fire the other!

A smile of malignant triumph parted Vetranio's lips, as he now arose and extinguished the last lamp burning besides his own. That done, he grasped the torch. His eyes, as he raised it, wandered dreamily over the array of his treasures, and the forms of his dead or insensible fellow-patricians around him, to be consumed by his act in annihilating fire. The sensation of his solemn night-solitude in his fated palace began to work in vivid and varying impressions on his mind, which was partially recovering some portion of its wonted acuteness, under the bodily reaction now produced in him by the very extravagance of the night's excess. His memory began to retrace, confusedly, the scenes with which the dwelling that he was about to destroy, had been connected, at distant or at recent periods. At one moment the pomp of former banquets, the jovial congregation of guests, since departed or dead, revived before him; at another, he seemed to be acting over again his secret departure from his dwelling on the night before his last feast, his stealthy return with the corpse that he had dragged from the street; his toil in setting it up in mockery behind the black curtain, and inventing the dialogue to be spoken before it by the hunchback. Now, his thoughts reverted to the minutest circumstances of the confusion and dismay among the members of his household, when the first extremities of the famine began to be felt in the city; and now, without visible connection or cause, they turned suddenly to the morning when he had hurried through the most solitary paths in his grounds to meet the betrayer Ulpius, at Numerian's garden gate. Once more the image of Antonina — so often present to his imagination, since the original was lost to his eyes — grew palpable before him. He thought of her, as listening at his knees to the sound of his lute; as awakening, bewildered and terrified, in his arms; as flying distractedly before her father's wrath; as now too surely lying dead in her beauty and her innocence, amid the thousand victims of the famine and the plague.

These and other reflections, while they crowded in whirlwind rapidity on his mind, wrought no alteration in the deadly purpose which they suspended. His delay in lighting the torch was the unconscious delay of the suicide, secure in his resolution ere he lifts the poison to his lips, — when Life rises before him as a thing that is past, and he stands for one tremendous moment in the dark gap between the present and the future, — no more the pilgrim of Time — not yet the inheritor of Eternity!

So, in the dimly-lighted hall, surrounded by the victims whom he had hurried before him to their doom, stood the lonely master of the great palace; and so spoke within him the mysterious voices of his last earthly thoughts. Gradually they sank and ceased, and stillness and vacancy closed like dark veils over his mind. Starting like one awakened from a trance, he once more felt the torch in his hand, and once more the expression of fierce desperation appeared in his eyes, as he lit it steadily at the lamp above him.

The dew was falling pure to the polluted earth; the light breezes sang their low, daybreak anthem among the leaves, to the Power that bade them forth; night had expired, and morning was already born of it, as Vetranio, with the burning torch in his hand, advanced towards the funeral pile.

He had already passed the greater part of the length of the room, when a faint sound of footsteps ascending a private staircase, which led to the palace gardens, and communicated with the lower end of the banqueting hall by a small door of inlaid ivory, suddenly attracted his attention. He hesitated in his deadly purpose, listening to the slow, regular, approaching sound, which, feeble though it was, struck mysteriously impressive upon his ear, in the dreary silence of all things around him. Holding the torch high above his head, as the footsteps came nearer, he fixed his eyes in intense expectation upon the door. It opened, and the figure of a young girl clothed in white stood before him. One moment he looked upon her with startled eyes, the next the torch dropped from his hand, and smouldered unheeded on the marble floor. It was Antonina.

Her face was overspread with a strange transparent paleness; her once soft, round cheeks had lost their girlish beauty of form; her expression, ineffably mournful, hopeless and subdued, threw a simple, spiritual solemnity over her whole aspect. She was changed, awfully changed, to the profligate senator, from the being of his former admiration; but still there remained in her despairing eyes enough of the old look of gentleness and patience, surviving through all anguish and dread, to connect her, even as she was now, with what she had been. She stood in the chamber of debauchery and suicide, between the funeral pile and the desperate man who was vowed to fire it, a feeble, helpless creature; yet powerful in the influence of her presence, at such a moment and in such a form, as a saving and reproving spirit, armed with the omnipotence of Heaven to mould the purposes of man.

Awed and astounded, as if he beheld an apparition from the tomb, Vetranio looked upon this young girl — whom he had loved with the least selfish passion that ever inspired him; whom he had lamented as long since lost and dead with the sincerest grief he had ever felt; whom he now saw standing before him, at the very moment ere he doomed himself to death, altered, desolate, supplicating — with emotions which held him speechless in wonder, and even in dread. While he still gazed upon her in silence, he heard her speaking to him in low, melancholy, imploring accents, which fell upon his ear, after the voices of terror and desperation that had risen around him throughout the night, like tones never addressed to it before.

"Numerian, my father, is sinking under the famine;" she began, "if no help is given to him, he may die even before sunrise! You are rich and powerful; I have come to you, having nothing now but *his* life to live for, to beg sustenance for him!" She paused, overpowered for the moment; and bent her eyes wistfully on the senator's face. Then, seeing that he vainly endeavoured to answer her, her head drooped upon her breast, and her voice sank lower as she continued: —

"I have striven for patience, under much sorrow and pain, through the long night that is passed; my eyes were heavy and my spirit was faint; I could have rendered up my soul willingly, in my loneliness and feebleness, to God who gave it; but that it was my duty to struggle for my life and my father's, now that I was restored to him after I had lost all beside! I could not think, or move, or weep; as, looking forth upon your palace, I watched and waited through the hours of darkness; but as morning dawned, the heaviness at my heart was lightened; I remembered that the palace I saw before me was yours; and though the gates were closed, I knew that I could reach it through your garden that joins to my father's land. I had none in Rome to ask mercy of but you! so I set forth hastily, ere my weakness should overpower me; remembering that I had inherited much misery at your hands, but hoping that you might pity me for what I had suffered, when you saw me again. I came wearily through the garden; it was long before I found my way hither; will you send me back as helpless as I came? You first taught me to disobey my father in giving me the lute; will you refuse to aid me in succouring him now? He is all that I have left in the world! Have mercy upon *him!* — have mercy upon *me!*"

Again she looked up in Vetranio's face. His trembling lips moved; but still no sound came from them. The expression of confusion and awe yet prevailed over his features, as he pointed slowly towards the upper end of the banqueting table. To *her* this simple action was eloquent beyond all power of speech; she turned her feeble steps instantly in the direction he had indicated.

He watched her, by the light of the single lamp that still burnt, passing — strong in the shielding inspiration of her good purpose — amid the bodies of his suicide companions, without pausing on her way. Having gained the upper end of the room, she took from the table a flask of wine; and from the wooden stand behind it, the bowl of offal disdained by the guests at the fatal banquet, returning immediately to the spot where Vetranio still stood. Here she stopped for a moment, as if about to speak once more; but her emotions overpowered her. From the sources which despair and suffering had dried up, the long-prisoned tears once more flowed forth at the bidding of gratitude and hope. She looked upon the senator, silent as himself; and her expression at that instant, was destined to remain on his memory, while memory survived. Then, with faltering and hasty steps she departed by the way she had come; and in the great palace, which his evil supremacy over the wills of others had made a hideous charnel-house, he was once more left alone.

He made no effort to follow or detain her as she left him. The torch still smouldered beside him on the floor, but he never stooped to take it up; he dropped down on a vacant couch, stupified by what he had beheld. That which no entreaties, no threats, no fierce violence of opposition could have effected in him, the appearance of Antonina had produced; it had forced him to pause at the very moment of the execution of his deadly design.

He remembered how, from the very first day when he had seen her, she had mysteriously influenced the whole progress of his life; how his ardour to possess her had altered his occupations, and even interrupted his amusements; how all his energy and all his wealth had been baffled in the attempt to discover her, when she fled from her father's house; how the first feeling of remorse that he' had ever known, had been awakened within him, by his knowledge of the share he had had in producing her unhappy fate. Recalling all this; reflecting that, had she approached him at an earlier period, she would have been driven back affrighted by the drunken clamour of his companions; and had she arrived at a later, would have found his palace in flames; thinking at the same time of her sudden presence in the banqueting-hall, when he had believed her to be dead, when her appearance at the moment before he fired the pile was most irresistible in its supernatural influence over his actions — that vague feeling of superstitious dread which exists intuitively in all men's minds, which had never before been aroused in his — thrilled through him. His eyes were fixed on the door by which she had departed, as if he expected her to return. Her destiny seemed to be portentously mingled with his own; his life seemed to move, his death to wait, at her bidding. There was no repentance, no moral purification in the emotions which now suspended his bodily faculties in inaction; he was struck for the time with a mental paralysis.

The restless moments moved onward and onward, and still he delayed the consummation of the ruin which the night's debauch had begun, Slowly the tender daylight grew and brightened in its beauty, warmed the cold prostrate bodies in the silent hall, and dimmed the faint glow of the wasting lamp; no black mist of smoke, no red glare of devouring fire arose to quench its fair lustre; no roar of flames interrupted the murmuring morning tranquillity of nature, or startled from their heavy repose the exhausted outcasts stretched upon the pavement of the street. Still the noble palace stood unshaken on its firm foundations; still the adornments of its porticos and its statues glittered as of old in the rays of the rising sun; and still the hand of the master who had sworn to destroy it, as he had sworn to destroy himself, hung idly near the torch which lay already extinguished in harmless ashes at his feet!

CHAPTER X.
The Last Efforts of the Besieged.

WE return to the street before the palace. The calamities of the siege had fallen fiercely on those who lay there during the night. From the turbulent and ferocious mob of a few hours since, not even the sound of a voice was now heard. Some, surprised in a paroxysm of hunger by exhaustion and insensibility, lay with their hands half forced into their mouths, as if in their ravenous madness they had endeavoured to prey upon their own flesh. Others, now and then wearily opened their languid eyes upon the street, no longer regardful, in the present extremity of their sufferings, of the building whose destruction they had assembled to behold, but watching for a fancied realisation of the visions of richly-spread tables and speedy relief called up before them, as if in mockery, by the delirium of starvation and disease.

The sun had as yet but slightly risen above the horizon, when the attention of the few among the populace who still preserved some perception of outward events, was suddenly attracted by the appearance of an irregular procession — composed partly of citizens and partly of officers of the senate, and headed by two men — which slowly approached from the end ot the street leading into the interior of the city. This assembly of persons stopped opposite Vetranio's palace; and then, such members of the mob who watched them as were not yet entirely abandoned by hope, heard the inspiring news that the procession they beheld was a procession of peace, and that the two men who headed it were the Spaniard, Basilius, a governor of a province; and Johannes, the chief of the Imperial notaries, — appointed ambassadors to conclude a treaty with the Goths.

As this intelligence reached them, men who had before appeared incapable of the slightest movement, now rose painfully, yet resolutely, to their feet, and crowded round the two ambassadors as round two angels descended to deliver them from bondage and death. Meanwhile, some officers of the senate, finding the front gates of the palace closed against them, proceeded to the garden entrances at the back of the building, to obtain admission to its owner. The absence of Vetranio and his friends from the deliberations of the government, had been attributed to their disgust at the obstinate and unavailing resistance offered to the Goths. Now, therefore, when submission had been resolved upon, it had been thought both expedient and easy to recal them peremptorily to their duties. In addition to this motive for seeking the interior of the palace, the servants of the senate had another errand to perform there. The widely-rumoured determination of Vetranio and his associates to destroy themselves by fire, in the frenzy of a last debauch —

disbelieved, or disregarded, while the more imminent perils of the city were under consideration — became a source of some apprehension and anxiety to the acting members of the Roman council, now that their minds were freed from part of the responsibility which had weighed on them, by their resolution to treat for peace.

Accordingly, the persons now sent into the palace were charged with the duty of frustrating its destruction, if such an act had been really contemplated, as well as the duty of recalling its inmates to their appointed places in the senate-house. How far they were enabled, at the time of their entrance into the banqueting-hall, to accomplish their double mission, the reader is well able to calculate. They found Vetranio still in the place which he had occupied since Antonina had quitted him. Startled by their approach from the stupor which had hitherto weighed on his faculties, the desperation of his purpose returned; he made an effort to tear from its place the lamp which still feebly burnt, and to fire the pile in defiance of all opposition. But his strength, already taxed to the utmost, failed him. Uttering impotent threats of resistance and revenge, he fell, swooning and helpless, into the arms of the officers of the senate who held him back. One of them was immediately dismissed, while his companions remained in the palace, to communicate with the leaders of the assembly outside. His report concluded, the two ambassadors moved slowly onward, separating themselves from the procession which had accompanied them, and followed only by a few chosen attendants — a mournful and a degraded embassy, sent forth by the people who had once imposed their dominion, their customs, and even their language, on the Eastern and Western worlds, to bargain with the barbarians whom their fathers had enslaved, for the purchase of a disgraceful peace.

On the departure of the ambassadors, all the spectators, still capable of the effort, repaired to the Forum to await their return, and were joined there by members of the populace from other parts of the city. It was known that the first intimation of the result of the embassy would be given from this place; and in the eagerness of their anxiety to hear it, in the painful intensity of their final hopes of deliverance, even death itself seemed for awhile to be arrested in its fatal progress through the ranks of the besieged. In silence and apprehension they counted the tardy moments of delay, and watched with sickening gaze the shadows lessening and lessening, as the sun gradually rose in the heavens to the meridian point.

At length, after an absence that appeared of endless duration, the two ambassadors re-entered Rome. Neither of them spoke as they hurriedly passed through the ranks of the people; but their looks of terror and despair were all-eloquent to every beholder — their mission had failed.

For some time, no member of the government appeared to have resolution enough to come forward and harangue the people on the subject of the unsuccessful embassy. After a long interval, however, the Prefect Pompeianus himself, urged partly by the selfish entreaties of his friends, and partly by the childish love of display which still adhered to him through all his present anxieties and apprehensions, stepped into one of the lower balconies of the senate-house to address the citizens beneath him.

The chief magistrate of Rome was no longer the pompous and portly personage, whose intrusion on Vetranio's privacy during the commencement of the siege, has been described previously. The little superfluous flesh still remaining on his face hung about it like an ill-fitting garment; his tones had become lachrymose; the oratorical gestures with which he was wont to embellish profusely his former speeches, were all abandoned; nothing remained of the original man but the bombast of his language, and the impudent complacency of his self-applause, which now appeared in contemptible contrast to his crest-fallen demeanour, and his disheartening narrative of degradation and defeat.

"Men of Rome, let each of you exercise in his own person the heroic virtues of a Regulus or a Cato!" the Prefect began. "A treaty with the barbarians is out of our power! It is the scourge of the empire, Alaric himself, who commands the invading forces! Vain were the dignified remonstrances of the grave Basilius, futile was the persuasive rhetoric of the astute Johannes, addressed to the slaughtering and vain-glorious Goth! On their admission to his presence, the ambassadors, anxious to awe him into a capitulation, enlarged, with sagacious and commendable patriotism, on the expertness of the Romans in the use of arms, their readiness for war, and their vast numbers within the city walls. I blush to repeat the barbarian's reply. Laughing immoderately, he answered, '*The thicker the grass, the easier it is to cut!*' Still undismayed, the ambassadors, changing their tactics, talked indulgently of their willingness to purchase a peace. At this proposal, his insolence burst beyond all bounds of barbarous arrogance. 'I will not relinquish the siege,' he cried, 'until I have delivered to me all the gold and silver in the city, all the household goods in it, and all the slaves from the northern countries.' 'What then, oh King, will you leave us?' asked our amazed ambassadors. 'YOUR LIVES!' answered the implacable Goth. Hearing this, even the resolute Basilius and the wise Johannes despaired. They asked time to communicate with the senate, and left the camp of the enemy without further delay. Such was the end of the embassy; such the arrogant ferocity of the barbarian foe!"

Here the Prefect paused, from sheer weakness and want of breath. His oration, however, was not concluded. He had disheartened the people by his narrative of what had occurred to the ambassadors: he now proceeded to console them by his relation of what had occurred to himself, when, after an interval, he thus resumed: —

"But even yet, oh citizens of Rome, it is not time

to despair! There is another chance of deliverance still left to us; and that chance has been discovered by *me*. It was my lot, during the absence of the ambassadors, to meet with certain men of Tuscany, who had entered Rome a few days before the beginning of the siege, and who spoke of a project for relieving the city which they would communicate to the Prefect alone. Ever anxious for the public welfare, daring all treachery from strangers for advantage of my office, I accorded to these men a secret interview. They told me of a startling and miraculous event. The town of Neveia, lying, as you well know, in the direct road of the barbarians when they marched upon Rome, was protected from their pillaging bands by a tempest of thunder and lightning terrible to behold. This tempest arose not, as you may suppose, from an accidental convulsion of the elements, but was launched over the heads of the invaders by the express interference of the tutelary deities of the town, invocated by the inhabitants, who returned in their danger to the practice of their ancient manner of worship. So said the men of Tuscany; and such pious resources as those employed by the people of Neveia did they recommend to the people of Rome! For my part I acknowledge to you that I have faith in their project. The antiquity of our former worship is still venerable in my eyes. The prayers of the priests of our new religion have wrought no miraculous interference in our behalf: let us therefore imitate the example of the inhabitants of Neveia, and by the force of our invocations hurl the thunders of Jupiter on the barbarian camp! Let us trust for deliverance to the potent interposition of the gods whom our fathers worshipped — those gods who now, perhaps, avenge themselves for our desertion of their temples by our present calamities. I go without delay to propose to the Bishop Innocentius and to the senate, the puplic performance of solemn ceremonies of sacrifice at the Capitol! I leave you in the joyful assurance that the gods, appeased by our returning fidelity to our altars, will not refuse the supernatural protection which they accorded to the people of a provincial town, to the citizens of Rome!"

No sounds either of applause or disapprobation followed the Prefect's notable proposal for delivering the city from the besiegers by the public apostasy of the besieged. As he disappeared from their eyes, the audience turned away speechless. An universal despair now overpowered in them even the last energies of discord and crime; they resigned themselves to their doom with the gloomy indifference of beings in whom all mortal sensations, all human passions, good or evil, were extinguished. The Prefect departed on his ill-omened expedition to propose the practice of Paganism to the Bishop of a Christian church; but no profitable effort for relief was even suggested, either by the government or the people.

And so this day drew in its turn towards a close — more mournful and more disastrous, more fraught with peril, misery, and gloom, than the days that had preceded it.

The next morning dawned, but no preparations for the ceremonies of the ancient worship appeared at the Capitol. The senate and the bishop hesitated to incur the responsibility of authorising a public restoration of Paganism; the citizens, hopeless of succour, heavenly or earthly, remained unheedful as the dead of all that passed around them. There was one man in Rome who might have succeeded in rousing their languid energies to apostasy; but where, and how employed, was he?

Now, when the opportunity for which he had laboured resolutely, though in vain, through a long existence of suffering, degradation, and crime, had gratuitously presented itself more tempting and more favourable than even he in his wildest visions of success had ever dared to hope, — where was Ulpius? Hidden from men's eyes, like a foul reptile, in his lurking-place in the deserted temple — now raving round his idols in the fury of madness, now prostrate before them in idiot adoration — weaker for the interests of his worship, at the crisis of its fate, than the weakest child crawling famished through the streets, — the victim of his own evil machinations at the very moment when they might have led him to triumph, — the object of that worst earthly retribution, by which the wicked are at once thwarted, doomed and punished, here as hereafter, through the agency of their own sins.

Three more days passed. The senate, their numbers fast diminishing in the pestilence, occupied the time in vain deliberations or moody silence. Each morning the weary guards looked forth from the ramparts, with the fruitless hope of discerning the long-promised legions of Ravenna on their way to Rome; and each morning devastation and death gained ground afresh among the hapless besieged. At length, on the fourth day, the senate abandoned all hope of further resistance and determined on submission, whatever might be the result. It was resolved that another embassy composed of the whole acting senate, and followed by a considerable train should proceed to Alaric: that one more effort should be made to induce him to abate his ruinous demands on the conquered; and that if this failed, the gates should be thrown open, and the city and the people abandoned to his mercy in despair.

As soon as the procession of this last Roman embassy was formed in the Forum, its numbers were almost immediately swelled, in spite of opposition, by those among the mass of the people who were still able to move their languid and diseased bodies, and who, in the extremity of their misery, had determined, at all hazards, to take advantage of the opening of the gates, and fly from the city of pestilence, in which they were immured, careless whether they perished on the swords of the Goths, or languished unaided on the open plains. All power of enforcing order had long since been lost; the few soldiers gathered about the senators made one abortive effort to drive the people back, and then resigned any further resistance to their will.

Feebly and silently the spirit-broken assembly now moved along the great highways, so often trodden to the roar of martial music, and the shouts of applauding multitudes, by the triumphal processions of victorious Rome; and from every street, as it passed on, the wasted forms of the people stole out like spectres to join it. Among these, as the embassy approached the Pincian Gate, were two, hurrying forth to herd with their fellow-sufferers, on whose fortunes in the fallen city our more particular attention has been fixed. To explain their presence on the scene (if such an explanation be required), it is necessary to digress for a moment from the progress of events during the last days of the siege to the morning when Antonina departed from Vetranio's palace to return with her succour of food and wine to her father's house.

The reader is already acquainted, from her own short and simple narrative, with the history of the closing hours of her mournful night-vigil by the side of her sinking parent, and with the motives which prompted her to seek the palace of the senator, and entreat assistance in despair from one whom she only remembered as the profligate destroyer of her tranquillity under her father's roof. It is now, therefore, most fitting to follow her on her way back through the palace gardens. No living creature but herself trod the grassy paths, along which she hastened with faltering steps — those paths which she dimly remembered to have first explored, when in former days she ventured forth to follow the distant sounds of Vetranio's lute. In spite of her vague, heavy sensations of solitude and grief, this recollection remained painfully present to her mind, unaccountably mingled with the dark and dreary apprehensions which filled her heart as she hurried onward, until she once more entered her father's dwelling; and then, as she again approached his couch, every other feeling became absorbed in a faint, overpowering fear, lest, after all her perseverance and success in her errand of filial devotion, she might have returned too late.

The old man still lived — his weary eyes opened gladly on her, when she aroused him to partake of the treasured gifts from the senator's banqueting-table. The wretched food which the suicide-guests had disdained, and the simple flask of wine which they would have carelessly quaffed at one draught, were viewed both by parent and child as the saving and invigorating sustenance of many days. After having consumed as much as they dared of their precarious supply, the remainder was carefully husbanded. It was the last sign and promise of life to which they looked — the humble, yet precious store, in which alone they beheld the earnest of their security, for a few days longer, from the pangs of famine and the separation of death.

And now, with their small provision of food and wine set like a beacon of safety before their sight, a deep, dream-like serenity — the sleep of the oppressed and wearied faculties — arose over their minds. Under its mysterious and tranquillising influence, all impressions of the gloom and misery in the city, of the fatal evidences around them of the duration of the siege, faded away before their perceptions as dim, retiring objects which the eye loses in vacancy. Gradually, as the day of the first unsuccessful embassy declined, their thoughts began to flow back gently to the world of bygone events which had crumbled into oblivion beneath the march of time. Her first recollections of her earliest childhood revived in Antonina's memory, and then mingled strangely with tearful remembrances of the last words and looks of the young warrior who had expired by her side, and with calm, solemn thoughts that the beloved spirit, emancipated from the sphere of shadows, might now be hovering near the quiet garden-grave where her bitterest tears of loneliness and affliction had been shed; or moving around her — an invisible and blessed presence — as she sat at her father's feet, and mourned their earthly separation!

In the emotions thus awakened, there was nothing of bitterness or agony — they calmed and purified the heart through which they moved. She could now speak to the old man, for the first time, of her days of absence from him, of the brief joys and long sorrows of her hours of exile, without failing in her melancholy tale. Sometimes her father listened to her in sorrowful and speechless attention; or spoke, when she paused, of consolation and hope, as she had heard him speak among his congregation, while he was yet strong in his resolution to sacrifice all things for the reformation of the church. Sometimes resigning himself to the influence of his thoughts, as they glided back to the times that were gone, he again revealed to her the changing events of his past life — not as before, with unsteady accents and wandering eyes; but now with a calmness of voice, and a coherence of language, which forbade her to doubt the strange and startling narrative that she heard. Once more he spoke of the image of his lost brother (as he had parted from him in his boyhood) still present to his mind; of the country that he had quitted in after years; of the name that he had changed — from Cleander to Numerian — to foil his former associates, if they still pursued him; and of the ardent desire to behold again the companion of his first home, which now, when his daughter was restored to him, when no other earthly aspiration but this was unsatisfied, remained, at the close of his life, the last longing wish of his heart.

Such was the communion in which father and daughter passed the hours of their short reprieve from the judgment of famine pronounced against the city of their sojourn; so did they live, as it were, in a quiet interval of existence, in a tranquil pause between the toil that is over and the toil that is to come in the hard labour of life.

But the term to these short days of repose after long suffering and grief, was fast approaching. The little hoard of provision diminished as rapidly as the stores that had been anxiously collected before it; and, on the morning of the second embassy to Alaric, the flask of wine and the bowl of food were both emptied. The brief dream of security was over and gone; the terrible realities of the struggle for life had begun again!

Where, or to whom, could they now turn for help? The siege still continued; the food just exhausted, was the last food that had been left on the senator's table; to seek the palace again would be to risk refusal, perhaps insult, as the result of a second entreaty for aid, where all power of conferring it might now but too surely be lost. Such were the thoughts of Antonina as she returned the empty bowl to its former place; but she gave them no expression in words. She saw, with horror, that the same expression of despair, almost of frenzy, which had distorted her father's features on the day of her restoration to him, now marked them again. Once more he tottered towards the window, murmuring in his bitter despondency against the delusive security and hope, which had held him idle for the interests of his child during the few days that were past. But, as he now looked out on the beleaguered city, he saw the populace hastening along the gloomy street beneath, as rapidly as their wearied limbs would carry them, to join the embassy. He heard them encouraging each other to proceed, to seize the last chance of escaping through the open gates from the horrors of famine and plague; and caught the infection of the recklessness and despair which had seized his fellow sufferers from one end of Rome to the other.

Turning instantly, he grasped his daughter's hand,

and drew her from the room, commanding her to come forth with him, and join the citizens in their flight, ere it was too late. Startled by his words and actions, she vainly endeavoured, as she obeyed, to impress her father with the dread of the Goths, which her own bitter experience taught her to feel, now that her only protector among them lay cold in the grave. With Numerian, as with the rest of the people, all apprehension, all doubt, all exercise of reason, was overpowered by the one eager idea of escaping from the fatal precincts of Rome.

So they mingled with the throng, herding affrightedly together in the rear of the embassy, and followed in their ranks as best they might. The sun shone down brightly from the pure blue sky, the wind bore into the city the sharp threatening notes of the trumpets from the Gothic camp, as the Pincian Gate was opened to the ambassadors and their train. With one accord the crowd instantly endeavoured to force their way out after them in a mass; but they now moved in a narrow space, and were opposed by a large reinforcement of the city guard. After a short struggle they were overpowered, and the gates were closed. Some few of the strongest and the foremost of their numbers succeeded in following the ambassadors; the greater part, however, remained on the inner side of the gate, pressing closely up to it in their impatience and despair, like prisoners awaiting their deliverance, or preparing to force their escape.

Among these — feeblest amid the most feeble —

were Numerian and Antonina — hemmed in by the surrounding crowd, and shut out either from flight from the city, or a return to home.

CHAPTER XI.
The Grave and the Camp.

WHILE the second and last embassy from the senate proceeds towards the tent of the Gothic king; while the streets of Rome are deserted by all but the dead, and the living populace crowd together in speechless expectation behind the barrier of the Pincian Gate, an opportunity is at length afforded of turning our attention towards a scene from which it has been long removed. Let us now revisit the farm-house in the suburbs; and look once more on the quiet garden and on Hermanric's grave.

The tranquility of the bright warm day is purest around the retired path leading to the little dwelling. Here the fragrance of wild flowers rises pleasantly from the waving grass: the lulling, monotonous hum of insect life pervades the light, steady air; the sunbeams, intercepted here and there by the clustering trees, fall in irregular patches of brightness on the shady ground; and saving the birds which occasionally pass overhead, singing in their flight, no living creature appears on the quiet scene, until gaining the wicket-gate which leads into the farm-house garden, we look forth upon the prospect within. There, following the small circular footpath which her own persevering steps have day by day already traced, appears the form of a solitary woman, pacing slowly about the mound of grassy earth which marks the grave of the young Goth.

For some time she proceeds on her circumscribed round with as much undeviating, mechanical regularity, as if beyond that narrow space rose a barrier which caged her from ever setting foot on the earth beyond. At length she pauses in her course when it brings her nearest to the wicket, advances a few steps towards it, then recedes, and recommences her monotonous progress, and then again breaking off on her round, finally succeeds in withdrawing herself from the confines of the grave, passes through the gate, and following the path to the high road, slowly proceeds towards the eastern limits of the Gothic camp. The fixed, ghastly, unfeminine expression on her features, marks her as the same woman whom we last beheld as the assassin at the farm-house; but beyond this she is hardly recognisable again. Her formerly powerful and upright frame is bent and lean; her hair waves in wild, white locks about her shrivelled face; all the rude majesty of her form has departed; there is nothing to shew that it is still Goisvintha haunting the scene of her crime, but the savage expression debasing her countenance, and betraying the evil heart within, unsubdued as ever in its yearning for destruction and revenge.

Since the period when we last beheld her, removed in the custody of the Huns from the dead body of her kinsman, the farm-house had been the constant scene

of her pilgrimage from the camp, the chosen refuge
where she brooded in solitude over her fierce desires.
Scorning to punish a woman whom he regarded as
insane, for an absence from the tents of the Goths,
which was of no moment either to the army or to
himself, Alaric had impatiently dismissed her from his
presence when she was brought before him. The
soldiers who had returned to bury the body of their
chieftain in the garden of the farm-house, found means
to inform her secretly of the charitable act which they
had performed at their own peril; but beyond this no
further intercourse was held with her by any of her
former associates.

All her actions favoured their hasty belief that her
faculties were disordered; and others shunned *her* as
she shunned *them*. Her daily allowance of food was
left for her to seek at a certain place in the camp, as
it might have been left for an animal too savage to be
cherished by the hand of man. At certain periods she
returned secretly from her wanderings, to take it. Her
shelter for the night was not the shelter of her people
before the walls of Rome; her thoughts were not their
thoughts. Widowed, childless, friendless, the assassin
of her last kinsman, she moved apart in her own secret
world of bereavement, desolation, and crime.

Yet there was no madness, no remorse for her share
in accomplishing the fate of Hermanric, in the dark
and solitary existence which she now led. From the
moment when the young warrior had expiated with his
death his disregard of the enmities of his nation and

the wrongs of his kindred, she thought of him only as of one more victim whose dishonour and ruin she must live to requite on the Romans with Roman blood; and matured her schemes of revenge with a stern resolution which time, and solitude, and bodily infirmity were all powerless to disturb.

She would pace for hours and hours together, in the still night and in the broad noonday, round and round the warrior's grave, nursing her vengeful thoughts within her, until a ferocious anticipation of triumph quickened her steps and brightened her watchful eyes. Then she would enter the farm-house, and, drawing the knife from its place of concealment in her garments, would pass its point slowly backwards and forwards over the hearth on which she had mutilated Hermanric with her own hand, and from which he had advanced, without a tremor, to meet the sword-points of the Huns. Sometimes, when darkness had gathered over the earth, she would stand, — a boding and menacing apparition — upon the grave itself, and chaunt, moaning to the moaning wind, fragments of obscure northern legends, whose hideous burden was ever of anguish and crime, of torture in prison vaults, and death on the annihilating sword — mingling with them the gloomy story of the massacre at Aquileia, and her fierce vows of vengeance against the households of Rome. The forager, on his late return past the farm-house to the camp, heard the harsh, droning accents of her voice, and quickened his onward step. The venturesome peasant from the country beyond, approaching under cover of the night to look from afar on the Gothic camp, beheld her form, shadowy and threatening, as he neared the garden, and fled affrighted from the place. Neither stranger nor friend intruded on her dread solitude. The foul presence of cruelty and crime violated undisturbed the scenes once sacred to the interests of tenderness and love, once hallowed by the sojourn of youth and beauty!

But now the farm-house garden is left solitary; the haunting-spirit of evil has departed from the grave; the footsteps of Goisvintha have traced to their close the same paths from the suburbs, over which the young Goth once eagerly hastened on his night-journey of love; and already the walls of Rome rise — dark, near, and hateful — before her eyes. Along these useless bulwarks of the fallen city she now wanders, as she has often wandered before, watching for the first opening of the long-closed gates. Let us follow her on her way.

Her attention was now fixed only on the broad ramparts, while she passed slowly along the Gothic tents towards the encampment at the Pincian Gate. Arrived there, she was aroused for the first time from her apathy by an unwonted stir and confusion prevailing around her. She looked towards the tent of Alaric, and beheld before it the wasted and crouching forms of the followers of the embassy, awaiting their sentence from the captain of the northern hosts. In a few moments she gathered enough from the words of the Goths congregated about this part of the camp, to assure her that it was the Pincian Gate which had given egress to the Roman suppliants, and which would therefore, in all probability, be the entrance again thrown open to admit their return to the city. Remembering this, she began to calculate the numbers of the conquered enemy grouped together before the king's tent, and then mentally added to them those who might be present at the interview proceeding within — mechanically withdrawing herself, while thus occupied, nearer and nearer to the waste ground before the city walls.

Gradually she turned her face towards Rome: she was realising a daring purpose, a fatal resolution, long cherished during the days and nights of her solitary wanderings. "The ranks of the embassy," she muttered, in a deep, thoughtful tone, "are thickly filled. Where there are many there must be confusion and haste; they march together, and know not their own numbers; they mark not one more or one less among them."

She stopped. Strange and dark changes of colour and expression passed over her ghastly features. She drew from her bosom the bloody helmet-crest of her husband, which had never quitted her since the day of his death; her face grew livid under an awful expression of rage, ferocity, and despair, as she gazed on it. Suddenly she looked up at the city — fierce and defiant, as if the great walls before her were mortal enemies against whom she stood at bay in the death-struggle. "The widowed and the childless shall drink of thy blood!" she cried, stretching out her skinny hand towards Rome, "though the armies of her nation barter their wrongs with thy people for bags of silver and gold! I have pondered on it in my solitude, and dreamed of it in my dreams! I have sworn that I would enter Rome, and avenge my slaughtered kindred, alone among thousands! Now, now I will hold to my oath! Thou blood-stained city of the coward and the traitor, the enemy of the defenceless, and the murderer of the weak! thou who didst send forth to Aquileia the slayers of my husband and the assassins of my children, I wait no longer before thy walls! This day will I mingle, daring all things, with thy returning citizens, and penetrate, amid Romans, the gates of Rome! Through the day will I lurk, cunning and watchful, in thy solitary haunts, to steal forth on thee at night, a secret minister of death! I will watch for thy young and thy weak ones in unguarded places; I will prey, alone in the thick darkness, upon thy unprotected lives; I will destroy *thy* children, as their fathers destroyed at Aquileia the children of the Goths! Thy rabble will discover me and arise against me; they will tear me in pieces, and trample my mangled body on the pavement of the streets; but it will be *after* I have seen the blood that I have sworn to shed, flowing under my knife! My vengeance will be complete, and torments and death will be to me as guests that I welcome, and as deliverers whom I await!"

Again she paused — the wild triumph of the fanatic on the burning pile, was flashing on her face — suddenly, her eyes fell once more upon the stained helmet crest; then, her expression changed again to despair, and her voice grew low and moaning, when she thus resumed: "I am weary of my life; when the vengeance is done, I shall be delivered from this prison of the earth — in the world of shadows I shall see my husband; and my little ones will gather round my knees again. The living have no part in me; I yearn towards the spirits who wander in the halls of the dead."

For a few minutes more she continued to fix her tearless eyes on the helmet crest. But soon the influence of the evil spirit revived in all its strength; she raised her head suddenly, remained for an instant absorbed in deep thought, then began to retrace her steps rapidly in the direction by which she had come.

Sometimes she whispered softly, "I must be doing, ere the time fail me: my face must be hidden, and my garments changed. Yonder, among the houses, I must search; and search quickly!" Sometimes she reiterated her denunciations of vengeance, her ejaculations of triumph in her frantic project. At the recapitulation of these, the remembrance of Antonina was aroused; and then, a bloodthirsty superstition darkened her thoughts, and threw a vague and dreamy character over her speech.

When she spoke now, it was to murmur to herself, that the victim who had twice escaped her might yet be alive; that the supernatural influences which had often guided the old Goths, on the day of retribution, might still guide *her;* might still direct the stroke of her destroying weapon — the last stroke ere she was discovered and slain — straight to the girl's heart. Thoughts such as these — wandering and obscure — arose in close, quick succession, within her; but whether she gave them expression in word and action, or whether she suppressed them in silence, she never wavered or halted in her rapid progress. Her energies were braced to all emergencies; and her strong will suffered them not for an instant to relax.

She gained a retired street in the deserted suburbs; and looking round her to see that she was unobserved, entered one of the houses abandoned by its inhabitants on the approach of the besiegers. Passing quickly through the outer halls she stopped at length in one of the sleeping apartments; and here she found, among other possessions left behind in the flight, the store of wearing apparel belonging to the owner of the room.

From this she selected a Roman robe, upper mantle, and sandals — the most common in colour and texture that she could find; and folding them up into the smallest compass, hid them under her own garments. Then, avoiding all those whom she met on her way, she returned in the direction of the King's tent; but when she approached it, branched off stealthily towards Rome, until she reached a ruined building half way between the city and the camp. In this concealment she clothed herself in her disguise, drawing the mantle closely round her head and face; and from this point — calm, vigilant, determined; her hand on the knife beneath her robe; her lips muttering the names of her murdered husband and children — she watched the high road to the Pincian Gate.

There, for a short time, let us leave her, and enter the tent of Alaric, while the senate yet plead before the Arbiter of the Empire for mercy and peace.

At the moment of which we write, the embassy had already exhausted its powers of intercession, apparently without moving the leader of the Goths from his first pitiless resolution of fixing the ransom of Rome at the price of every possession of value which the city contained. There was a momentary silence now in the great tent. At one extremity of it, congregated in a close and irregular group, stood the wearied and broken-spirited members of the senate, supported by such of their attendants as had been permitted to follow them; at the other appeared the stately forms of Alaric and the warriors who surrounded him as his council of war. The vacant space in the middle of the tent was strewn with martial weapons, separating the representatives of the two nations one from the other; and thus accidentally, yet palpably, typifying the fierce hostility which had sundered in years past, and was still to sunder for years to come, the people of the North and the people of the South.

The Gothic King stood a little in advance of his warriors, leaning on his huge, heavy sword. His steady eye wandered from man to man among the broken-spirited senators, contemplating, with cold and cruel penetration, all that suffering and despair had altered for the worse in their outward appearance. Their soiled robes, their wan cheeks, their trembling limbs were each marked in turn by the cool, sarcastic examination of the conqueror's gaze. Debased and humiliated as they were, there were some among the ambassadors who felt the insult thus silently and deliberately inflicted on them the more keenly for their very helplessness. They moved uneasily in their places, and whispered among each other in low and bitter accents. At length one of their number raised his downcast eyes and broke the silence. The old Roman spirit, which long years of voluntary frivolity and degradation had not yet entirely depraved, flushed his pale, wasted face, as he spoke thus: —

"We have entreated, we have offered, we have promised — men can do no more! Deserted by our Emperor and crushed by pestilence and famine, nothing is now left to us but to perish in unavailing resistance beneath the walls of Rome! It was in the power of Alaric to win everlasting renown by moderation to the unfortunate of an illustrious nation; but he has preferred to attempt the spoiling of a glorious city and the subjugation of a suffering people! Yet let him remember, though destruction may sate his vengeance, and pillage enrich his hoards, the day of retribution will yet come. There are still soldiers in the empire, and heroes who will lead them confidently to battle, though the bodies of their countrymen lie slaughtered around them in the streets of pillaged Rome!"

A momentary expression of wrath and indignation appeared on Alaric's features, as he listened to this bold speech; but it was almost immediately replaced by a smile of derision. "What! ye have still soldiers before whom the barbarian must tremble for his conquests!" he cried. "Where are they? Are they on their march, or in ambush, or hiding behind strong walls, or have they lost their way on the road to the Gothic camp? Ha! here is one of them!" he exclaimed, advancing towards an enfeebled and disarmed guard of the senate, who quailed beneath his fierce glance. "Fight, man!" he loudly continued — "fight, while there is yet time, for Imperial Rome! Thy sword is gone — take mine, and be a hero again!"

With a rough laugh, echoed by the warriors behind him, he flung his ponderous weapon, as he spoke, towards the wretched object of his sarcasm. The hilt struck heavily against the man's breast — he staggered and fell helpless to the ground. The laugh was redoubled among the Goths; but now their leader did not join in it. His eye glowed in triumphant scorn, as he pointed to the prostrate Roman, exclaiming — "So does the South fall beneath the sword of the North! So shall the Empire bow before the rule of the Goth! Say, as ye look on these Romans before us, are we not avenged of our wrongs? They die not fighting on our swords; they live to entreat our pity, as children that are in terror of the whip!"

He paused. His massive and noble countenance gradually assumed a thoughtful expression. The ambassadors moved forward a few steps — perhaps to make a final entreaty, perhaps to depart in despair;

but he signed with his hand, in command to them to be silent and remain where they stood. The marauder's thirst for present plunder, and the conqueror's lofty ambition of future glory, now stirred in strong conflict within him. He walked to the opening of the tent, and, thrusting aside its curtain of skins looked out upon Rome in silence. The dazzling majesty of the temples and palaces of the mighty city, as they towered before him, gleaming in the rays of the unclouded sunlight, fixed him long in contemplation. Gradually, dreams of future dominion amid those unrivalled structures, which now waited but his word to be pillaged and destroyed, filled his aspiring soul, and saved the city from his wrath. He turned again toward the ambassadors — in a voice and look superior to them as a being of a higher sphere — and spoke thus: —

"When the Gothic conqueror reigns in Italy, the palaces of her rulers shall be found standing for the places of his sojourn. I will ordain a lower ransom; I will spare Rome."

A murmur arose among the warriors behind him. The rapine and destruction which they had eagerly anticipated, was denied them for the first time by their chief. As their muttered remonstrances caught his ear, Alaric instantly and sternly fixed his eyes upon them; and repeating in accents of deliberate command — "I will ordain a lower ransom; I will spare Rome," steadily scanned the countenances of his ferocious followers. Not a word of dissent fell from their lips; not a gesture of impatience appeared in their ranks; they preserved perfect silence, as the king again advanced towards the ambassadors, and continued: —

"I fix the ransom of the city at five thousand pounds of gold; at thirty thousand pounds of silver." — Here he suddenly ceased, as if pondering further on the terms he should exact. The hearts of the senate, lightened for a moment by Alaric's unexpected announcement that he would moderate his demands, sank within them again, as they thought on the tribute required of them, and remembered their exhausted treasury. But it was no time now to remonstrate, or to delay; and they answered with one accord, ignorant though they were of the means of performing their promise, "The ransom shall be paid!"

The king looked at them when they spoke, as if in astonishment that men whom he had deprived of all freedom of choice, ventured still to assert it, by intimating their acceptance of terms which they dared not decline. The mocking spirit revived within him while he thus gazed on the helpless and humiliated embassy; and he laughed once more as he resumed, partly addressing himself to the silent array of the warriors behind him: —

"The gold and silver are but the first dues of the tribute — my army shall be rewarded with more than the wealth of the enemy. You men of Rome have laughed at our rough bear-skins and our heavy armour, you shall clothe us with your robes of festivity! I will add to the gold and silver of your ransom, four thousand garments of silk, and three thousand pieces of scarlet cloth. My barbarians shall be barbarians no longer! I will make patricians, epicures, Romans of them!"

The members of the ill-fated embassy looked up as he paused, in mute appeal to the mercy of the triumphant conqueror; but they were not yet to be released from the crushing infliction of his rapacity and scorn.

"Hold!" he cried, "I will have more — more still! You are a nation of feasters; — we will rival you in your banquets, when we have stripped you of your banqueting robes! To the gold, the silver, the silk, and the cloth, I will add yet more — three thousand pounds weight of pepper, your precious merchandise, bought from far countries with your lavish wealth! — see that you bring it hither, with the rest of the ransom, to the last grain! The flesh of *our* beasts shall be seasoned for us like the flesh of *yours!*"

He turned abruptly from the senators, as he pronounced the last words, and began to speak in jesting tones and in the Gothic language to the council of warriors around him. Some of the ambassadors bowed their heads in silent resignation; others, with the utter thoughtlessness of men bewildered by all that they had seen and heard during the interview that was now closed, unhappily revived the recollection of the broken treaties of former days, by mechanically inquiring, in the terms of past formularies, what security the besiegers would require for the payment of their demands.

"Security!" cried Alaric fiercely, instantly relapsing as they spoke into his sterner mood. "Behold yonder the future security of the Goths for the faith of Rome!" and flinging aside the curtain of the tent, he pointed proudly to the long lines of his camp, stretching round all that was visible of the walls of the fallen city.

The ambassadors remembered the massacre of the hostages of Aquileia, and the evasion of the payment of tribute-money promised in former days; and were silent as they looked through the opening of the tent.

"Remember the conditions of the ransom," pursued Alaric in warning tones, "remember my security that the ransom shall be quickly paid! So shall you live for a brief space in security; and feast and be merry again, while your territories yet remain to you. Go — I have spoken — it is enough!"

He withdrew abruptly from the senators; and the curtain of the tent fell behind them as they passed out. The ordeal of the judgment was over; the final sentence had been pronounced; the time had already arrived to go forth and obey it.

The news that terms of peace had been at last settled, filled the Romans who were waiting before the tent with emotions of delight, equally unalloyed by reflections on the past, or forebodings for the future. Barred from their reckless project of flying to the open country, by the Goths surrounding them in the camp; shut out from retreating to Rome by the gates through which they had rashly forced their way; exposed in their helplessness to the brutal jeers of the enemy, while they waited in a long agony of suspense for the close of the perilous interview between Alaric and the senate, they had undergone every extremity of suffering, and had yielded unanimously to despair, when the intelligence of the concluded treaty sounded like a promise of salvation in their ears.

None of the apprehensions aroused in the minds of their superiors by the vastness of the exacted tribute, now mingled with the unreflecting ecstasy of their joy at the prospect of the removal of the blockade. They arose to return to the city from which they had fled in dismay, with cries of impatience and delight. They fawned like dogs upon the ambassadors; and even upon the ferocious Goths. On their departure from Rome, they had mechanically preserved some regularity in their progress; but now they hurried onward without distinction of place, or discipline of march — senators, guards, plebeians, all huddled together in the disorderly equality of a mob.

Not one of them, in their new-born security, marked the ruined building on the high road; not one of them observed the closely-robed figure that stole out from it to join them in their rear; and then, with stealthy footstep and shrouded face, soon mingled in the thickest of their ranks. The attention of the ambassadors was still engrossed by their forebodings of failure in collecting the ransom; the eyes of the people were fixed only on the Pincian Gate; their ears were open to no sounds, but their own ejaculations of delight. Not one disguised stranger only, but many, might now have joined them in their tumultuous progress, unquestioned and unobserved.

So they hastily re-entered the city; where thousands of heavy eyes were strained to look on them, and thousands of attentive ears drank in their joyful news from the Gothic camp. Then were heard in all directions the sounds of hysterical weeping and idiotic laughter; the low groans of the weak who died victims of their sudden transport, and the confused outbursts of the strong who had survived all extremities, and at last beheld their deliverance in view. Still silent and serious, the ambassadors now slowly penetrated the throng on their way back to the Forum; and as they proceeded the crowd gradually dispersed on either side of them. Enemies, friends, and strangers, all whom the ruthless famine had hitherto separated in interests and sympathies, were now united together as one family, by the expectation of speedy relief.

But there was one among the assembly that was now separating, who stood alone in her unrevealed emotions, amid the rejoicing thousands around her. The women and children in the throng as, pre-occupied by their own feelings, they unheedfully passed her by, saw not the eager, ferocious attention in her eyes, as she watched them steadily till they were out of sight. Within their gates the stranger and the enemy waited for the treacherous darkness of night; and waited unobserved. Where she had first stood when the thick

crowd hemmed her in, there she still continued to
stand, after they slowly moved past her, and space
grew free. Yet beneath this outward calm and silence
lurked the wildest passions that ever raged against
the weak restraint of human will — even the firm
self-possession of Goisvintha was shaken, when she
found herself within the walls of Rome.

No glance of suspicion had been cast upon her;
not one of the crowd had approached to thrust her
back when she passed through the gates with the
heedless citizens around her. Shielded from detection,
as much by the careless security of her enemies as by
the stratagem of her disguise, she stood on the pavement
of Rome, as she had vowed to stand, afar from
the armies of her people; alone as an avenger of
blood!

It was no dream; no fleeting, deceitful vision. The
knife was under her hand; the streets stretched before
her; the living beings who thronged them were Romans;
the hours of the day were already on the wane; the
approach of her vengeance was as sure as the approach
of darkness that was to let it loose. A wild
exultation quickened in her the pulses of life, while
she thought on the dread projects of secret assassination
and revenge which now opposed her, a solitary
woman, in deadly enmity against the defenceless population
of a whole city. As her eyes travelled slowly
from side to side over the moving throng; as she
thought on the time that might still elapse ere the discovery
and death — the martyrdom in the cause of

blood — which she expected and defied, would overtake her; her hands trembled beneath her robe; and she reiterated in whispers to herself: — "Husband, children, brother — there are five deaths to avenge! Remember Aquileia! Remember Aquileia!"

Suddenly, as she looked from group to group among the departing people, her eyes became arrested by one object; she instantly stepped forward; then abruptly restrained herself and moved back where the crowd was still thick; gazing fixedly ever in the same direction. She saw the victim twice snatched from her hands — at the camp and in the farm-house — a third time offered to her grasp in the streets of Rome. The chance of vengeance last expected, was the chance that had first arrived. A vague, oppressing sensation of awe mingled with the triumph at her heart — a supernatural guidance seemed to be directing her with fell rapidity, through every mortal obstacle, to the climax of her revenge!

She screened herself behind the people; she watched the girl from the most distant point; but concealment was now vain — their eyes had met. The robe had slipped aside when she suddenly stepped forward, and in that moment Antonina had seen her.

Numerian, moving slowly with his daughter through the crowd, felt her hand tighten round his, and saw her features stiffen into sudden rigidity; but the change was only for an instant. Ere he could speak, she caught him by the arm, and drew him forward with convulsive energy. Then, in accents hardly articulate, low, breathless, unlike her wonted voice, he heard her exclaim, as she struggled on with him, "She is there — there behind us! to kill *me*, as she killed *him!* Home! home!"

Exhausted already, through long weakness and natural infirmity, by the rough contact, of the crowd, bewildered by Antonina's looks and actions, and by the startling intimation of unknown peril, conveyed to him in her broken exclamations of affright, Numerian's first impulse, as he hurried onward by her side, led him to entreat protection and help from the surrounding populace. But, even could he have pointed out to them the object of his dread amid that motley throng of all nations, the appeal he now made would have remained unanswered. Of all the results of the frightful severity of privation suffered by the besieged, none were more common than those mental aberrations which produce visions of danger, enemies, and death, so palpable as to make the persons beholding them, implore assistance against the hideous creation of their own delirium. Accordingly, most of those to whom the entreaties of Numerian were addressed, passed without noticing them. Some few carelessly bid him remember that there were no enemies now, — that the days of peace were approaching, — and that a meal of good food, which he might soon expect to enjoy, was the only help for a famished man. No one, in that period of horror and suffering, which was now drawing to a close, saw anything extraordinary in the confusion of the father and the terror of the child.

So they pursued their feeble flight unprotected, and the footsteps of Goisvintha followed them as they went.

They had already commenced the ascent of the Pincian Hill, when Antonina stopped abruptly, and turned to look behind her. Many people yet thronged the street below; but her eyes penetrated among them, sharpened by peril, and instantly discerned the ample robe and the tall form, still at the same distance from them and pausing as they had paused. For one moment, the girl's eyes fixed in the wild, helpless stare of terror on her father's face; but the next, that mysterious instinct of preservation, which is co-existent with the instinct of fear, — which gifts the weakest animal with cunning to improve its flight, and takes the place of reason, reflection, and resolve, when all are banished from the mind — warned her against the fatal error of permitting the pursuer to track her to her home. "Not there! not there!" she gasped faintly, as Numerian endeavoured to lead her up the ascent. "She will see us as we enter the doors! — through the streets! Oh, father, if you would save me! we may lose her in the streets! — the guards, the people are there! Back! back!"

Numerian trembled as he marked the terror in her looks and gestures; but it was vain to question or oppose her. Nothing short of force could restrain her, — no commands or entreaties could draw from her more than the same breathless exclamation; "Onward, father; onward, if you would save me!" 'She was insensible to every sensation but fear, incapable of any other exertion than flight.

Turning and winding, hurrying forward ever at the same rapid pace, they passed unconsciously along the intricate streets that led to the river side; and still the avenger tracked the victim, constant as the shadow to the substance; steady, vigilant, unwearied, as a bloodhound on a hot scent.

And now, even the sound of the father's voice ceased to be audible in the daughter's ears; she no longer felt the pressure of his hand, no longer perceived his very presence at her side. At length, frail and shrinking, she again paused, and looked back. The street they had reached was very tranquil and desolate: two slaves were walking at its further extremity. While they were in sight, no living creature appeared in the roadway behind; but, as soon as they had passed away, a shadow stole slowly forward over the pavement of a portico in the distance, and the next moment Goisvintha appeared in the street.

The sun glared down fiercely over her dark figure as she stopped, and for an instant looked stealthily around her. She moved to advance, and Antonina saw no more. Again she turned to renew her hopeless flight; and again her father, — perceiving only as the mysterious cause of her dread a solitary woman, who, though she followed, attempted not to arrest, or even to address them, — prepared to accompany her to the last, in despair of all other chances of securing her safety. More and more completely did her terror now enchain her faculties, as she still unconsciously traced her rapid way through the streets that led to the Tiber. It was not Numerian, not Rome, not daylight in a great city, that was before her eyes: it was the storm, the assassination, the night at the farm-house, that she now lived through over again.

Still the quick flight and the ceaseless pursuit were continued, as if neither were ever to have an end; but the close of the scene was, nevertheless, already at hand. During the interval of the passage through the streets, Numerian's mind had gradually recovered from its first astonishment and alarm; at length he perceived the necessity of instant and decisive action, while there was yet time to save Antonina from sinking under the excess of her own fears. Though a vague, awful foreboding of disaster and death filled his heart, his resolution to penetrate at once, at all hazards, the dark mystery of impending danger indicated by his daughter's words and actions, did not fail him; for it was aroused by the only motive powerful enough to revive all that suffering and infirmity had not yet destroyed of the energy of his former days, — the preservation of his child. There was something of the old firmness and vigour of the intrepid reformer of the Church, in his dim eyes, as he now stopped, and inclosing Antonina in his arms, arrested her instantly in her flight.

She struggled to escape; but it was faintly, and only for a moment. Her strength and consciousness were beginning to abandon her. She never attempted to look back; she felt in her heart that Goisvintha was still behind, and dared not to verify the frightful conviction with her eyes. Her lips moved; but they expressed an altered and a vain petition: "Hermanric! oh, Hermanric!" was all they murmured now.

They had arrived at the long street that ran by the banks of the Tiber. The people had either retired to their homes or repaired to the Forum to be informed of the period when the ransom would be paid. No one but Goisvintha was in sight as Numerian looked around him; and she, after having carefully viewed the empty street, was advancing towards them at a quickened pace.

For an instant the father looked on her steadily as she approached, and in that instant his determination was formed. A flight of steps at his feet led to the narrow doorway of a small temple, the nearest building to him. Ignorant whether Goisvintha might not be secretly supported by companions in her ceaseless pursuit, he resolved to secure this place for Antonina, as a temporary refuge at least; while standing before it, he should oblige the woman to declare her purpose, if she followed them even there. In a moment he had begun the ascent of the steps, with the exhausted girl by his side. Arrived at the summit, he guided her before him into the doorway, and stopped on the threshold to look round again. Goisvintha was nowhere to be seen.

Not duped by the woman's sudden disappearance into the belief that she had departed from the street, — persisting in his resolution to lead his daughter to a place of repose, where she might most immediately feel herself secure, and might therefore most readily recover her self-possession, Numerian drew Antonina with him into the temple. He lingered there for a moment, ere he departed to watch the street from the portico outside.

The light in the building was dim, — it was admitted only from a small aperture in the roof, and through the narrow doorway, where it was intercepted by the overhanging bulk of the outer portico. A crooked pile of dark heavy-looking substances on the floor, rose high towards the ceiling, in the obscure interior. Irregular in form, flung together one over the other in strange disorder, for the most part dusky in hue, yet here and there gleaming at points with metallic brightness, these objects presented a mysterious, indefinite, and startling appearance. It was impossible, on a first view of their confused arrangement, to discover what they were, or to guess for what purpose they could have been piled together on the floor of a deserted temple. From the moment when they had first attracted Numerian's observation, his attention was fixed on them, and as he looked, a faint thrill of suspicion — vague, inexplicable, without apparent cause or object — struck chill to his heart.

He had moved a step forward to examine the hidden space at the back of the pile, when his further advance was instantly stopped by the appearance of a man who walked forth from it, dressed in the floating, purple-edged robe and white fillet of the Pagan priests.

Before either father or daughter could speak, even before they could move to depart, he stepped up to them, and placing his hand on the shoulder of each, confronted them in silence.

At the moment when the stranger approached, Numerian raised his hand to thrust him back, and in so doing fixed his eyes on the man's countenance, as a ray of light from the doorway floated over it. Instantly his arm remained outstretched and rigid, then it dropped to his side, and the expression of horror on the face of the child became reflected, as it were, on the face of the parent. Neither moved under the hand of the dweller in the temple when he laid it heavily on each, and both stood before him speechless as himself.

CHAPTER XII.
The Temple and the Church.

It was Ulpius. The Pagan was changed in bearing and countenance as well as in apparel. He stood more firm and upright; a dull, tawny hue overspread his face; his eyes, so sunken and lustreless in other days, were now distended, and bright with the glare of insanity. It seemed as if his bodily powers had renewed their vigour, while his mental faculties had declined towards their ruin.

No human eye had ever beheld by what foul and secret means he had survived through the famine; on what unnatural sustenance he had satisfied the cravings of inexorable hunger; but there, in his gloomy shelter, the madman and the outcast had lived, and moved, and suddenly and strangely strengthened, after the people of the city had exhausted all their united resources, lavished in vain all their united wealth, and drooped and died by thousands around him!

His grasp still lay heavy on the father and daughter, and still both confronted him — silent, as if death-struck by his gaze; motionless, as if frozen at his touch. His presence was exerting over them a fatal fascination. The power of action, suspended in Antonina as she entered their ill-chosen refuge, was now arrested in Numerian also; but with *him*, no thought of the enemy in the street had part, at this moment, in the resistless influence which held him helpless before the enemy in the temple. It was a feeling of deeper awe and darker horror. For now, as he looked upon the hideous features of Ulpius, as he saw the forbidden robe of priesthood in which the Pagan was arrayed, he beheld not only the traitor who had successfully plotted against the prosperity of his household, but the madman as well, — the moral leper of the whole human family — the *living* Body, and the *dead* Soul — the Disinherited of that Divine Light of Life which it is the awful privilege of mortal man to share with the angels of God.

He still clasped Antonina to his side, but it was unconsciously. To all outward appearance he was helpless as his helpless child, when Ulpius slowly removed his grasp from their shoulders, separated them, and locking the hand of each in his cold, bony fingers, began to speak.

His voice was deep and solemn, but his accents, in their hard, unvarying tone, seemed to express no human emotion. His eyes, far from brightening as he spoke, relapsed into a dull, vacant insensibility. The connection between the action of speech and the accompanying and explaining action of look which is observable in all men, seemed lost in *him*. It was fearful to behold the deathlike face, and to listen at the same moment to the living voice.

"Lo! the votaries come to the Temple!" murmured the Pagan. "The good servants of the mighty worship gather at the voice of the Priest! In the far provinces, where the enemies of the gods approach to profane the sacred groves, behold the scattered people congregating by night, to journey to the shrine of Serapis! Adoring thousands kneel beneath the lofty porticos, while within, in the secret hall where the light is dim, where the air quivers round the breathing deities on their pedestals of gold, the High Priest Ulpius reads the destinies of the Future, that are unrolled before his eyes like a book!"

As he ceased, and still holding the hands of his captives, looked on them fixedly as ever, his eyes brightened and dilated again; but they expressed not the slightest recognition either of father or daughter. The delirium of his imagination had transported him to the Temple at Alexandria; the days were revived when his glory had risen to its culminating point, when the Christians trembled before him as their fiercest enemy, and the Pagans surrounded him as their last hope. The victims of his former and forgotten treachery, were but as two among the throng of votaries allured by the fame of his eloquence; by the triumphant notoriety of his power to protect the adherents of the ancient creed. But it was not always thus that his madness declared itself; there were moments when it rose to appalling frenzy. Then, he imagined himself to be again hurling the Christian assailants from the topmost walls of the besieged temple — in that past time, when the image of Serapis was doomed, by the Bishop of Alexandria to be destroyed. His yells of fury, his frantic execrations of defiance were heard afar, in the solemn silence of pestilence-stricken Rome. Those who, during the most fatal days of the Gothic blockade, dropped famished on the pavement before the little temple, as they endeavoured to pass it on their onward way, presented a dread reality of death, to embody the madman's visions of battle and slaughter. As these victims of famine lay expiring in the street, they heard above them his raving voice cursing them for Christians; triumphing over them as defeated enemies destroyed by his hand; exhorting his imaginary adherents to fling the slain above on the dead below, until the bodies of the besiegers of the temple were piled, as barriers against their living comrades, round its walls. Sometimes his frenzy gloried in the fancied revival of the foul and sanguinary ceremonies of Pagan superstition. Then he bared his arms, and shouted aloud for the sacrifice; he committed dark and nameless atrocities — for now again, the dead and the dying lay before him, to give substance to the shadow of his evil thoughts; and Plague and Hunger were as creatures of his will, and slew the victim for the altar ready to his hands.

At other times, when the raving fit had passed away, and he lay panting in the darkest corner of the interior of the temple, his insanity assumed another and a mournful form. His voice grew low and moaning; the wreck of his memory — wandering and uncontrollable — floated back, far back, on the dark waters of the past; and his tongue uttered fragments of words and phrases that he had murmured at his father's knees — farewell, childish wishes that he had breathed in his mother's ear — innocent, anxious questions which he had addressed to Macrinus, the high priest, when he first entered the service of the gods at Alexandria. His boyish reveries — the gentleness of speech and poetry of thought of his first youthful days, were now, by the unsearchable and arbitrary influences of his disease, revived in his broken words; renewed in his desolate old age of madness and crime, breathed out in unconscious mockery by his lips, while the foam still gathered about them, and the last flashes of frenzy yet lightened in his eyes.

This unnatural calmness of language and vividness of memory; this treacherous appearance of thoughtful, melancholy self-possession, would often continue through long periods, uninterrupted; but, sooner or later, the sudden change came; the deceitful chain of thought snapped asunder in an instant; the word was left half uttered; the wearied limbs started convulsively into renewed action; and as the dream of violence returned and the dream of peace vanished, the madman rioted afresh in his fury; and journeyed as his visions led him, round and round his temple sanctuary, and hither and thither, when the night was dark and death was busiest in Rome, among the expiring in deserted houses, and the lifeless in the silent streets.

But there were other later events in his existence, that never revived within him. The old, familiar image of the idol Serapis, which had drawn him into the temple when he re-entered Rome, absorbed in itself and in its associated remembrances, all that remained active of his paralysed faculties. His betrayal of his trust in the house of Numerian, his passage through the rifted wall, his crushing repulse in the tent of Alaric, never for a moment occupied his wandering thoughts. The clouds that hung over his mind, might open to him parting glimpses of the toils and triumphs of his early career; but they descended in impenetrable darkness on all the after-days of his dreary life.

Such was the being to whose will, by a mysterious fatality, the father and child were now submitted — such the existence — solitary, hopeless, loathsome — of their stern and wily betrayer of other days!

Since he had ceased speaking, the cold, death-like grasp of his hand had gradually strengthened; and he had begun to look slowly and inquiringly round him,

15*

from side to side. Had this change marked the approaching return of his raving paroxysm, the lives of Numerian and Antonina would have been sacrificed the next moment; but all that it now denoted was the quickening of the lofty and obscure ideas of celebrity and success; of priestly honour and influence; of the splendour and glory of the gods, which had prompted his last words. He moved suddenly, and drew the victims of his dangerous caprice a few steps further into the interior of the temple; then led them close up to the lofty pile of objects which had first attracted Numerian's eyes on entering the building. "Kneel and adore!" cried the madman fiercely, replacing his hands on their shoulders and pressing them to the ground — "You stand before the Gods, in the presence of their High Priest!"

The girl's head sunk forward, and she hid her face in her hands; but her father looked up tremblingly at the pile. His eyes had insensibly become more accustomed to the dim light of the temple, and he now saw more distinctly the objects composing the mass that rose above him. Hundreds of images of the gods, in gold, silver, and wood — many in the latter material being larger than life; canopies, vestments, furniture, utensils, all of ancient pagan form, were heaped together, without order or arrangement on the floor, to a height of full fifteen feet. There was something at once hideous and grotesque in the appearance of the pile. The monstrous figures of the idols, with their rude carved draperies and symbolic weapons, lay in every wild variety of position, and presented every startling eccentricity of line, more especially towards the higher portions of the mass, where they had evidently been flung up from the ground by the hand that had raised the structure. The draperies mixed among the images and the furniture, were here coiled serpent-like around them, and there hung down towards the ground, waving slow and solemn in the breezes that wound through the temple doorway. The smaller objects of gold and silver, scattered irregularly over the mass, shone out from it like gleaming eyes; while the pile itself, seen in such a place under a dusky light, looked like some vast, mis-shapen monster — the gloomy embodiment of the bloodiest superstitions of Paganism, the growth of damp airs and teeming ruin, of shadow and darkness, of accursed and infected solitude!

Even in its position, as well as in the objects of which it was composed, the pile wore an ominous and startling aspect; its crooked outline, expanding towards the top, was bent over fearfully in the direction of the doorway; it seemed as if a single hand might sway it in its uncertain balance, and hurl it instantly in one solid mass to the floor.

Many toilsome hours had passed away, long secret labour had been expended in the erection of this weird and tottering structure; but it was all the work of one hand. Night after night had the Pagan entered the deserted temples in the surrounding streets, and pillaged them of their contents to enrich his favoured shrine:

the removal of the idols from their appointed places, which would have been sacrilege in any meaner man, was in his eyes the dread privilege of the high priest alone. He had borne heavy burdens, and torn asunder strong fastenings, and journeyed and journeyed again for hours together over the same gloomy streets, without loitering in his task; he had raised treasures and images one above another, he had strengthened the base and heightened the summit of this precious and sacred heap; he had repaired and rebuilt, whenever it crumbled and fell, this new Babel that he longed to rear to the Olympus of the temple roof, with a resolute patience and perseverance that no failure or fatigue could overcome. It was the dearest purpose of his dreamy superstition to surround himself with innumerable deities, as well as to assemble innumerable worshippers; to make the sacred place of his habitation a mighty Pantheon, as well as a point of juncture for the scattered congregations of the Pagan world. This was the ambition in which his madness expanded to the fiercest fanaticism; and as he now stood erect with his captives beneath him, his glaring eyes looked awestruck when he fixed them on his idols; he uplifted his arms in solemn, ecstatic triumph, and in low tones poured forth his invocations, wild, intermingled, and fragmentary, as the barbarous altar which his solitary exertions had reared.

Whatever was the effect on Numerian of his savage and confused ejaculations, they were unnoticed, even unheard, by Antonina; for now, while the madman's voice softened to an undertone, and while she hid all surrounding objects from her eyes, her senses were awakened to sounds in the temple which she had never remarked before.

The rapid current of the Tiber washed the foundation walls of one side of the building, within which the clear, lulling bubble of the water was audible with singular distinctness. But besides this another and a shriller sound caught the ear. On the summit of the temple roof still remained several rows of little gilt bells, originally placed there, partly with the intention of ornamenting this portion of the outer structure, partly in order that the noise they produced, when agitated by the wind, might scare birds from settling in their flight on the consecrated edifice. The sounds produced by these bells were silvery and high pitched; now, when the breeze was strong, they rang together merrily and continuously; now, when it fell, their notes were faint, separate, and irregular — almost plaintive in their pure metallic softness. But however their tone might vary under the capricious influences of the wind, it seemed always wonderfully mingled, within the temple, with the low, eternal bubbling of the river, which filled up the slightest pauses in the pleasant chiming of the bells, and ever preserved its gentle and monotonous harmony just audible beneath them.

There was something in this quaint, unwonted combination of sounds, as they were heard in the vaulted interior of the little building, strangely simple, attractive, and spiritual; the longer they were listened to, the more completely did the mind lose the recollection of their real origin, and gradually shape out of them wilder and wilder fancies, until the bells, as they rang their small peal, seemed like happy voices of a heavenly stream, borne lightly onward on its airy bubbles, and ever rejoicing over the gliding current that murmured to them as it ran.

Spite of the peril of her position, and of the terror which still fixed her speechless and crouching on the ground, the effect on Antonina of the strange mingled music of the running water and the bells was powerful enough, when she first heard it, to suspend all her other emotions in a momentary wonder and doubt. She withdrew her hands from her face, and glanced round mechanically to the doorway, as if imagining that the sounds proceeded from the street.

When she looked, the declining sun, gliding between two of the outer pillars which surrounded the temple, covered with a bright glow the smooth pavement before the entrance. A swarm of insects flew drowsily round and round in the warm mellow light — their faint monotonous humming deepened, rather than interrupted, the perfect silence prevailing over all things without. But a change was soon destined to appear in the repose of the quiet, vacant scene; hardly a minute had elapsed while Antonina still looked on it, before she saw stealing over the sunny pavement, a dark shadow, the same shadow that she had last beheld when she stopped in her flight to look behind her in the empty street. At first it slowly grew and lengthened, then it remained stationary, then it receded and vanished as gradually as it had advanced, — and then the girl heard, or fancied that she heard, a faint sound of footsteps, retiring along the lateral colonnades towards the river side of the building.

A low cry of horror burst from her lips, as she sank back towards her father; but it was unheeded. The voice of Ulpius had resumed in the interval its hollow loudness of tone; he had raised Numerian from the ground; his strong, cold grasp, which seemed to penetrate to the old man's heart, which held him motionless and helpless as if by a fatal spell, was on his arm — "Hear it! hear it!" cried the Pagan, waving his disengaged hand, as if he were addressing a vast concourse of people — "I advance this man to be one of the servants of the High Priest! He has travelled from a far country to the sacred shrine; he is docile and obedient before the altar of the gods; the lot is cast for his future life; his dwelling shall be in the temple to the day of his death! He shall minister before me in white robes, and swing the smoking censer, and slay the sacrifice at my feet!

He stopped. A dark and sinister expression appeared in his eyes, as the word "sacrifice" passed his lips; he muttered doubtingly to himself — "the sacrifice! — is it yet the hour of the sacrifice?" — and looked round towards the doorway.

The sun still shone gaily on the outer pavement; the insects still circled slowly in the mellow light; no shadow was now visible; no distant footsteps were heard; there was nothing audible but the happy music of the bubbling water, and the chiming, silvery bells For a few moments, the madman looked out anxiously towards the street, without uttering a word or moving a muscle. The raving fit was near possessing him again, as the thought of the sacrifice flashed over his darkened mind; but once more its approach was delayed. He slowly turned his head in the direction of the interior of the temple. "The sun is still bright in the outer courts," he murmured, in an under tone, "the hour of the sacrifice is not yet! Come!" he continued, in a louder voice, shaking Numerian by the arm, "It is time that the servant of the temple should behold the place of the sacrifice, and sharpen the knife for the victim before sunset! Arouse thee, bondman, and follow me!"

As yet, Numerian had neither spoken, nor attempted to escape. The preceding events, though some space has been occupied in describing them, passed in so short a period of time, that he had not hitherto recovered from the first overwhelming shock of the meeting with Ulpius. But now, awed though he still was, he felt that the moment of the struggle for freedom had arrived.

"Leave me, and let us depart! — there can be no fellowship between us again!" he exclaimed with the reckless courage of despair, taking the hand of Antonina, and striving to free himself from the madman's grasp. But the effort was vain; Ulpius tightened his hold, and laughed in triumph. "What! the servant of the Temple is in terror of the High Priest, and shrinks from walking in the place of the sacrifice!" he cried. "Fear not, bondman! The mighty one, who rules over life and death, and time, and futurity, deals kindly with the servant of his choice! Onward, onward! to the place of darkness and doom, where I alone am omnipotent, and all others are creatures who tremble and obey! To thy lesson, learner! by sunset the victim must be crowned!"

He looked round on Numerian for an instant, as he prepared to drag him forward; and their eyes met. In the fierce command of his action, and the savage exultation of his glance, the father saw repeated in a wilder form, the very attitude and expression which he had beheld in the Pagan on the morning of the loss of his child. All the circumstances of that miserable hour — the vacant bedchamber — the banished daughter — the triumph of the betrayer — the anguish of the betrayed — rushed over his mind, and rose up before it vivid as a pictured scene before his eyes. He struggled no more; the powers of resistance in mind and body were crushed alike. He made an effort to remove Antonina from his side, as if, in forgetfulness of the hidden enemy without, he designed to urge her flight through the open door, while the madman's attention was yet distracted from her. But, beyond this last exertion of the strong instinct of paternal love, every other active emotion seemed dead within him.

Vainly had he striven to disentangle the child from the fate that might be in store for the parent. To *her* the dread of the dark shadow on the pavement was superior to all other apprehensions. She now clung more closely to her father, and tightened her clasp round his hand. So, when the Pagan advanced into the interior of the temple, it was not Numerian alone who followed him to the place of sacrifice, but Antonina as well.

They moved to the back of the pile of idols. Behind it appeared a high partition of gilt and inlaid wood reaching to the ceiling, and separating the outer from the inner part of the temple. A low archway passage, protected by carved gates similar to those at the front of the building, had been formed in the partition; and through this, Ulpius and his prisoners now passed into the recess beyond.

This apartment was considerably smaller than the first hall of the temple which they had just left. The ceiling and the floor both sloped downwards together; and here the rippling of the waters of the Tiber was more distinctly audible to them than in the outer division of the building. At the moment when they entered it, the place was very dark; the pile of idols intercepted even the little light that could have been admitted through its narrow entrance; but the dense obscurity was soon dissipated. Dragging Numerian after him to the left side of the recess, Ulpius drew back a sort of wooden shutter, and a vivid ray of light immediately streamed in through a small circular opening pierced in this part of the temple.

 Then, there became apparent, at the lower end of the apartment, a vast yawning cavity in the wall, high enough to admit a man without stooping, but running downwards almost perpendicularly to some lower region, which it was impossible to see, for no light shot upwards from this precipitous artificial abyss, in the darkness of which, the eye was lost after it had penetrated to the distance of a few feet only from the opening. At the base of the confined space thus visible, appeared the commencement of a flight of steps, evidently leading far downwards into the cavity. On the abruptly sloping walls which bounded it on all sides, were painted, in the brilliant hues of ancient fresco, representations of the deities of the mythology — all in the attitude of descending into the vault; and all followed by figures of nymphs bearing wreaths of flowers, beautiful birds, and other similar adjuncts of the votive ceremonies of Paganism. The repulsive contrast between the bright colours and graceful forms presented by the frescos, and the perilous and gloomy appearance of the cavity which they decorated, increased remarkably the startling significance in the character of the whole structure. Its past evil uses seemed ineradicably written over every part of it, as past crime and torment remain ineradicably written on the human face: the mind imbibed from it terrifying ideas of deadly treachery; of secret atrocities; of frightful refinements of torture, which no uninitiated eye had ever beheld and no human resolution had ever been powerful enough to resist.

But the impressions thus received, were not produced only by what was *seen* in and around this strange vault; but by what was *heard* there besides. The wind penetrated the cavity at some distance, and through some opening that could not be beheld, and was apparently intercepted in its passage; for it whistled upwards towards the entrance in shrill, winding notes; sometimes producing another and nearer sound, resembling the clashing of many small metallic substances violently shaken together. The noise of the wind, as well as the bubbling of the current of the Tiber, seemed to proceed from a greater distance than appeared compatible with the narrow extent of the back part of the temple, and the proximity of the river to its low foundation walls. It was evident that the vault only reached its outlet, after it had wound backwards, underneath the building, in some strange complication of passages, or labyrinth of artificial caverns, which might have been built long since as dungeons for the living, or as sepulchres for the dead.

"The place of the sacrifice — aha! the place of the sacrifice!" cried the Pagan exultingly; as he drew Numerian to the entrance of the cavity; and solemnly pointed into the darkness beneath.

The father gazed steadily into the chasm, never turning now to look on Antonina; never moving to renew the struggle for freedom. Earthly loves and earthly hopes began to fade away from his heart — he was praying. The solemn words of Christian supplication fell in low, murmuring sounds from his lips, in the place of idolatry and bloodshed; and mingled with the incoherent ejaculations of the madman who kept him captive; and who now bent his glaring eyes on the darkness of the vault, half forgetful in the gloomy fascination which it exercised even over *him*, of the prisoners whom he held at its mouth.

The single ray of light, admitted from the circular aperture in the wall, fell wild and fantastic over the widely-differing figures of the three, as they stood so strangely united together before the abyss that opened beneath them. The shadows were above and the shadows were around; there was no light in the ill-omened place, but the one vivid ray that streamed over the gaunt figure of Ulpius, as he still pointed into the darkness; over the rigid features of Numerian, praying in the bitterness of expected death; and over the frail youthful form of Antonina as she nestled trembling at her father's side. It was an unearthly and a solemn scene!

Meanwhile the shadow which the girl had observed on the pavement before the doorway of the temple, now appeared there again, but not to retire as before; for, the instant after, Goisvintha stealthily entered the outer apartment of the building left vacant by its first occupants. She passed softly around the pile of idols, looked into the inner recess of the temple, and saw the three figures standing together in the ray of light, gloomy and motionless, before the mouth of the cavity. Her first glance fixed on the Pagan — whom she instinctively doubted and dreaded; whose purpose in keeping captive the father and daughter she could not divine; her next was directed on Antonina.

The girl's position was a guarded one; still holding her father's hand, she was partly protected by his body; and stood unconsciously beneath the arm of Ulpius, as it was raised while he grasped Numerian's shoulder. Marking this, and remembering that Antonina had twice escaped her already, Goisvintha hesitated for a moment, and then, with cautious step and lowering brow, began to retire again towards the doorway of the building, "Not yet — not yet the time!" she muttered, as she resumed her former lurking place; "they stand where the light is over them — the girl is watched and shielded — the two men are still on either side of her! Not yet the moment of the blow; the stroke of the knife must be sure and safe! *Sure*, for this time she must die by my hand! *Safe*, for I have other vengeance to wreak besides the vengeance on *her!* I, who have been patient and cunning since the night when I escaped from Aquileia, will be patient and cunning still! If she passes the door, I slay her as she goes out; if she remains in the temple —"

At the last word, Goisvintha paused and gazed upward; the setting sun threw its fiery glow over her haggard face; her eye brightened fiercely in the full light as she looked. "The darkness is at hand!" she continued; "the night will be thick and black in the dim halls of the temple; I shall see *her* when she shall not see *me!* — the darkness is coming; the vengeance is sure!"

She closed her lips, and with fatal perseverance continued to watch and wait, as she had resolutely watched and waited already. The Roman and the Goth; the opposite in sex, nation, and fate; the madman who dreamed of the sanguinary superstitions of Paganism before the temple altar, and the assassin who brooded over the chances of bloodshed beneath the temple portico; were now united in a mysterious identity of expectation, uncommunicated and unsuspected by either — the hour when the sun vanished from the heaven, was *the hour of the sacrifice* for both!

* * * * *

There is now a momentary pause in the progress of events. Occurrences to be hereafter related, render it necessary to take advantage of this interval to inform the reader of the real nature and use of the vault in the temple wall, the external appearance of which we have already described.

The marking peculiarity in the construction of the Pagan religion, may be most aptly compared to the marking peculiarity in the construction of the Pagan temples. Both were designed to attract the general eye by the outward effect only, which was in both the false delusive reflection of the inward substance. In the temple, the people, as they worshipped beneath the long colonnades, or beheld the lofty porticos from the street, were left to imagine the corresponding majesty and symmetry of the interior of the structure, and were not admitted to discover how grievously it disappointed the brilliant expectations which the exterior was so well calculated to inspire; how little the dark, narrow halls of the idols, the secret vaults and gloomy recesses within, fulfilled the promise of the long flights of steps, the broad extent of pavement, the massive sun-brightened pillars without. So in the religion, the votary was allured by the splendour of processions; by the pomp of auguries; by the poetry of the superstition which peopled his native woods with the sportive Dryads, and the fountains from which he drank with their guardian Naiads; which gave to mountain and lake, to sun and moon and stars, to all things around and above him, their fantastic allegory, or their gracious legend of beauty and love: but beyond this, his first acquaintance with his worship was not permitted to extend, here his initiation concluded. He was kept in ignorance of the dark and dangerous depths which lurked beneath this smooth and attractive surface; he was left to imagine that what was displayed, was but the prelude to the future discovery of what was hidden of beauty, in the rites of Paganism; he was not admitted to behold the wretched impostures, the loathsome orgies, the hideous incantations, the bloody human sacrifices perpetrated in secret, which made the foul real substance of the fair exterior form. His first sight of the temple was not less successful in deceiving his eye, than his first impression of the religion in deluding his mind.

With these hidden and guilty mysteries of the Pagan worship, the vault before which Ulpius now stood with his captives, was intimately connected.

The human sacrifices offered among the Romans were of two kinds; those publicly and those privately performed. The first were of annual recurrence in the early years of the Republic; were prohibited at a later date; were revived by Augustus, who sacrificed his prisoners of war at the altar of Julius Cæsar; and were afterwards — though occasionally renewed for particular purposes under some subsequent reigns — wholly abandoned as part of the ceremonies of Paganism during the latter periods of the empire.

The sacrifices perpetrated in private were much longer practised. They were connected with the most secret mysteries of the mythology; were concealed from the supervision of government; and lasted probably until the general extinction of heathen superstition in Italy and the provinces. Many and various were the receptacles constructed for the private immolation of human victims in different parts of the empire — in its crowded cities as well as in its solitary woods — and among all, one of the most remarkable and the longest preserved, was the great cavity pierced in the wall of the temple which Ulpius had chosen for his solitary lurking-place in Rome.

It was not merely as a place of concealment for the act of immolation, and for the corpse of the victim, that the vault had been built. A sanguinary artifice had complicated the manner of its construction, by placing in the cavity itself the instrument of the sacrifice; by making it, as it were, not merely the receptacle, but the devourer also, of its human prey. At the bottom of the flight of steps leading down into it (the top of which, as we have already observed, was alone visible from the entrance in the temple recess), was fixed the image of a dragon formed in brass.

The body of the monster, protruding opposite the steps almost at a right angle from the wall, was moved in all directions by steel springs, which communicated with one of the lower stairs, and also with a sword placed in the throat of the image to represent the dragon's tongue. The walls around the steps narrowed so as barely to admit the passage of the human body, when they approached the dragon. At the slightest pressure on the stair with which the spring communicated, the body of the monster bent forward, and the sword instantly protruded from its throat, at such a height from the steps as ensured that it should transfix in a vital part the person who descended. The corpse, then dropping by its own weight off the sword, fell through a tunnelled opening beneath the dragon, running downward in an opposite direction to that taken by the steps above; and was deposited on an iron grating washed by the waters of the Tiber, which ran under the arched foundations of the temple. The grating was approached by a secret subterranean passage, leading from the front of the building, by which the sacrificing priests were enabled to reach the dead body; to fasten weights to it; and opening the grating, to drop it into the river, never to be beheld again by mortal eyes.

In the days when this engine of destruction was permitted to serve the purpose for which the horrible ingenuity of its inventors had constructed it, its principal victims were young girls. Crowned with flowers, and clad in white garments, they were lured into immolating themselves, by being furnished with rich offerings, and told that the sole object of their fatal expedition down the steps of the vault was to realise the pictures adorning its walls (which we have described a few pages back), by presenting their gifts at the shrine of the idol below.

At the period of which we write, the dragon had for many years — since the first prohibitions of Paganism — ceased to be fed with its wonted prey. The scales forming its body grew gradually corroded and loosened by the damp; and when moved by the wind which penetrated to them from beneath, whistling up in its tortuous course through the tunnel that ran in one direction below, and the vault of the steps that ascended in another above, produced the clashing sound which has been mentioned as audible at intervals from the mouth of the cavity. But the springs which moved the deadly apparatus of the whole machine, being placed within it, under cover, continued to resist the slow progress of time and neglect; and still remained as completely fitted as ever, to execute the fatal purpose for which they had been designed.

The ultimate destiny of the dragon of brass was the destiny of the religion whose bloodiest superstitions it embodied; it fell beneath the resistless advance of Christianity. Shortly after the date of our narrative, the interior of the building beneath which it was placed having suffered from an accident, which will be related further on, the exterior was dismantled, in order that its pillars might furnish materials for a church. The vault in the wall was explored by a monk, who had been present at the destruction of other Pagan temples, and who volunteered to discover its contents. With a torch in one hand, and an iron bar in the other, he descended into the cavity, sounding the walls and the steps before him as he proceeded. For the first and the last time the sword protruded harmless from the monster's throat, when the monk pressed the fatal stair, before stepping on it, with his iron bar. The same day the machine was destroyed and cast into the Tiber, where its victims had been thrown before it in former years.

* * * * * * *

Some minutes have elapsed since we left the father and daughter standing by the Pagan's side, before the mouth of the vault; and as yet there appears no change in the several positions of the three. But already, while Ulpius still looks down stedfastly into the cavity at his feet, his voice, as he continues to speak, grows louder, and his words become more distinct. Fearful recollections associated with the place are beginning to stir his weary memory, to lift the darkness of oblivion from his idle thoughts.

"They go down, far down there!" he abruptly exclaimed, pointing into the black depths of the vault, "and never arise again to the light of the upper earth! The great Destroyer is watchful in his solitude beneath, and looks through the darkness for their approach! Hark! the hissing of his breath is like the clash of weapons in a deadly strife!"

At this moment the wind moved the loose scales of the dragon. During an instant Ulpius remained silent, listening to the noise they produced. For the first time an expression of dread appeared in his face. His memory was obscurely reviving the incidents of his discovery of the deadly machinery in the vault, when he first made his sojourn in the temple, when — filled with the confused remembrance of the mysterious rites and incantations, the secret sacrifices which he had witnessed and performed at Alexandria — he had found and followed the subterranean passage which led to the iron grating beneath the dragon. As the wind lulled again, and the clashing of the metal ceased with it, he began to give these recollections expression in words, uttering them in slow, solemn accents to himself.

"I have seen the Destroyer; the Invisible has revealed himself to *me!*" he murmured. "I stood on the iron bars; the restless waters toiled and struggled beneath my feet, as I looked up into the place of darkness. A voice called to me, 'Get light, and behold me from above! Get light! get light!' Sun, and moon, and stars gave no light *there!* but lamps burnt in the city, in the houses of the dead, when I walked by them in the night time; and the lamp gave light, when sun, and moon, and stars gave none! From the top steps I looked down, and saw the Powerful One in his golden brightness; and approached not, but watched and listened in fear. The voice again! — the voice was heard again! 'Sacrifice to me in secret, as thy brethren sacrifice! Give me the living where the living are! and the dead where the dead!' The air came up cold, and the voice ceased, and the lamp was like sun, and moon, and stars — it gave no light in the place of darkness!"

While he spoke, the loose metal again clashed in the vault, for the wind was strengthening as the evening advanced. "Hark! the signal to prepare the sacrifice!" cried the Pagan, turning abruptly to Numerian. "Listen, bondman! the living and the dead are within our reach. The breath of the Invisible strikes them in the street and in the house; they stagger in the highways, and drop at the temple steps. When the hour comes, we shall go forth and find them. Under *my* hand they go down into the cavern beneath. Whether they are hurled dead, or whether they go down living, they fall through to the iron bars, where the water leaps and rejoices to receive them! It is mine to sacrifice them above, and thine to wait for them below, to lift the bars, and give them to the river to be swallowed up! The dead drop down first; the living that are slain by the Destroyer follow after!"

Here he paused suddenly. Now, for the first time, his eye rested on Antonina, whose very existence he seemed hitherto to have forgotten. A revolting smile of mingled cunning and satisfaction instantly changed the whole character of his countenance, as he gazed on her, and then looked round significantly to the vault. "Here is one!" he whispered to Numerian, taking her by the arm. "Keep her captive — the hour is near!"

Numerian had hitherto stood unheedful while he spoke; but when he touched Antonina, the bare action was enough to arouse the father to resistance — hopeless though it was — once more. He shook off the grasp of Ulpius from the girl's arm, and drew back with her — breathless, vigilant, desperate — to the side wall behind him.

The madman laughed in proud approval. "My bondman obeys me and seizes the captive!" he cried. "He remembers that the hour is near, and loosens not his hold! Come!" he continued, "Come out into the hall beyond! — it is time that we watch for more victims for the sacrifice till the sun goes down. The Destroyer is mighty and must be obeyed!"

He walked to the entrance leading into the first apartment of the temple, and then waited to be followed by Numerian, who — now for the first time separated from Ulpius — remained stationary in the position he had last occupied, and looked eagerly around him. No chance of escape presented itself; the mouth of the vault on one side, and the passage through the partition on the other, were the only outlets to the place. There was no hope but to follow the Pagan into the great hall of the temple, to keep carefully at a distance from him, and to watch the opportunity of flight through the doorway. The street, so desolate when last beheld, might now afford more evidence that it was inhabited. Citizens, guards might be passing by, and might be summoned into the temple — help might be at hand.

As he moved forward with Antonina, such thoughts passed rapidly through the father's mind, unaccompanied at the moment by the recollection of the stranger who had followed them from the Pincian Gate, or of the apathy of the famished populace in aiding each other in any emergency. Seeing that he was followed as he had commanded, Ulpius passed on before them to the pile of idols; but a strange and sudden alteration appeared in his gait. He had hitherto walked with the step of a man — young, strong, and resolute of purpose; now he dragged one limb after the other, as slowly and painfully as if he had received a mortal hurt. He tottered with more than the infirmity of his age; his head dropped upon his breast; and he moaned and murmured inarticulately, in low, long-drawn cries.

He had advanced to the side of the pile, half way towards the door way of the temple, when Numerian, who had watched with searching eyes the abrupt change in his demeanour, forgetting the dissimulation which might still be all-important, abandoned himself to his first impulse, and hurriedly pressing forward with Antonina, attempted to pass the Pagan, and escape. But at the moment, Ulpius stopped in his slow progress, reeled, threw out his hands convulsively, and seizing Numerian by the arm, staggered back with him against the side wall of the temple. The fingers of the tortured wretch closed as if they were never to be unlocked again — closed as if with the clutch of death, with the last frantic grasp of a drowning man.

For days and nights past he had toiled incessantly under the relentless tyranny of his frenzy, building up higher and higher his altar of idols, and pouring forth his invocations before his gods in the place of the sacrifice; and now, at the moment when he was most triumphant in his ferocious activity of purpose, when his fancied bondman and his fancied victim were most helpless at his command, — now, when his strained faculties were strung to their highest pitch, the long-deferred paroxysm had seized him, which was the precursor of his repose, of the only repose granted by his awful fate, — a change (the mournful change already described) in the form of his insanity. For at those rare periods when he slept, his sleep was not unconsciousness, not rest: it was a trance of hideous dreams — his tongue spoke, his limbs moved, when he slumbered as when he spoke! It was only when his visions of the pride, the power, the fierce conflicts, and daring resolutions of his maturer years gave place to his dim, quiet, waking dreams of his boyish days, that his wasted faculties reposed, and his body rested with them in the motionless languor of perfect fatigue. Then, if words were still uttered by his lips, they were as murmurs of an infant, happy sleep; for the innocent phrases of his childhood which they then revived, seemed for a time to bring with them the innocent tranquillity of his childhood as well.

"Go! go! — fly while you are yet free!" cried Numerian, dropping the hand of Antonina, and pointing to the door. But, for the second time the girl refused to move forward a step. No horror, no peril in the temple, could banish for an instant her remembrance of the night at the farm-house in the suburbs. She kept her head turned towards the vacant entrance, fixed her eyes on it in the unintermitting watchfulness of terror, and whispered affrightedly, "Goisvintha! Goisvintha!" when her father spoke.

The clasp of the Pagan's fingers remained fixed and death-like as at first; he leaned back against the wall, as still as if life and action had for ever departed from him. The paroxysm had passed away; his face, distorted but the moment before, was now in repose, but it was a repose that was awful to look on. Tears rolled slowly from his half-closed eyes over his seamed and wrinkled cheeks, — tears which wore not the impressive expression of mental anguish, (for a vacant, unchanging smile was on his lips,) but the mere mechanical outburst of the physical weakness that the past crisis of agony had left behind it. Not the slightest appearance of thought or observation was perceptible in his features: his face was the face of an idiot.

Numerian, who had looked on him for an instant, shuddered, and averted his eyes, recoiling from the sight before him. But a more overpowering trial of his resolution was approaching, which he could not avoid. Ere long the voice of Ulpius grew audible once more; but now its tones were weak, piteous, almost childish, and the words they uttered were quiet words of love and gentleness, which, dropping from such lips, and pronounced in such a place, were fearful to hear. The temple, and all that was in it, vanished from his sight, as from his memory. Swayed by the dread and supernatural influences of his disease, the madman passed back in an instant over the dark valley of life's evil pilgrimage to the long-quitted precincts of his boyish home. While in bodily presence he stood in the place of his last crimes, the outcast of reason and humanity, in mental consciousness he lay in his mother's arms, as he had lain there ere yet he had departed to the temple at Alexandria; and *his* heart communed with *her* heart, and his eyes looked on her as they had looked before his father's fatal ambition had separated for ever parent and child!

"Mother! — come back, mother!" he whispered. "I was not asleep, I saw you when you came in, and sat by my bedside, and wept over me when you kissed me! Come back, and sit by me still! I am going away, far away, and may never hear your voice again! How happy we should be, mother, if I stayed with you always! But it is my father's will that I should go to the temple in another country, and live there to be a priest; and his will must be obeyed. I may never return; but we shall not forget one another! I shall remember *your* words, when we used to talk together happily, and you will remember *mine!*"

Hardly had the first sentence been uttered by Ulpius, when Antonina felt her father's whole frame suddenly tremble at her side. She turned her eyes from the doorway, on which they had hitherto been fixed, and looked on him. The Pagan's hand had fallen from his arm: he was free to depart, to fly as he had longed to fly but a few minutes before, and yet he never stirred. His daughter touched him, spoke to him; but he neither moved nor answered. It was not merely the shock of the abrupt transition in the language of Ulpius from the ravings of crime to the murmurs of love, — it was not merely astonishment at hearing from him, in his madness, revelations of his early life which had never passed his lips during his days of treacherous servitude in the house on the Pincian Hill, that thus filled Numerian's inmost soul with awe, and struck his limbs motionless. There was more in all that he heard than this. The words seemed as words that had doomed him at once and for ever.

His eyes, directed full on the face of the madman, were dilated with horror; his deep, gasping convulsive breathings mingled heavily, during the moment of silence that ensued, with the chiming of the bells above, and the bubbling of the water below, — the lulling music of the temple, playing its happy evening hymn at the pleasant close of day!

"We shall remember, mother! — we shall remember!" continued the Pagan softly, "and be happy in our remembrances! My brother, who loves *me* not, will love *you* when I am gone! You will walk in my little garden, and think on me as you look at the flowers that we have planted and watered together in the evening hours, when the sky was glorious to behold, and the earth was all quiet around us! Listen, mother, and kiss me! When I go to the far country, I will make a garden there like my garden here, and plant the same flowers that we have planted here; and in the evening I will go out and give them water, at the hour when you go out to give my flowers water at home; and so though we see each other no more, it will yet be as if we laboured together in the garden, as we labour now!"

The girl still fixed her eager gaze on her father. His eyes presented the same rigid expression of horror; but he was now wiping off with his own hand, mechanically, as if he knew it not, the foam which the paroxysms had left round the madman's lips; and, amid the groans that burst from him, she could hear such words as, "Lord God! — Mercy, Lord God!

Thou, who hast *thus* restored him to me — *thus*, worse than dead! — Mercy! mercy!"

The light on the pavement beneath the portico of the temple was fading visibly, — the sun had gone down.

For the third time the madman spoke, but his tones were losing their softness; they were complaining, plaintive, unutterably mournful; his dreams of the past were already changing. "Farewell, brother, farewell for years and years!" he cried. "You have not given *me* the love that I gave *you;* the fault was not mine that our father loved me the best, and chose me to be sent to the Temple, to be a priest at the altar of the gods! The fault was not mine that I partook not in your favoured sports, and joined not the companions whom *you* sought; it was our father's will that I should not live as *you* lived, and I obeyed it! You have spoken to me in anger, and turned from me in disdain; but farewell again, Cleander, farewell in forgiveness and in love!"

He might have spoken more, but his voice was drowned in one long shriek of agony which burst from Numerian's lips, and echoed discordantly through the hall of the temple, and he sank down with his face to the ground, at the Pagan's feet. The dark and terrible destiny was fulfilled! The enthusiast for the right, and the fanatic for the wrong; the man who had toiled to reform the Church, and the man who had toiled to restore the Temple; the master who had received and trusted the servant in his home, and the servant who in that home had betrayed the master's trust; the two characters, separated hitherto in the sublime disunion of good and bad, now struck together in tremendous contact, as brethren who had drawn their life from one source; who, as children, had been sheltered under the same roof!

Not in the hour when the good Christian succoured the forsaken Pagan, wandering homeless in Rome, was the secret disclosed; no chance word of it was uttered when the deceiver told the feigned relation of his life to the benefactor whom he was plotting to deceive; or when, on the first morning of the siege, the machinations of the servant triumphed over the confidence of the master: — it was reserved to be revealed in the words of delirium, at the closing years of madness, when he who discovered it was unconscious of all that he spoke, and his eyes were blinded to the true nature of all that he saw; when earthly voices that might once have called him back to repentance, to recognition, and to love, were become to him as sounds that have no meaning; when, by a ruthless and startling fatality, it was on the brother who had wrought for the true faith, that the whole crushing weight of the terrible disclosure fell, unpartaken by the brother who had wrought for the false! But the judgments pronounced in Time, go forth from the tribunal of that Eternity to which the mysteries of life tend, and in which they shall be revealed — neither waiting on human seasons nor abiding by human justice, but speaking to the soul in the language of immortality, which is heard in the world that is now, and interpreted in the world that is to come.

Lost, for an instant, even the recollection that Goisvintha might still be watching her opportunity from without, calling despairingly on her father, and vainly striving to raise him from the ground, Antonina remembered not, in the overwhelming trial of the moment the revelations of Numerian's past life that had been disclosed to her in the days when the famine was at its worst in Rome. The name of "Cleander," which she had then heard her father pronounce, as the name that he had abandoned when he separated himself from the companions of his sinful choice, passed unheeded by her when the Pagan unconsciously uttered it. She saw the whole scene but as a fresh menace of danger, as a new vision of terror, more ominous of ill than all that had preceded it.

Thick as was the darkness in which the lulling and involuntary memories of the past had enveloped the perceptions of Ulpius, the father's piercing cry of anguish seemed to have penetrated it, as with a sudden ray of light. The madman's half-closed eyes opened instantly, and fixedly, dreamily at first, on the altar of idols. He waved his hands to and fro before him, as if he were parting back the folds of a heavy veil that obscured his sight; but his wayward thoughts did not resume, as yet, their old bias towards ferocity and crime. When he spoke again, his speech was still inspired by the visions of his early life — but now of his early life in the Temple at Alexandria. His expressions were more abrupt, more disjointed than before; yet they continued to display the same evidence of the mysterious, instinctive vividness of recollection, which was the result of the sudden change in the nature of his insanity. His language wandered (still as if the words came from him undesignedly and unconsciously) over the events of his boyish introduction to the service of the gods, and, though confusing them in order, still preserved them in substance, as they have been already related in the history of his "apprenticeship to the Temple."

Now, he was, in imagination, looking down once more from the summit of the temple of Serapis on the glittering expanse of the Nile and the wide country around it; and now, he was walking proudly through the streets of Alexandria by the side of his uncle, Macrinus, the High Priest. Now, he was wandering at night, in curiosity and awe, through the gloomy vaults and subterranean corridors of the sacred place; and now, he was listening, well pleased, to the kindly greeting, the inspiring praises of Macrinus during their first interview. But at this point, and while dwelling on this occasion, his memory became darkened again; it vainly endeavoured to retrace the circumstances attending the crowning evidence of the High Priest's interest in his pupil, and anxiety to identify him completely with his new protector and his new duties, which had been displayed when he conferred on the trembling boy the future distinction of one of his own names.

And here let it be remembered, as a chief link in the mysterious chain of fatalities which had united to keep the brothers apart as brethren after they had met as men, that both had, from widely different causes, abandoned in after-life the names which they bore in their father's house; that while one, by his own act and for his own purpose, transformed himself from Cleander, the associate of the careless and the criminal, to Numerian, the preacher of the Gospel and reformer of the Church; the other had (to quote the words of the fourth chapter) "become from the boy Emilius the student Ulpius," by the express and encouraging command of his master, Macrinus, the High Priest.

While the Pagan still fruitlessly endeavoured to revive the events connected with the change in his name on his arrival in Alexandria, and, chafing under the burden of oblivion that weighed upon his thoughts, attempted for the first time to move from the wall against which he had hitherto leaned — while Antonina still strove in vain to recal her father to the recollection of the terrible exigencies of the moment, as he crouched prostrate at the madman's feet — the doorway of the temple was darkened once more by the figure of Goisvintha. She stood on the threshold, a gloomy and indistinct form in the fading light, looking intently into the deeply-shadowed interior of the building. As she marked the altered positions of the father and daughter, she uttered a suppressed ejaculation of triumph; but, while the sound passed her lips, she heard, or thought she heard, a noise in the street behind. Even now her vigilance and cunning, her deadly, calculating resolution to await in immovable patience the fit time for striking the blow deliberately and with impunity, did not fail her. Turning instantly, she walked to the top step of the temple, and stood there for a few moments, watchfully surveying the open space before her.

But, in those few moments, the scene in the building changed once more. The madman, while he still wavered between relapsing into the raving fit and continuing under the influence of the tranquil mood, in which he had been prematurely disturbed, caught sight of Goisvintha, when her approach suddenly shadowed the entrance to the temple. Her presence, momentary though it was, was for *him* the presence of a figure that had not appeared before; that had stood in a strange position between the shade within and the faint light without; it was a new object, presented to his eyes while they were straining to recover such imperfect faculties of observation as had been their wont, and its ascendancy over him was instantaneous and all-powerful.

He started bewildered, like a deep sleeper suddenly awoke; violent shudderings ran for a moment over his frame; then it strengthened again with its former unnatural strength: the demon raged within him in renewed fury, as he tore his robe which Numerian held as he lay at his feet, from the feeble grasp that confined it; and, striding up to the pile of idols, stretched out his hands in solemn deprecation.

"The High Priest has slept before the altar of the gods!" he cried loudly, "but they have been patient with their well-beloved; their thunder has not struck him for his crime! Now the servant returns to his service — the rites of Serapis begin!"

Numerian still remained prostrate, spirit-broken; he slowly clasped his hands together on the floor, and his voice was now to be heard, still supplicating in low and stifled accents, as if in unceasing prayer lay his last hope of preserving his own reason. "God! Thou art the God of Mercy; be merciful to *him!*" he murmured. "Thou acceptest of repentance; grant repentance to *him*. If at any time I have served Thee without blame, let the service be counted to *him;* let the vials of thy wrath be poured out on *me!*"

"Hark! the trumpet blows for the sacrifice!" interrupted the raving voice of the Pagan, as he turned from the altar, and extended his arms in frenzied inspiration. "The roar of music and the voice of exultation soar upward from the highest mountain-tops! The incense smokes; and in and out, and round and round, the dancers whirl about the pillars of the Temple! The ox for the sacrifice is without spot; his horns are gilt; the crown and fillet adorn his head; the Priest stands before him, naked from the waist upwards; he heaves the libation out of the cup; the blood flows over the altar! Up! up! tear forth with reeking hands the heart while it is yet warm, futurity is before you in the quivering entrails, look on them and read! read!"

While he spoke, Goisvintha had entered the temple. The street was still desolate; no help was at hand.

Not advancing at once, she concealed herself near the door, behind a projection in the pile of idols, watching from it until Ulpius, in the progress of his frenzy, should turn away from Antonina, whom he stood fronting at this instant. But she had not entered unperceived; Antonina had seen her again. And now the bitterness of death, when the young die unprotected in their youth, came over the girl; and she cried in a low wailing voice, as she knelt by Numerian's side — "I must die, father, I must die, as Hermanric died! Look up at me, and speak to me before I die!"

Her father was still praying; he heard nothing, for his heart was bleeding in atonement at the shrine of his boyish home, and his soul still communed with its Maker. The voice that followed hers was the voice of Ulpius.

"Oh, beautiful are the gardens round the sacred altars, and lofty the trees that embower the glittering shrines!" he exclaimed, rapt and ecstatic in his new visions. "Lo, the morning breaks, and the spirits of light are welcomed by a sacrifice! The sun goes down behind the mountain, and the beams of evening tremble on the victim beneath the knife of the adoring Priest! The moon and stars shine high in the firmament, and the Genii of Night are saluted in the still hours with blood!"

As he paused, the lament of Antonina was continued in lower and lower tones — "I must die, father, I must die!" And with it murmured the supplicating accents of Numerian — "God of Mercy! deliver the helpless, and forgive the afflicted! Lord of Judgment! deal gently with thy servants who have sinned!" While, mingling with both in discordant combination, the strange music of the temple still poured on its lulling sound — the rippling of the running waters, and the airy chiming of the bells!

"Worship! — Emperors, armies, nations, glorify and worship *me!*" shouted the madman, in thunder-tones of triumph and command, as his eye for the first time encountered the figure of Numerian prostrate at his feet. "Worship the demi-god who moves with the deities through spheres unknown to man! I have heard the moans of the unburied who wander on the shores of the Lake of the Dead — worship! I have looked on the river whose black current roars and howls in its course through the caves of everlasting night — worship! I have seen the furies lashed by serpents on their wrinkled necks; and followed them as they hurled their torches over the pining ghosts! I have stood unmoved in the hurricane-tumult of hell — worship! worship! worship!"

He turned round again towards the altar of idols, calling upon his gods to proclaim his deification; and, at the moment when he moved, Goisvintha sprang forward. Antonina was kneeling with her face turned from the door, as the assassin seized her by her long hair, and drove the knife into her neck. The moaning accents of the girl, bewailing her approaching fate, closed in one faint groan; she stretched out her arms, and fell forward over her father's body.

In the ferocious triumph of the moment, Goisvintha raised her arm to repeat the stroke; but at that instant the madman looked round. "The sacrifice! — the sacrifice!" he shouted, leaping at one spring, like a wild beast, at her throat. She struck ineffectually at him with the knife, as he fastened his long nails in her flesh, and hurled her backwards to the floor. Then he yelled and gibbered in frantic exultation, set his foot on her breast, and spat on her as she lay beneath him.

The contact of the girl's body when she fell — the short but terrible tumult of the attack that passed almost over him — the shrill, deafening cries of the madman — awoke Numerian from his trance of despairing remembrance, aroused him in his agony of supplicating prayer — he looked up.

The scene that met his eyes was one of those scenes which crush every faculty but the faculty of mechanical action — before which, thought vanishes from men's minds, utterance is suspended on their lips, expression is paralysed on their faces. The coldness of the tomb seemed breathed over Numerian's aspect by the contemplation of the terrible catastrophe; his eyes were glassy and vacant, his lips parted and rigid; even the remembrance of the discovery of his brother seemed lost to him, as he stooped over his daughter and bound a fragment of her robe round her neck.

The mute, soulless, ghastly stillness of death looked settled on his features, as, unconscious now of weakness or age, he rose with her in his arms, stood motionless for one moment before the doorway, and looked slowly round on Ulpius; then he moved forward with heavy regular steps. The Pagan's foot was still on Goisvintha's breast, as the father passed him; his gaze was still fixed on her; but his cries of triumph were calmed; he laughed and muttered incoherently to himself.

The moon was rising, soft, faint and tranquil, over the quiet street, as Numerian descended the temple steps with his daughter in his arms: and, after an instant's pause of bewilderment and doubt, instinctively pursued his slow, funereal course along the deserted roadway in the direction of home. Soon, as he advanced, he beheld in the moonlight, down the long vista of the street at its termination, a little assemblage of people walking towards him with calm and regular progress. As they came nearer, he saw that one of them held an open book, that another carried a crucifix, and that others followed these two with clasped hands and drooping heads. And then, after an interval, the fresh breezes that blew towards him bore onward these words, slowly and reverently pronounced: —

"*Know, therefore, that God exacteth of thee less than thine iniquity deserveth.*"

"*Canst thou, by searching, find out God? Canst thou find out the Almighty to perfection?*"

Then the breeze fell; the words grew indistinct,

but the procession still moved forward. As it came nearer and nearer, the voice of the reader was again plainly heard:

"*If iniquity be in thy hand, put it far away, and let not wickedness dwell in thy tabernacles.*

"*For then shalt thou lift up thy face without spot; yea, thou shalt be steadfast, and shalt not fear;*

"*Because thou shalt forget thy misery, and remember it as waters that pass away:*

"*And thine age shall be clearer than the noonday; thou shalt shine forth, thou shalt be as the morning.*"

The reader stopped and closed the book; for now Numerian had met the members of the little procession, and they looked on him standing voiceless before them in the clear moonlight, with his daughter's head drooping over his shoulder, as he carried her in his arms.

There were some among those who gathered round him, whose features he would have recognised at another time, as the features of the surviving adherents of his former congregation. The assembly he had met, was composed of the few sincere Christians in Rome, who had collected, on the promulgation of the news that Alaric had ratified terms of peace, to make a pilgrimage through the city, in the hopeless endeavour, by reading from the Bible and passing exhortation, to awaken the reckless populace to a feeling of contrition for their sins, and of devout gratitude for their approaching deliverance from the horrors of the siege.

But now, when Numerian confronted them, neither

by word nor look did he express the slightest recognition of any who surrounded him. To all the questions addressed to him, he replied by hurried gestures that none could comprehend. To all the promises of help and protection heaped upon him in the first outbreak of the grief and pity of his adherents of other days, he answered but by the same dull, vacant glance. It was only when they relieved him of his burden, and gently prepared to carry the senseless girl among them back to her father's house, that he spoke; and then, in faint entreating tones, he besought them to let him hold her hand as they went, so that he might be the first to feel her pulse beat — if it yet moved.

They turned back by the way they had come,— a sorrowful and slow-moving procession! As they passed on, the reader again opened the Sacred Book; and then, these words rose through the soothing and heavenly tranquillity of the first hours of night: —

"*Behold, happy is the man whom God correcteth; therefore despise not thou the chastening of the Almighty:*

"*For he maketh sore, and bindeth up; he woundeth, and his hands make whole.*"

CHAPTER XIII.
Retribution.

As, in the progress of Life, each man pursues his course with the passions, good and evil, set, as it were, on either side of him; and, viewing their results in the actions of his fellow-men, finds his attention, while still attracted by the spectacle of what is noble and virtuous, suddenly challenged by the opposite display of what is mean and criminal — so, in the progress of this narrative, which aims to be the reflection of Life, the reader who has journeyed with us thus far, and who may now be inclined still to follow the little procession of Christian devotees, to walk by the side of the afflicted father, and to hold with him, the hand of his ill-fated child, is yet, in obedience to the conditions of the story, required to turn back for awhile to the contemplation of its darker passages of guilt and terror — he must enter the Temple again; but he will enter it for the last time.

The scene before the altar of idols was fast proceeding to its fatal climax.

The Pagan's frenzy had exhausted itself in its own fury — his insanity was assuming a quieter and a more dangerous form; his eye grew cunning and suspicious; a stealthy deliberation and watchfulness appeared in all his actions. He now slowly lifted his foot from Goisvintha's breast, and raised his hands at the same time, to strike her back if she should attempt to escape. Seeing that she lay senseless from her fall, he left her; retired to one of the corners of the temple, took from it a rope that lay there, and returning, bound her arms behind her, at the hands and wrists. The rope cut deep through the skin — the pain restored her to her senses; she suffered the sharp agony in her own body, in the same place where she had inflicted it on the young chieftain, at the farm-house beyond the suburbs.

The minute after, she felt herself dragged along the ground, further into the interior of the building. The madman drew her up to the iron gates of the passage through the partition; and, fastening the end of the rope to them, left her there. This part of the temple was enveloped in total darkness — her assailant addressed not a word to her — she could not obtain even a glimpse of his form; but she could hear him still laughing to himself, in hoarse, monotonous tones, that sounded now near, and now distant again.

She abandoned herself as lost — prematurely devoted to the torment and death that she had anticipated: but, as yet, her masculine resolution and energy did not decline. The very intensity of the anguish she suffered from the bindings at her wrists, producing a fierce bodily effort to resist it, strengthened her iron-strung nerves. She neither cried for help, nor appealed to the Pagan for pity. The gloomy fatalism which she had inherited from her savage ancestors, sustained her in a suicide pride.

Ere long the laughter of Ulpius, while he moved slowly hither and thither in the darkness of the temple, was overpowered by the sound of her voice — deep, groaning, but yet steady — as she uttered her last words — words, poured forth like the wild dirges, the fierce death-songs of the old Goths, when they died deserted on the bloody battle-field; or were cast bound into deep dungeons, a prey to the viper and the asp. Thus she spoke: —

"I swore to be avenged! while I went forth from Aquileia with the child that was killed and the child that was wounded; while I climbed the high wall in the night time, and heard the tumult of the beating waves near the bank where I buried the dead; while I wandered in the darkness over the naked heath, and through the lonely forest; while I climbed the pathless sides of the mountains, and made my refuge in the cavern by the waters of the dark lake.

"I swore to be avenged! while the warriors approached me on their march, and the roaring of the trumpets and the clash of the armour sounded in my ears; while I greeted my kinsman, Hermanric, a mighty chieftain, at the King's side, among the invading hosts; while I looked on my last child, dead like the rest, and knew that he was buried afar from the land of his people, and from the others that the Romans had slain before him.

"I swore to be avenged! while the army encamped before Rome, and I stood with Hermanric, looking on the great walls in the misty evening; while the daughter of the Roman was a prisoner in our tent, and I eyed her as she lay on my knees; while for her sake my kinsman turned traitor, and withheld my hand from the blow; while I passed unseen into the lonely farmhouse, to deal judgment on him with my knife; while I saw him die the death of a deserter at my feet, and knew that it was a Roman who had lured him from his people, and blinded him to the righteousness of revenge.

"I swore to be avenged! while I walked round the grave of the chieftain who was the last of my race; while I stood alone out of the army of my people, in the city of the slayers of my babes; while I tracked the footsteps of the Roman who had twice escaped me, as she fled through the street; while I watched and was patient among the pillars of the temple, and waited till the sun went down, and the victim was unshielded, for the moment to strike.

"I swore to be avenged! and my oath has been fulfilled — the knife that still bleeds, drops with *her* blood — the chief vengeance has been wreaked! The rest that were to be slain remain for others, and not for me! For now I go to my husband and my children; now the hour is near at hand when I shall herd with their spirits in the Twilight World of Shadows, and make my long abiding-place with them in the Valley of Eternal Repose! The Destinies have willed it — it is enough!"

Her voice trembled and grew faint, as she pronounced the last words. The anguish of the fastenings at her wrists was at last overpowering her senses, conquering, spite of all resistance, her stubborn endurance.

For a little while yet she spoke at intervals; but her speech was fragmentary and incoherent. At one moment she still gloried in her revenge, at another she exulted in the fancied contemplation of the girl's body still lying before her; and her hands writhed beneath their bonds, in the effort to repossess themselves of the knife, and strike again. But soon all sounds ceased to proceed from her lips, save the loud, thick, irregular breathings, which showed that she was yet conscious, and yet lived.

Meanwhile the madman had passed into the inner recess of the temple, and had drawn the shutter over the opening in the wall, through which light had been admitted into the place when Numerian and Antonina first entered it. Even the black chasm formed by the mouth of the vault of the dragon now disappeared, with all other objects, in the thick darkness. But no obscurity could confuse the senses of Ulpius in the temple, whose every corner he visited in his restless wanderings by night and by day alike. Led as if by a mysterious penetration of sight, he traced his way unerringly to the entrance of the vault, knelt down before it; and placing his hands on the first of the steps by which it was descended, listened, breathless and attentive, to the sounds that rose from the abyss — listened, rapt and unmoving, a formidable and unearthly figure, — like a magician waiting for a voice from the oracles of Hell, — like a spirit of Night looking down into the mid caverns of the earth, and watching the mysteries of subterranean creation, the giant pulses of Action and Heat, which are the lifesprings of the rolling world.

The fitful wind whistled up, wild and plaintive; the river chafed and bubbled through the iron grating below; the loose scales of the dragon clashed as the night breezes reached them: and these sounds were still to *him* as the language of his gods, which filled him with a fearful rapture, and inspired him, in the terrible degradation of his being, as with a new soul. He listened and listened yet. Fragments of wild fancies — the vain yearnings of the disinherited mind to recover its divine birthright of boundless thought — now thrilled through him, and held him still and speechless where he knelt.

But at length, through the gloomy silence of the recess, he heard the voice of Goisvintha raised once more, and in hoarse, wild tones calling aloud for light and help. The agony of pain and suspense, the awful sense of darkness and stillness, of solitary bondage and slow torment, had at last effected that which no open peril, no common menace of violent death could have produced. She yielded to fear and despair, — sank prostrate under a paralysing, superstitious dread. The misery that she had inflicted on others recoiled in retribution on herself, as she now shuddered under the consciousness of the first emotions of helpless terror that she had ever felt.

Ulpius instantly rose from the vault, and advanced straight through the darkness to the gates of the partition; but he passed his prisoner without stopping for an instant, and hastening into the outer apartment of the temple, began to grope over the floor for the knife which the woman had dropped when he bound her. He was laughing to himself once more, for the evil spirit was prompting him to a new project, tempting him to a pitiless refinement of cruelty and deceit.

He found the knife, and returning with it to Goisvintha, cut the rope that confined her wrists. Then she became silent when the first sharpness of her suffering was assuaged; he whispered softly in her ear, "Follow me, and escape!"

Bewildered and daunted by the darkness and mystery around her, she vainly strained her eyes to look through the obscurity, as Ulpius drew her on into the recess. He placed her at the mouth of the vault, and here she strove to speak; but low, inarticulate sounds alone proceeded from her powerless utterance. Still, there was no light; still, the burning, gnawing agony at her wrists (relieved but for an instant when the rope was cut) continued and increased; and still she felt the presence of the unseen being at her side, whom no darkness could blind, and who bound and loosed at his arbitrary will.

By nature fierce, resolute, and vindictive under injury, she was a terrible evidence of the debasing power of crime, as she now stood, enfeebled by the weight of her own avenging guilt, upraised to crush her in the hour of her pride; by the agency of Darkness, whose perils the innocent and the weak have been known to brave; by Suspense, whose agony they have resisted;

by Pain, whose infliction they have endured in patience.

"Go down, far down the steep steps, and escape!" whispered the madman, in soft, beguiling tones. "The darkness above leads to the light below! Go down, far down!"

He quitted his hold of her as he spoke. She hesitated, shuddered and drew back, but again she was urged forward, and again she heard the whisper, "The darkness above leads to the light below! Go down, far down!"

Despair gave the firmness to proceed, and dread the hope to escape. Her wounded arms trembled as she now stretched them out, and felt for the walls of the vault on either side of her. The horror of death in utter darkness, from unseen hands, and the last longing aspiration to behold the light of heaven once more, were at their strongest within her, as she began slowly and cautiously to tread the fatal stair.

While she descended, the Pagan dropped into his former attitude at the mouth of the vault, and listened breathlessly. Minutes seemed to elapse between each step, as she went lower and lower down. Suddenly he heard her pause, as if panic-stricken in the darkness, and her voice ascended to him, groaning, "Light! light! Oh, where is the light!" He rose up, and stretched out his hands to hurl her back if she should attempt to return; but she descended again. Twice he heard her heavy footfall on the steps, — then there was an interval of deep silence, — then a sharp, grinding clash of metal echoed piercingly through the vault, followed by the noise of a dull, heavy fall, faintly audible far beneath,—and then the old familiar sounds of the place were heard again, and were not interrupted more. The sacrifice to the Dragon was achieved!

* * * * *

The madman stood on the steps of the sacred building, and looked out on the street shining before him in the bright Italian moonlight. No remembrance of Numerian and Antonina, and of the earlier events in the temple, remained within him. He was pondering imperfectly, in vague pride and triumph, over the sacrifice that he had offered up at the shrine of the Dragon of Brass. Thus secretly exulting, he now remained inactive. Absorbed in his wandering meditations, he delayed to trace the subterranean passages leading to the iron grating where the corpse of Goisvintha lay washed by the waters, as they struggled onward through the bars, and waiting but his hand to be cast into the river, where all past sacrifices had been engulphed before it.

His tall solitary figure was lit by the moonlight streaming through the pillars of the portico; his loose robes waved slowly about him in the wind, as he stood firm and erect before the door of the temple: he looked more like the spectral genius of departed Paganism than a living man. But, lifeless though he seemed, his quick eye was still on the watch, still directed by the restless suspicion of insanity. Minute after minute quietly elapsed, and as yet nothing was presented to his rapid observation but the desolate roadway, and the high, gloomy houses that bounded it on either side. It was soon, however, destined to be attracted by objects far different from these, — by objects which startled the repose of the tranquil street with the tumult of action and life.

He was still gazing earnestly on the narrow view before him, vaguely imagining to himself, the while, Goisvintha's fatal descent into the vault, and thinking triumphantly of her dead body that now lay on the grating beneath it, when a red glare of torchlight, thrown wildly on the moon-brightened pavement, whose purity it seemed to stain, caught his eye.

The light appeared at the end of the street leading from the more central portion of the city, and ere long displayed clearly a body of forty or fifty people advancing towards the temple. The Pagan looked eagerly on them as they came nearer and nearer. The assembly was composed of priests, soldiers, and citizens, — the priests bearing torches, the soldiers carrying hammers, crowbars, and other similar tools, or bending under the weight of large chests secured with iron fastenings, close to which the populace walked, as if guarding them with jealous care. This strange procession was preceded by two men, who were considerably in advance of it — a priest and a soldier. An expression of impatience and exultation appeared on their pale, famine-wasted countenances, as they approached the temple with rapid steps.

Ulpius never moved from his position, but fixed his

piercing eyes on them as they advanced. Not vainly did he now stand, watchful and menacing, before the entrance of his gloomy shrine. He had seen the first degradations heaped on fallen Paganism, and he was now to see the last. He had immolated all his affections and all his hopes, all his faculties of body and mind, his happiness in boyhood, his enthusiasm in youth, his courage in manhood, his reason in old age, at the altar of his gods; and now they were to exact from him, in their defence, lonely, criminal, maddened, as he already was in their cause, more than all this! The decree had gone forth from the senate which devoted to legalised pillage the treasures in the temples of Rome!

Rulers of a people impoverished by former exactions, and comptrollers only of an exhausted treasury, the government of the city had searched vainly among all ordinary resources for the means of paying the heavy ransom exacted by Alaric as the price of peace. The one chance of meeting the emergency that remained, was to strip the Pagan temples of the mass of jewelled ornaments and utensils, the costly robes, the idols of gold and silver which they were known to contain, and which, under that mysterious, hereditary influence of superstition, whose power it is the longest labour of truth to destroy, had remained untouched and respected, alike by the people and the senate, after the worship that they represented had been interdicted by the laws, and abandoned by the nation.

This last expedient for freeing Rome from the

blockade, was adopted almost as soon as imagined. The impatience of the starved populace for the immediate collection of the ransom, allowed the government little time for the tedious preliminaries of deliberation. The soldiers were provided at once with the necessary implements for the task imposed on them; certain chosen members of the senate and the people followed them, to see that they honestly gathered in the public spoil; and the priests of the Christian churches volunteered to hallow the expedition by their presence, and led the way with their torches into every secret apartment of the temples where treasure might be contained. At the close of the day, immediately after it had been authorised, this strange search for the ransom was hurriedly commenced. Already much had been collected; votive offerings of price had been snatched from the altars, where they had so long hung undisturbed; hidden treasure-chests of sacred utensils had been discovered and broken open; idols had been stripped of their precious ornaments, and torn from their massive pedestals; and now the procession of gold-seekers, proceeding along the banks of the Tiber, had come in sight of the little temple of Serapis, and were hastening forward to empty it, in its turn, of every valuable that it contained.

The priest and the soldier, calling to their companions behind to hurry on, had now arrived opposite the temple steps; and saw confronting them in the pale moonlight, from the eminence on which he stood, the weird and solitary figure of Ulpius — the apparition of a Pagan in the gorgeous robes of his priesthood, bidden back from the tombs to stay the hand of the spoiler before the shrine of his gods.

The soldier dropped his weapon to the ground; and, trembling in every limb, refused to proceed. But the priest, a tall, stern, emaciated man, went on defenceless and undaunted. He signed himself solemnly with the cross as he slowly ascended the steps; fixed his unflinching eyes on the madman, who glared back on him in return; and called aloud in a harsh, steady voice: "Man, or demon! in the name of Christ, whom thou deniest, stand back!"

For an instant, as the priest approached him, the Pagan averted his eyes and looked on the concourse of people and the armed soldiers rapidly advancing. His fingers closed round the hilt of Goisvintha's knife, which he had hitherto held loosely in his hand, as he exclaimed in low, concentrated tones, "Aha! the siege — the siege of Serapis!" The priest now standing on the same step with him, stretched out his arm to thrust him back, and at that moment received the stroke of the knife. He staggered, lifted his hand again to sign his forehead with the cross; and, as he raised it, rolled back dead on the pavement of the street.

The soldier, standing motionless with superstitious terror a few feet from the corpse, called to his companions for help. Hurling his bloody weapon at them in defiance, as they ran in confusion to the base of the temple steps, Ulpius entered the building, and locked and chained the gates.

Then the assembled people thronging round the corpse of the priest, heard the madman shouting in his frenzy, as if to a great body of adherents round him, to pour down the molten lead and the scorching sand; to hurl back every scaling ladder planted against the walls; to massacre each prisoner who was seized mounting the ramparts to the assault; and as they looked up to the building from the street, they saw at intervals through the bars of the closed gates, the figure of Ulpius passing swift and shadowy; his arms extended, his long grey hair and white robes streaming behind him, as he rushed round and round the temple reiterating his wild, Pagan war-cries as he went. The enfeebled, superstitious populace trembled while they gazed — a spectre driven on a whirlwind would not have been more terrible to their eyes.

But the priests among the crowd, roused to fury by the murder of one of their own body, revived the courage of those around them. Even the shouts of Ulpius were now overpowered by the sound of their voices, raised to the highest pitch, promising heavenly and earthly rewards — salvation, money, absolution, promotion — to all who would follow them up the steps, and burst their way into the temple. Animated by the words of the priests, and growing gradually confident in their own numbers, the boldest in the throng seized a piece of timber lying by the river-side, and, using it as a battering-ram, assailed the gate.

But they were weakened with famine; they could gain little impetus, from the necessity of ascending the temple steps to the attack; the iron quivered as they struck it; but hinge and lock remained firm alike. They were preparing to renew the attempt, when a tremendous shock — a crash as if the whole heavy roof of the building had fallen in — drove them back in terror to the street.

Recalled by the sight of the armed men, the priests and the attendant crowd of people advancing to invade his sanctuary, to the days when he had defended the great Temple of Serapis at Alexandria, against enemies similar in appearance, though far superior in numbers; persuaded in the revival of these, the most sanguinary visions of his insanity, that he was still resisting the Christian fanatics, supported by his adherents in his sacred fortress of former years, the Pagan displayed none of his accustomed cunning and care in moving through the darkness around him. He hurried hither and thither, encouraging his imaginary followers, and glorying in his dreams of slaughter and success, forgetful in his frenzy of all that the temple contained.

As he pursued his wild course round and round the altar of idols, his robe became entangled, and was torn, by the projecting substances at one corner of it. The whole overhanging mass tottered at the moment, but did not yet fall. A few of the smaller idols, however, at the outside dropped to the ground; and with them an image of Serapis, which they happened partially to support — a heavy monstrous figure, carved life-size in wood, and studded with gold, silver, and precious stones — fell at the Pagan's feet. But this was all — the outer materials of the perilous structure had been detached only at one point; the pile itself still remained in its place.

The madman seized the image of Serapis in his arms, and passed blindly onward with it through the passage in the partition into the recess beyond. At that instant the shock of the first attack on the gates resounded through the building. Shouting, as he heard it, "A sally! a sally! men of the Temple, the gods and the high priest lead you on!" and still holding the idol before him, he rushed straight forward to the entrance, and struck in violent collision against the backward part of the pile.

The ill-balanced, top-heavy mass of images and furniture of many temples swayed, parted and fell over against the gates and the wall on either side of them. Maimed and bleeding, struck down by the lower part of the pile, as it was forced back against the partition when the upper part fell, the fury of Ulpius was but increased by the crashing ruin around him. He struggled up again into an erect position; mounted on the top of the fallen mass — now spread out at the sides over the floor of the building, but confined at one end by the partition, and at the other by the opposite wall and the gates — and still clasping the image of Serapis in his arms, called louder and louder to "the men of the Temple," to mount with him the highest ramparts, and pour down on the besiegers the molten lead!

The priests were again the first men to approach the gates of the building after the shock that had been heard within it. The struggle for the possession of the temple had assumed to them the character of a holy warfare against heathenism and magic — a sacred conflict to be sustained by the Church, for the sake of her servant who had fallen a martyr at the outset of the strife. Strong in their fanatical boldness, they advanced with one accord close to the gates. Some of the smaller images of the fallen pile had been forced through the bars, behind which appeared the great idols, the broken masses of furniture, the long robes and costly hangings, all locked together in every wild variety of position — a chaos of distorted objects heaped up by an earthquake! Above and further inward, the lower part of the Pagan's robe was faintly discernible through the upper interstices in the gate, as he stood, commanding, on the summit of his prostrate altar, with his idol in his arms.

The priests felt an instant conviction of certain triumph when they discerned the cause of the shock that had been heard within the temple. One of their number snatched up a small image that had fallen through to the pavement where he stood; and holding it before the people below, exclaimed exultingly: —

"Children of the Church, the mystery is revealed! Idols more precious than this lie by hundreds on the floor of the temple! It is no demon, but a man, one

man, who still defies us within! — a robber who would
defraud the Romans of the ransom of their lives! —
the pillage of many temples is around him; remember
now, that the nearer we came to this place the fewer
were the spoils of idolatry that we gathered in; the
treasure which is yours, the treasure which is to free
you from the famine, has been seized by the assassin
of our holy brother; it is *there*, scattered at his feet
To the gates! To the gates again! Absolution for al
their sins to the men who burst in the gates!"

Again the mass of timber was taken up; again the
gates were assailed; and again they stood firm — they
were now strengthened, barricaded by the fallen pile
It seemed hopeless to attempt to break them down
without a reinforcement of men, without employing
against them the heaviest missiles, the strongest engine
of war.

The people gave vent to a cry of fury, as they
heard from the temple the hollow laughter of the mad
man triumphing in their defeat. The words of th
priest, in allaying their superstitious fears, had aroused
the deadly passions that superstition brings forth.
few among the throng hurried to the nearest guard
house for assistance, but the greater part pressed closel
round the temple; some pouring forth impotent ex
crations against the robber of the public spoil; som
joining the priests in calling on him to yield. But tl
clamour lasted not long, it was suddenly and strangel
stilled by the voice of one man in the crowd, callir
loudly to the rest to fire the temple!

The words were hardly spoken ere they were repeated triumphantly on all sides. "Fire the temple!" cried the people, ferociously. "Burn it over the robber's head! A furnace — a furnace! to melt down the gold and silver ready to our hands! Fire the temple! Fire the temple!"

Those who were most active among the crowd (which was now greatly increased by stragglers from all parts of the city) entered the houses behind them, and returned in a few minutes with every inflammable substance that they could collect in their hands. A heap of fuel, two or three feet in height, was raised against the gates immediately, and soldiers and people pressed forward with torches to light it. But the priest who had before spoken, waved them back. "Wait!" he cried; "the fate of his body is with the people, but the fate of his soul is with the Church!"

Then, turning to the temple, he called solemnly and sternly to the madman. "Thy hour is come! repent, confess, and save thy soul!"

"Slay on! Slay on!" answered the raving voice from within. "Slay, till not a Christian is left! Victory! Serapis! See, they drop from our walls! — they writhe bleeding on the earth beneath us! There is no worship but the worship of the gods! Slay! Slay on!"

"Light!" cried the priest. "His damnation be on his own head! Anathema! Maranatha! Let him die accursed!"

The dry fuel was fired at once at all points — it was an anticipation of an "Auto da Fé;" a burning of a heretic, in the fifth century! As the flames rose, the people fell back and watched their rapid progress. The priests, standing before them in a line, stretched out their hands in denunciation against the temple, and repeated together the awful excommunication service of the Roman Church.

* * * * * * *

The fire at the gates had communicated with the idols inside. It was no longer on his prostrate altar, but on his funeral pile that Ulpius now stood; and the image that he clasped was the stake to which he was bound. A red glare, dull at first, was now brightening and brightening below him; flames, quick and noiseless, rose and fell, and rose again, at different points, illuminating the interior of the Temple with fitful and changing light. The grim, swarthy forms of the idols seemed to sway and writhe like living things in torment, as fire and smoke alternately displayed and concealed them. A deadly stillness now overspread the face and form of the Pagan, as he looked down steadfastly on the deities of his worship engendering his destruction beneath him. His cheek — the cheek which had rested in boyhood on his mother's bosom — was pressed against the gilded breast of the god, Serapis, his taskmaster in life — his pillow in death!

"I rise! I rise to the world of light, with my deities whom I have served!" he murmured; "the brightness of their presence is like a flaming fire; the smoke of their breath pours forth around me like the smoke of incense! I minister in the Temples of the Clouds; and the glory of eternal sunlight shines round me while I adore! I rise! I rise!"

The smoke whirled in black volumes over his head; the fierce voice of the fast-spreading fire roared on him; the flames leapt up at his feet — his robes kindled, burst into radiant light, as the pile yawned and opened under him.

* * * * * * *

Time had passed. The strife between the Temple and the Church was ended. The priests and the people had formed a wider circle round the devoted building; all that was inflammable in it had been burnt; smoke and flame now burst only at intervals through the gates, and gradually both ceased to appear. Then the crowd approached nearer to the Temple, and felt the heat of the furnace they had kindled, as they looked in.

The iron gates were red hot — from the great mass behind (still glowing bright in some places, and heaving and quivering with its own heat) a thin, transparent vapour rose slowly to the stone roof of the building, now blackened with smoke. The priests looked eagerly for the corpse of the Pagan; they saw two dark, charred objects closely united together, lying in a chasm of ashes near the gate, at a spot where the fire had already exhausted itself, but it was impossible to discern which was the man and which was the idol.

The necessity of providing means for entering the temple had not been forgotten while the flames were raging. Proper implements for forcing open the gates were now at hand, and already the mob began to dip their buckets in the Tiber, and pour water wherever any traces of the fire remained. Soon all obstacles were removed; the soldiers crowded into the building with spades in their hands, trampled on the black, watery mire of cinders which covered what had once been the altar of idols, and throwing out into the street the refuse ashes and the stone images which had remained unconsumed, dug in what was left as in a new mine, for the gold and silver which the fire could not destroy.

The Pagan had lived with his idols, had perished with his idols! — and now where *they* were cast away, there *he* was cast away with them. The soldiers, as they dug into fragments the black ruins of his altar, mingled *him* in fragments with it! The people, as they cast the refuse thrown out to them into the river, cast what remained of *him* with what remained of his gods! And when the temple was deserted, when the citizens had borne off all the treasure they could collect, when nothing but a few heaps of dust was left of all that had been burnt, the night-wind blew away before it the ashes of Ulpius with the ashes of the deities that Ulpius had served!

CHAPTER XIV.
The Vigil of Hope.

A NEW prospect now opens before us. The rough paths through which we have hitherto threaded our way grow smoother as we approach their close. Rome, so long dark and gloomy to our view, brightens at length like a landscape when the rain is past, and the first rays of returning sunlight stream through the parting clouds. Some days have elapsed, and in those days the temples have yielded all their wealth; the conquered Romans have bribed the triumphant barbarians to mercy; the ransom of the fallen city has been paid.

The Gothic army is still encamped round the walls, but the gates are opened, markets for food are established in the suburbs, boats appear on the river and waggons on the high roads, laden with provisions, and proceeding towards Rome. All the hidden treasure kept back by the citizens is now bartered for food; the merchants who hold the market reap a rich harvest of spoil, but the hungry are filled, the weak are revived, every one is content.

It is the end of the second day since the free sale of provisions and the liberty of egress from the city have been permitted by the Goths. The gates are closed for the night, and the people are quietly returning, laden with their supplies of food, to their homes. Their eyes no longer encounter the terrible traces of the march of pestilence and famine through every street; the corpses have been removed, and the sick are watched and sheltered. Rome is cleansed from her pollutions, and the virtues of household life begin to revive wherever they once existed. Death has thinned every family, but the survivors again assemble together in the social hall. Even the veriest criminals, the lowest outcasts of the population, are united harmlessly for a while in the general participation of the first benefits of peace.

To follow the citizens to their homes; to trace in their thoughts, words, and actions, the effect on them of their deliverance from the horrors of the blockade; to contemplate in the people of a whole city, now recovering as it were from a deep swoon, the varying forms of the first reviving symptoms in all classes, in good and bad, rich and poor — would afford matter enough in itself for a romance of searching human interest, for a drama of the passions, moving absorbingly through strange, intricate, and contrasted scenes. But another employment than this now claims our care. It is to an individual, and not to a divided source of interest that our attention turns; we relinquish all observations on the general mass of the populace, to revert to Numerian and Antonina alone — to penetrate once more into the little dwelling on the Pincian Hill.

The apartment where the father and daughter had suffered the pangs of famine together, during the period of the blockade, presented an appearance far different from that which it had displayed on the occasion when they had last occupied it. The formerly bare walls were now covered with rich, thick hangings; and the simple couch and scanty table of other days, had been exchanged for whatever was most luxurious and complete in the household furniture of the age. At one end of the room three women, attended by a little girl, were engaged in preparing some dishes of fruit and vegetables; at the other, two men were occupied in low, earnest conversation, occasionally looking round anxiously to a couch placed against the third side of the apartment, on which Antonina lay extended, while Numerian watched by her in silence. The point of Goisvintha's knife had struck deep, but, as yet, the fatal purpose of the assassination had failed.

The girl's eyes were closed; her lips were parted in the languor of suffering; one of her hands lay listless on her father's knee. A slight expression of pain, melancholy in its very slightness, appeared on her pale face, and occasionally a long-drawn, quivering breath escaped her — nature's last touching utterance of its own feebleness! The old man, as he sat by her side, fixed on her a wistful, inquiring glance. Sometimes he raised his hand, and gently and mechanically moved to and fro the long locks of her hair, as they spread over the head of the couch, but he never turned to communicate with the other persons in the room — he sat as if he saw nothing save his daughter's figure stretched before him, and heard nothing save the faint, fluttering sound of her breathing, close at his ear.

It was now dark, and one lamp, hanging from the ceiling, threw a soft equal light over the room. The different persons occupying it presented but little evidence of health and strength in their countenances, to contrast them in appearance with the wounded girl; all had undergone the wasting visitation of the famine, and all were pale and languid, like her. A strange, indescribable harmony prevailed over the scene. Even the calmness of absorbing expectation and trembling hope, expressed in the demeanour of Numerian, seemed reflected in the actions of those around him, in the quietness with which the women pursued their employment, in the lower and lower whispers in which the men continued their conversation. There was something pervading the air of the whole apartment that conveyed a sense of the solemn, unworldly stillness, which we attach to the abstract idea of religion.

Of the two men cautiously talking together, one was the patrician, Vetranio; the other, a celebrated physician of Rome.

Both the countenance and manner of the senator gave melancholy proof that the orgy at his palace had altered him for the rest of his life. He looked what he was, a man changed for ever in constitution and character. A fixed expression of anxiety and gloom appeared in his eyes; his emaciated face was occasionally distorted by a nervous, involuntary contraction of the muscles; it was evident that the paralysing effect of the debauch which had destroyed his companions would remain with him to the end of his existence.

No remnant of his careless self-possession, his easy, patrician affability, appeared in his manner, as he now listened to his companion's conversation; years seemed to have been added to his life, since he had headed the table at "The Banquet of Famine."

"Yes," said the physician, a cold, calm man, who spoke much, but pronounced all his words with emphatic deliberation, "Yes, as I have already told you, the wound, in itself, was not mortal. If the blade of the knife had entered near the centre of the neck, she must have died when she was struck. But it passed outwards and backwards; the large vessels escaped; no vital part has been touched."

"And yet you persist in declaring that you doubt her recovery!" exclaimed Vetranio, in low, mournful tones.

"I do," pursued the physician. "She must have been exhausted in mind and body, when she received the blow — I have watched her carefully; I know it! There is nothing of the natural health and strength of youth to oppose the effects of the wound. I have seen the old die from injuries that the young recover, because life, in them, was losing its powers of resistance; *she* is in the position of the old!"

"*They* have died before me, and *she* will die before me! I shall lose all — all!" sighed Vetranio bitterly to himself.

"The resources of our art are exhausted," continued the other, "nothing remains, but to watch carefully and wait patiently; the chances of life or death will be decided in a few hours; they are equally balanced now."

"I shall lose all! — all!" repeated the senator, mournfully, as if he heeded not the last words.

"If she dies," said the physician, speaking in warmer tones, for he was struck with pity, in spite of himself, at the spectacle of Vetranio's utter dejection, "if she dies, you can at least remember that all that could be done to secure her life has been done by *you*. Her father, helpless in his lethargy and his age, was fitted only to sit and watch her, as he has sat and watched her day after day; but you have spared nothing, forgotten nothing. Whatever I have asked for, that you have provided; the hangings round the room, and the couch that she lies on, are yours; the first fresh supplies of nourishment from the newly-opened markets were brought here from you; I told you that she was thinking incessantly of what she had suffered, that it was necessary to preserve her against her own recollections, that the presence of women about her might do good, that a child appearing sometimes in the room might soothe her fancy, might make her look at what was passing, instead of thinking of what had passed, — you found them, and sent them! I have seen parents less anxious for their children, lovers for their mistresses, than you for this girl."

"My destiny is with her," interrupted Vetranio, looking round superstitiously to the frail form on the couch. "I know nothing of the mysteries that the Christians call their 'Faith;' but I believe now in the soul; I believe that one soul contains the fate of another, and that *her* soul contains the fate of mine!"

The physician shook his head derisively. His calling had determined his philosophy — he was as ardent a materialist as Epicurus himself.

"Listen," said Vetranio; "since I first saw her, a change came over my whole being; it was as if her life was mingled with mine! I had no influence over her, save an influence for ill: I loved her, and she was driven defenceless from her home! I sent my slaves to search Rome night and day; I exerted all my power, I lavished my wealth to discover her; and, for the first time, in this one effort, I failed in what I had undertaken. I felt that through *me* she was lost — dead! Days passed on; life weighed weary on me; the famine came. You know in what way I determined that my career should close; the rumour of the Banquet of Famine reached you as it reached others!"

"It did," replied the physician. "And I see before me, in your face," he added, after a momentary pause, "the havoc which that ill-omened banquet has worked. My friend, be advised! — abandon for ever the turmoil of your Roman palace, and breathe in tranquillity the air of a country home. The strength you once had, is gone never to return — if you would yet live, husband what is still left."

"Hear me," pursued Vetranio, in low, gloomy tones, "I stood alone in my doomed palace; the friends whom I had tempted to their destruction lay lifeless around me; the torch was in my hand that was to light our funeral pile, to set us free from the loathsome world! I approached triumphantly to kindle the annihilating flames, when *she* stood before me — *she*, whom I had sought as lost, and mourned as dead! A strong hand seemed to wrench the torch from me; it dropped to the ground! She departed again; but I was powerless to take it up; her look was still before me; her face, her figure, — she, herself, appeared ever watching between the torch and me!"

"Lower! — speak lower!" interrupted the physician, looking on the senator's agitated features with unconcealed astonishment and pity, "You retard your own recovery, — you disturb the girl's repose by discourse such a this."

"The officers of the senate," continued Vetranio, sadly resuming his gentler tones, "when they entered the palace, found me still standing on the place where we had met! Days passed on again: I stood, looking out upon the street, and thought of my companions, whom I had lured to their death, and of my oath to partake their fate, which I had never fulfilled. I would have driven my dagger to my heart; but her face was yet before me, my hands were bound! In that hour I saw her for the second time; saw her carried past me — wounded, assassinated! She had saved me once; she had saved me twice! I knew that now the chance was offered me, after having wrought her ill, to work her good; after failing to discover her when she was lost, to succeed in saving her when she was dying; after having survived the deaths of my friends at my own table, to survive to see life restored under my influence, as well as destroyed! These were my thoughts; these are my thoughts still — thoughts felt only since I saw *her!* Do you know now why I believe that her soul contains the fate of mine? Do you see me, weakened, shattered, old before my time; my friends lost, my fresh feelings of youth gone for ever; and can you not now comprehend that *her* life is *my* life? — that if she dies, the one good purpose of my existence is blighted? — that I lose all I have henceforth to live for? — all, all!"

As he pronounced the concluding words, the girl's eyes half unclosed, and turned languidly towards her father. She made an effort to lift her hand caressingly from his knee to his neck; but her strength was unequal even to this slight action. The hand was raised only a few inches ere it sank back again to its old position; a tear rolled slowly over her cheek as she closed her eyes again, but she never spoke.

"See," said the physician, pointing to her, "the current of life is at its lowest ebb! If it flows again, it must flow to-night."

Vetranio made no answer: he dropped down on the seat near him, and covered his face with his robe.

The physician, beholding the senator's situation, and reflecting on the strange hurriedly-uttered confession which had just been addressed to him, began to doubt whether the scenes through which his patron had lately passed, had not affected his brain. Philosopher though he was, the man of science had never observed the outward symptoms of the first working of good and pure influences in elevating a degraded mind; he had never watched the denoting signs of speech and action which mark the progress of mental revolution while the old nature is changing for the new; such objects of contemplation existed not for *him*. He gently touched Vetranio on the shoulder. "Rise," said he, "and let us depart. Those are around her who can watch her best. Nothing remains for us but to wait and hope. With the earliest morning we will return."

He delivered a few farewell directions to one of the women in attendance, and then, accompanied by the senator, who, without speaking again, mechanically rose to follow him, quitted the room.

After this, the silence was only interrupted by the sound of an occasional whisper, and of quick, light footsteps passing backwards and forwards. Then the cooling, reviving draughts which had been prepared for the night, were poured ready into the cups; and the women approached Numerian, as if to address him, but he waved his hand impatiently when he saw them; and then they too, in their turn, departed, to wait in an adjoining apartment until they should be summoned again.

Nothing changed in the manner of the father when he was left alone in the chamber of sickness, which the lapse of a few hours might convert into the chamber of death. He sat watching Antonina, and touching the outspread locks of her hair from time to time, as had been his wont. It was a fair, starry night; the fresh air of the soft winter climate of the South blew gently over the earth, the great city was sinking fast into tranquillity, calling voices were sometimes heard faintly from the principal streets, and the distant notes of martial music sounded cheerily from the Gothic camp as the sentinels were posted along the line of watch; but soon these noises ceased, and the stillness of Rome was as the stillness round the couch of the wounded girl.

Day after day, and night after night, since the assassination in the temple, Numerian had kept the same place by his daughter's side. Each hour as it passed, found him still absorbed in his long vigil of hope; his life seemed suspended in its onward course by the one influence that now enthralled it. At the brief intervals when his bodily weariness overpowered him on his melancholy watch, it was observed by those around him that, even in his short dreaming slumbers, his face remained ever turned in the same direction, towards the head of the couch, as if drawn thither by some irresistible attraction, by some powerful ascendancy, felt even amid the deepest repose of sensation, the heaviest fatigue of the overlaboured mind, and the worn, sinking heart. He held no communication, save by signs, with the friends about him; he seemed neither to hope, to doubt, nor to despair with them; all his faculties were strung up to vibrate at one point only, and were dull and unimpressible in every other direction.

But twice he had been heard to speak more than the fewest, simplest words. The first time, when Antonina uttered the name of Goisvintha, on the recovery of her senses after her wound, he answered eagerly by reiterated declarations that there was nothing henceforth to fear; for he had seen the assassin dead under the Pagan's foot, on leaving the temple. The second time, when mention was incautiously made before him of rumours circulated through Rome of the burning of an unknown Pagan priest, hidden in the temple of Serapis, with vast treasures around him, the old man was seen to start and shudder, and heard to pray for the soul that was now waiting before the dread Judgment seat; to murmur about a vain restoration, and a discovery made too late; to mourn over horror that thickened round him, over hope fruitlessly awakened, and bereavement more terrible than mortal had ever suffered before; to entreat that the child, the last left of all, might be spared, — with many words more, which ran on themes like these, and which were counted by all who listened to them, but as the wanderings of a mind whose higher powers were fatally prostrated by feebleness and grief.

One long hour of the night had already passed away since parent and child had been left together, and neither word nor movement had been audible in the melancholy room. But, as the second hour began, the girl's eyes unclosed again, and she moved painfully on the couch. Accustomed to interpret the significance of her slightest actions, Numerian rose and brought her one of the reviving draughts that had been left ready for use. After she had drunk, when her eyes met her father's, fixed on her in mute and mournful enquiry, her lips closed, and formed themselves into an expression which he remembered they had always assumed, when, as a little child, she used silently to hold up her face to him to be kissed. The miserable contrast between what she was now and what she had been then, was beyond the passive endurance, the patient resignation of the spirit-broken old man: the empty cup dropped from his hands, he knelt down by the side of the couch, and groaned aloud.

"Oh, father! father!" cried the weak, plaintive voice above him, "I am dying! Let us remember that our time to be together here grows shorter and shorter; and let us pass it as happily as we can!"

He raised his head, and looked up at her, vacant and wistful, forlorn already, as if the death-parting was over.

"I have tried to live humbly and gratefully," she sighed faintly. "I have longed to do more good on the earth than I have done! Yet you will forgive me now, father, as you have always forgiven me! You have been patient with me all my life; more patient than I have ever deserved! But I had no mother to teach me to love you as I ought, to teach me what I know now, when my death is near, and time and opportunity are mine no longer!"

"Hush! hush!" whispered the old man affrightedly; "you will live! God is good, and knows that we have suffered enough. The curse of the last separation is not pronounced against *us!* Live — live!"

"Father!" said the girl tenderly, "we have that

within us which not death itself can separate. In another world I shall still think of *you*, when you think of *me!* I shall see you even when I am no more here, when you long to see *me!* When you go out alone, and sit under the trees on the garden bank where I used to sit; when you look forth on the far plains and mountains that I used to look on: when you read at night in the Bible that we have read in together, and remember Antonina as you lie down sorrowful to rest; *then* I shall see you! *then* you will feel that I am looking on you! You will be calm and consoled, even by the side of my grave; for you will think, not of the body that is beneath, but of the spirit that is waiting for you, as I have often waited for you here when you were away, and I knew that the approach of the evening would bring you home again!"

"Hush! you will live! — you will live!" repeated Numerian in the same low, vacant tones. The strength that still upheld him was in those few simple words; they were the food of a hope that was born in agony and cradled in despair.

"Oh, if I *might* live!" said the girl softly, "if I might live but for a few days yet, how much I have to live for!" She endeavoured to bend her head towards her father as she spoke; for the words were beginning to fall faintly and more faintly from her lips — exhaustion was mastering her once again. She dwelt for a moment now on the name of Hermanric, on the grave in the farm-house garden; then reverted again to her father. The last feeble sounds she uttered were addressed to him; and their burden was still of consolation and of love.

Soon the old man, as he stooped over her, saw her eyes close again — those innocent, gentle eyes which even yet preserved their old expression while the face grew wan and pale around them — and darkness and night sank down over his soul while he looked. "She sleeps," he murmured in a voice of awe, as he resumed his watching position by the side of the couch. "They call death a sleep; but on *her* face there is no death!"

The night grew on. The women who were in attendance entered the room about midnight, wondering that their assistance had not yet been required. They beheld the solemn, unruffled composure on the girl's wasted face; the rapt attention of Numerian, as he ever preserved the same attitude by her side; and went out again softly without uttering a word, even in a whisper. There was something dread and impressive in the very appearance of this room; where Death, that destroys, was in mortal conflict with Youth and Beauty, that adorn; while the eyes of one old man watched in loneliness the awful progress of the strife.

Morning came; and still there was no change. Once, when the lamp that lit the room was fading out as the dawn appeared, Numerian had risen and looked close on his daughter's face — he thought at that moment that her features moved; but he saw that the flickering of the dying light on them had deceived him; the same stillness was over her. He placed his ear close to her lips for an instant, and then resumed his place, not stirring from it again. The slow current of his blood seemed to have come to a pause — he was waiting as a man waits with his head on the block, ere the axe descends — as a mother waits to hear that the breath of life has entered her new-born child.

The sun rose bright in a cloudless sky. As the fresh, sharp air of the early dawn warmed under its spreading rays, the women entered the apartment again, and partly drew aside the curtain and shutter from the window. The beams of the new light fell fair and glorifying on the girl's face; the faint, calm breeze ruffled the lighter locks of her hair. Once this would have awakened her; but it did not disturb her now.

Soon after the voice of the child who sojourned with the women in the house was heard beneath, in the hall, through the half-opened door of the room. The little creature was slowly ascending the stairs, singing her faltering morning song to herself. She was preceded on her approach by a tame dove, bought at the provision market outside the walls, but preserved for the child as a pet and plaything by its mother. The bird fluttered, cooing, into the room, perched upon the head of the couch, and began dressing its feathers there. The women had caught the infection of the old man's enthralling suspense; and moved not to bid the child retire, or to take away the dove from its place — they watched like him. But the soft, lulling notes of the bird were powerless over the girl's ear, as the light sunbeam over her face — still she never woke.

The child entered, and pausing in her song, climbed on to the side of the couch. She held out one little hand for the dove to perch upon, placed the other lightly on Antonina's shoulder, and pressed her fresh, rosy lips to the girl's faded cheek. "I and my bird have come to make Antonina well this morning," she said, gravely.

The still, heavily-closed eyelids moved! — they quivered, opened, closed, then opened again. The eyes had a faint, dreaming, unconscious look; but Antonina lived! Antonina was awakened at last to another day on earth!

Her father's rigid, straining gaze still remained fixed upon her as at first; but on his countenance there was a blank, an absence of all appearance of sensation and life. The women, as they looked on Antonina and looked on him, began to weep; the child resumed very softly its morning song, now addressing it to the wounded girl and now to the dove.

As this moment Vetranio and the physician appeared on the scene. The latter advanced to the couch, removed the child from it, and examined Antonina intently. At length, partly addressing Numerian, partly speaking to himself, he said: "She has slept long, deeply, without moving, almost without

20*

breathing — a sleep like death to all who looked on it."

The old man spoke not in reply, but the women answered eagerly in the affirmative.

"She is saved," pursued the physician, leisurely quitting the side of the couch, and smiling on Vetranino; "be careful of her for days and days to come."

"Saved! saved!" echoed the child joyfully, setting the dove free in the room, and running to Numerian to climb on his knees. The father glanced down, when the clear, young voice sounded in his ear. The springs of joy, so long dried up in his heart, welled forth again, as he saw the little hands raised towards him entreatingly; his grey head drooped — he wept.

At a sign from the physician the child was led from the room. The silence of deep and solemn emotion was preserved by all who remained; nothing was heard but the suppressed sobs of the old man, and the faint, retiring notes of the infant voice, still singing its morning song. And now one word, joyfully reiterated again and again, made all the burden of the music: —

"SAVED! SAVED!"

THE CONCLUSION.

"Ubi Thesaurus ibi Cor."

SHORTLY after the opening of the provision markets outside the gates of Rome, the Goths broke up their camp before the city, and retired to winter quarters in Tuscany. The negociations which ensued between Alaric and the Court and Government at Ravenna, were conducted with cunning moderation by the conqueror, and with infatuated audacity by the conquered, and ultimately terminated in a resumption of hostilities. Rome was besieged a second and a third time by "the barbarians." On the latter occasion the city was sacked; its palaces were burnt; its treasures were seized; the monuments of the Christian religion were alone respected.

But it is no longer with the Goths that our narrative is concerned; the connection with them which it has hitherto maintained, closes with the end of the first siege of Rome. We can claim the reader's attention for historical events no more, — the march of our little pageant, arrayed for his pleasure, is over. If, however, he has felt, and still retains some interest in Antonina, he will not refuse to follow us, and look on her again, ere we part.

More than a month had passed since the besieging army had retired to their winter quarters, when several of the citizens of Rome assembled themselves on the plains beyond the walls, to enjoy one of those rustic festivals of ancient times, which are still celebrated, under different usages, but with the same spirit, by the Italians of modern days.

The place was a level plot of ground beyond the Pincian Gate, backed by a thick grove of pine trees, and looking towards the north over the smooth extent of the country round Rome. The persons congregated were mostly of the lower class. Their amusements were dancing, music, games of strength and games of chance; and above all, to people who had lately suffered the extremities of famine, abundant eating and drinking, — long, serious, ecstatic enjoyment of the powers of mastication and the faculties of taste.

Among the assembly were some individuals whose dress and manner raised them, outwardly at least, above the general mass. These persons walked backwards and forwards together on different parts of the ground, as observers, not as partakers in the sports. One of their number, however, in whatever direction he turned, preserved an isolated position. He held an open letter in his hand, which he looked at from time to time, and appeared to be wholly absorbed in his own thoughts. This man we may advantageously particularise on his own account, as well as on account of the peculiarity of his accidental situation; for he was the favoured minister of Vetranio's former pleasures — "the industrious Carrio."

The freedman (who was last introduced to the reader in Chapter I. of this Vol., as exhibiting to Vetranio the store of offal which he had collected during the famine, for the consumption of the palace) had contrived of late greatly to increase his master's confidence in him. On the organisation of the Banquet of Famine, he had discreetly refrained from testifying the smallest desire to save himself from the catastrophe in which the senator and his friends had determined to involve themselves. Securing himself in a place of safety, he awaited the end of the orgy; and when he found that its unexpected termination left his master still living to employ him, appeared again as a faithful servant, ready to resume his customary occupation with undiminished zeal.

After the dispersion of his household during the famine, and amid the general confusion of the social system in Rome, on the raising of the blockade, Vetranio found no one near him that he could trust but Carrio — and he trusted him. Nor was the confidence misplaced: the man was selfish and sordid enough; but these very qualities ensured his fidelity to his master, as long as that master retained the power to punish and the capacity to reward.

The letter which Carrio held in his hand was addressed to him at a villa — from which he had just returned — belonging to Vetranio, on the shores of the Bay of Naples, and was written by the senator, from Rome. The introductory portions of this communication seemed to interest the freedman but little: they contained praises of his diligence in preparing the country-house for the immediate habitation of its' owner, and expressed his master's anxiety to quit

Rome as speedily as possible, for the sake of living in perfect tranquillity, and breathing the reviving air of the sea, as the physicians had counselled. It was the latter part of the letter that Carrio perused and reperused, and then meditated over with unwonted attention and labour of mind. It ran thus: —

"I have now to repose in you a trust, which you will execute with perfect fidelity as you value my favour, or respect the wealth from which you may obtain your reward. When you left Rome, you left the daughter of Numerian lying in danger of death: she has since revived. Questions that I have addressed to her during her recovery, have informed me of much in her history that I knew not before; and have induced me to purchase, for reasons of my own, a farm-house and its lands, beyond the suburbs. (The extent of the place and its situation, are written on the vellum that is within this). The husbandman who cultivated the property, has survived the famine; and will continue to cultivate it for me. But, it is my desire that the garden, and all that it contains, shall remain entirely at the disposal of Numerian and his daughter, who may often repair to it; and who must henceforth be regarded there, as occupying my place and having my authority. You will divide your time between overlooking the few slaves whom I leave at the palace in my absence, and the husbandman and his labourers whom I have installed at the farm; and you will answer to me for the due performance of your own duties, and the duties of those under you —

being assured that by well filling this office, you will serve your own interests in these, and in all things besides."

The letter concluded by directing the freedman to return to Rome on a certain day, and to go to the farm-house at an appointed hour, there to meet his master, who had further directions to give him, and who would visit the newly-acquired property before he proceeded on his journey to Naples.

Nothing could exceed the perplexity of Carrio, as he read the passage in his patron's letter which we have quoted above. Remembering the incidents attending Vetranio's early connexion with Antonina and her father, the mere circumstance of a farm having been purchased to flatter what was doubtless some accidental caprice on the part of the girl, would have little astonished him. But, that this act should be followed by the senator's immediate separation of himself from the society of Numerian's daughter; that she was to gain nothing after all from these lands which had evidently been bought at her instigation, but the authority over a little strip of garden; and yet, the inviolability of this valueless privilege should be insisted on in such serious terms, and with such an imperative tone of command as the senator had never been known to use before — these were inconsistencies which all Carrio's ingenuity failed to reconcile. The man had been born and reared in vice; vice had fed him, clothed him, freed him, given him character, reputation, power in his own small way — he lived in it, as in the atmosphere that he breathed; to show him an action referable only to a principle of pure integrity, was to set him a problem which it was hopeless to solve. And yet, it is impossible, in one point of view, to pronounce him utterly worthless. Ignorant of all distinctions between good and bad, he thought wrong from sheer inability to see right.

However his instructions might perplex him, he followed them now — and continued in after days to follow them — to the letter. If to serve one's own interests be an art, of that art Carrio deserved to be head professor. He arrived at the farm-house, not only punctually, but before the appointed time; and, calling the honest husbandman and the labourers about him, explained to them every particular of the authority that his patron had vested in him, with a flowing and peremptory solemnity of speech which equally puzzled and impressed his simple audience. He found Numerian and Antonina in the garden, when he entered it. The girl had been carried there daily, in a litter, since her recovery; and her father had followed. They were never separated now; the old man, when his first absorbing anxiety for her was calmed, remembered again more distinctly the terrible disclosure in the temple, and the yet more terrible catastrophe that followed it; and sought constant refuge from the horror of the recollection, in the presence of his child.

The freedman, during his interview with the father and daughter, observed, for once, an involuntary and unfeigned respect; but he spoke briefly, and left them together again almost immediately. Humble and helpless as they were, they awed him; they looked, thought, and spoke, like beings of another nature than his; they were connected, he knew not how, with the mystery of the grave in the garden — he would have been self-possessed in the presence of the emperor himself, but he was uneasy in theirs. So he retired to the more congenial scene of the public festival which was in the immediate neighbourhood of the farm-house, to await the hour of his patron's arrival, and to perplex himself afresh by a re-perusal of Vetranio's letter.

The time was now near at hand when it was necessary for the freedman to return to his appointed post. He carefully rolled up his note of instructions; stood for a few minutes vacantly regarding the amusements which had hitherto engaged so little of his attention; and then turning, proceeded through the pine-grove on his way back. We will follow him.

On leaving the grove, a footpath conducted over some fields to the farm-house. Arrived here, Carrio hesitated for a moment; then moved slowly onward to await his master's approach in the lane that led to the high-road. At this point we will part company with him, to enter the garden by the wicket-gate.

The trees, the flower-beds, and the patches of grass, all remained in their former positions; nothing had been added or taken away since the melancholy days that were past; but a change was visible in Hermanric's grave. The turf above it had been renewed;

and a border of small evergreen shrubs was planted over the track which Goisvintha's footsteps had traced. A white marble cross was raised at one end of the mound; the short Latin inscription on it signified, "PRAY FOR THE DEAD."

The sunlight was shining calmly over the grave, and over Numerian and Antonina, as they sat by it. Sometimes, when the mirth grew louder at the rustic festival, it reached them in faint, subdued notes; sometimes they heard the voices of the labourers in the neighbouring fields talking to each other at their work; but, besides these, no other sounds were loud enough to be distinguished. There was still an expression of the melancholy and feebleness that grief and suffering leave behind them, on the countenances of the father and daughter: but resignation and peace appeared there as well — resignation that was perfected by the hard teaching of woe, and peace that was purer for being imparted from the one to the other, like the strong and deathless love from which it grew.

There was something now in the look and attitude of the girl, as she sat thinking of the young warrior who had died in her defence and for her love, and training the shrubs to grow closer round the grave, which, changed though she was, recalled in a different form the old poetry and tranquillity of her existence when we first saw her singing to the music of her lute in the garden on the Pincian Hill. No thoughts of horror and despair were suggested to her as she looked on the farm-house scene. Hers was not the grief which shrinks selfishly from all that revives the remembrance of the dead: to *her*, their influence over the memory was a grateful and a guardian influence that gave a better purpose to the holiest life, and a nobler nature to the purest thoughts.

Thus they were sitting by the grave — sad, yet content: footsore already on the pilgrimage of life, yet patient to journey further if they might, when an unusual tumult, a noise of rolling wheels, mingled with a confused sound of voices, was heard in the lane behind them. They looked round, and saw that Vetranio was approaching them alone through the wicket-gate.

He came forward slowly; the stealthy poison instilled by the Banquet of Famine palpably displayed its presence within him, as the clear sunlight fell on his pale, wasted face. He smiled kindly as he addressed Antonina; but the bodily pain and mental agitation which that smile was intended to conceal, betrayed themselves in his troubled voice as he spoke.

"This is our last meeting for years — it may be our last meeting for life;" he said; "I linger at the outset of my journey, but to behold you as guardian of the one spot of ground that is most precious to you on earth, as mistress, indeed, of the little that I give you here —" he paused a moment and pointed to the grave: then continued: — "All the atonement that I owe to you, *you* can never know; *I* can never tell! — think only that I bear away with me a companion in the solitude to which I go, in the remembrance of you. Be calm, good, happy still, for my sake; and while you forgive the senator of former days, forget not the friend who now parts from you, in some sickness and sorrow, but also in much patience and hope! — Farewell!"

His hand trembled as he held it out; a flush overspread the girl's cheek while she murmured a few inarticulate words of gratitude; and, bending over it, pressed it to her lips. Vetranio's heart beat quick; the action revived an emotion that he dared not cherish; but he looked at the wan, downcast face before him, at the grave that rose mournful by his side, and quelled it again. Yet an instant he lingered to exchange a farewell with the old man, then turned quickly, passed through the gate, and they saw him no more.

Antonina's tears fell fast on the grass beneath, as she resumed her place. When she raised her head again, and saw that her father was looking at her, she nestled close to him and laid one of her arms round his neck: the other gradually dropped to her side, until her hand reached the topmost leaves of the shrubs that grew round the grave.

Shall we longer delay in the farm-house garden? No! For us, as for Vetranio, it is now time to depart! While peace still watches round the walls of Rome; while the hearts of the father and daughter still repose together in security, after the trials that have wrung them, let us quit the scene! Here, at last, the narrative that we have followed over a dark and stormy track, reposes on a tranquil field; and here let us cease to pursue it!

So the traveller who traces the course of a river, wanders through the day among the rocks and precipices that lead onward from its troubled source; and, when the evening is at hand, pauses and rests where the banks are grassy and the stream is smooth.

THE END.

www.ingramcontent.com/pod-product-compliance
Lightning Source LLC
Chambersburg PA
CBHW030739230426
43667CB00007B/777